WHAT IS CATHOLICISM?

*An Anglican responds
to the official teaching
of the Roman Catholic Church*

David L. Edwards

MOWBRAY

Mowbray
Villiers House
41/47 Strand
London, WC2N 5JE

387 Park Avenue South
New York, NY 10016–8810

First published 1994

British Library Cataloguing in Publication Data.
A catalogue entry for this book is available from the British Library.

Library of Congress Cataloging-in-Publication Data
Applied for.

ISBN 0–264–67325–5

Quotations from the *Catechism of the Catholic Church*, English translation for United Kingdom and Ireland, copyright © 1994 Geoffrey Chapman–Libreria Editrice Vaticana, are used by permission.

Typeset by York House Typographic Ltd
Printed and bound in Great Britain by
Biddles Ltd, Guildford and King's Lynn

Contents

PREFACE 1

To Anglicans

DEAR ANGLICANS,

We all know that this is difficult time. We claim to be Catholic Christians, Bible-based, valuing the sacraments and the orthodox creeds in our worship led by bishops, but we are also instructed by the Protestant Reformation and by modern knowledge and thought. In recent years this heritage has landed us in problem after problem. Our position is complicated and for that reason it is often criticized, abandoned or ignored by those who prefer, and it may be need, the grand simplicities. Indeed, we are eloquent in self-criticism; we disagree and debate between ourselves; and when we are true to ourselves we make no claim to have been in the past, or to be in the present, right at every point of belief or behaviour. A book of mine in 1958 was entitled *Not Angels but Anglicans*, for one may love without being blind. Our manifestly imperfect kind of Christianity, polluted by human failings and political entanglements, can easily be marginalized or ridiculed. It can be said to have been the product of expediency when the rulers of England struggled to keep the nation religiously united (even 'uniform'!). Outside England it can be dismissed as the church of an eccentric minority and the name 'Anglican' continues to suggest an English connection, even in countries where 'Episcopal Church' or 'Church of the Province' is preferred because it signals the strong tendency away from Englishness.

Since the Second World War the Anglican involvement in the ecumenical movement for Christian renewal and reunion has brought us fresh difficulties. Because we have a Catholic side to us, despite many efforts we have been unable to reach adequate agreement for reunion with any more definitely Protestant body outside China and the Indian sub-continent. And because we are not Catholics as Catholicism is defined in Rome, we have also found it impossible to secure the Roman Catholic Church's official acceptance of our priesthood or our doctrines. Recently we have incurred fresh disapproval in that quarter by the decisions of Anglican provinces including the Church of England to ordain women as priests. These disappointments do, and must, raise for us probing questions. Where, if anywhere, do we stand? Is our tradition merely an ambiguous compromise with little reference to truth? What, if anything, can we offer to other churches? In answer, some Anglicans have become Roman Catholics although it is not a one-way traffic.

I long to make a contribution now, if only because I have written this book on the eve of retirement from full-time work as an Anglican priest. I have been given so many privileges and joys since I was ordained forty years ago that I want to repay a little of the debt, believing that I am a priest.

It may seem strange that what I offer is a controversial book about the official teaching of the Roman Catholic Church. If it is noticed at all, such a book may seem to be an attempt to add to the problems in relationships between Christians who are, and those who are not, Roman Catholics. But as is (I trust) demonstrated at some length in my other books including the three volumes of my history of *Christian England*, I am not a Protestant fanatic. In 1997 we shall celebrate the sending of its first archbishop to Canterbury from Rome in 597 and in the sixteenth century the separate Anglican tradition began as part-acceptance and part-repudiation of medieval Catholicism. Ever since then our High Church movement has taken a special pride in our Catholic heritage. I believe that in the twenty-first century our true position will emerge as our connection develops with contemporary Roman Catholicism, officially or unofficially. Through this process we shall find some consolation for our own distresses in the discovery that thoughtful people in other churches cannot escape the challenges which have so troubled us. Even when the Vatican insists on the necessity of detailed assent to its teaching – as it has done very firmly in its response to the Anglican/RC International Commission of theologians in 1992, to give only one example – many other Roman Catholics, theologians and pastoral clergy as well as laity, hold other convictions and are not afraid to express them. We should not feel lonely in our own unsettlement, and perhaps some of our discussions and tentative conclusions may be of assistance. We shall certainly be enriched as we study and experience the vast and often glorious reality of the Roman Catholic Church, but we may also become clearer and more confident about the reasons which led previous generations to protest against some of the actions of the papacy and which have caused us to proceed against the wishes of the papacy in the new question about women priests. Many of those protests are now being accepted by Roman Catholics. We may also begin to see a realistic prospect of full communion with these fellow-Christians, without destroying our hopes of full communion with others.

I hope that my journalism and my other books would show that I have some awareness of the work of successive Anglican meetings such as the Lambeth Conferences, and of Anglican theologians far more eminent than myself, but I have not burdened this book by many quotations from such sources. In this restricted space I have had to adopt a personal approach to issues which have been explored over four centuries. This has, I think, some advantages. I have tried to avoid leaving any impression that Anglicans have already reached the final truth and perfect institution. I have tried to be honestly, perhaps tactlessly, specific about problems which can be buried temporarily in statements which come from meetings full of good will. I have also tried to address the official teaching of the Roman Catholic Church as it has been set out authoritatively in the 1980s and the 1990s, for as times have changed so positions have changed since the Anglican commentaries on Roman Catholicism made by Cranmer, Jewel, Hooker, Andrewes, Laud, Pusey, Maurice, Gore, Temple and Ramsey (to mention only ten great Englishmen). And I hope that my personal approach will have a further advantage. Other Anglicans could write different and better books. I should like to provoke them into doing so, since the Anglican position certainly needs a large-scale and rigorous restatement in the light of developments in the century which is now about to end. In previous books I tried to conduct dialogues with the Anglican Evangelical leader, Dr John Stott, and with Anglican theologians more radical than myself. In the one book (*Essentials*, in the US edition *Evangelical Essentials*) I was thought to be too liberal, and in the other (*Tradition and Truth*) too conservative, but the work was an education for me and for some others, and I dare to hope that this book also will be accepted as an attempt to contribute to the growth of understanding of the truth through dialogues.

At first my intention was to try to persuade a Roman Catholic to reply to me in this book, but I saw that when I had quoted the Roman Catholic Church's official teaching extensively, and I hope fairly, there would be no room for such a reply. Here, therefore, the dialogue comes as I comment on the teaching and I then have to leave it for the reader to judge. I still hope that elsewhere a Roman Catholic who agrees with this official teaching – or perhaps one who disagrees with some of it – will emerge to respond in public to the comments which I offer, but meanwhile I dedicate this book to a pope who may take action one day.

DAVID L. EDWARDS

PREFACE 2

To an unknown pope

DEAR AND HOLY FATHER,

You do not know me and I think it probable that if you ever read these words by that time I shall be dead. My only claim to attention is that I think I write on behalf of many millions of Christians, both outside the Roman Catholic Church and within it, who share my conviction that we Christians have in the past got many things wrong. In many ways we need a fresh start – and one necessary part of it, as it seems to many of us, is that . we should no longer refuse to receive the Holy Communion together.

I do not know your name. You will be pope after the time of John Paul II, the present Roman Pontiff. I hope you will be a great leader as he is, with a strong spirituality, a charismatic personality and extraordinary talents. This is a brief commentary on the two most important documents of his pontificate, the summary of official teaching called the *Catechism of the Catholic Church* approved by him and first published in French in 1992 (in English in 1994) and the *Code of Canon Law* of the Latin Church approved by him and first published in 1983. Mine is a commentary which mixes criticisms with praises, although there is much to praise, for I believe that the progress of our ecumenical movement for Christian unity has long passed the point where Christians were obliged to be nervously complimentary to each other all the time because the memories of bitter disputes and even persecutions in the past were so vivid and so shaming. We have reached a stage when we can behave as members of one family, gladly accepting one another but on that permanent basis sometimes arguing and always helping one another to grow.

You, Holy Father, do not need to be reminded – but perhaps I ought to show that I know – that 'catechesis' is a theological term meaning 'handing on the faith'. A 'catechism' may be a short collection of questions and answers, thought to be specially suitable for children to learn by heart. Such was the American 'Baltimore Catechism' of 1885 or the catechism (for long called the 'penny catechism') which was approved by the Roman Catholic hierarchy of England and Wales in 1889 and slightly revised in 1985. Or it may be a substantial book such as the Roman Catechism of 1566, intended and much used as the basis for teaching by parish priests, or the mostly American book called *The Teaching of Christ: A Catholic Catechism for Adults* published in 1976, revised in 1983 and translated into many languages. In his Apostolic Constitution *Depositum Fidei* John Paul II introduced the 'universal' catechism of 1992, which belongs to the second category. He wrote that 'the contents are often presented in a "new" way in order to respond to the questions of our age' and I am certainly one of those who admire the work done to make the new book more up-to-date and comprehensive than any previous manual of official doctrine.

The new catechism was proposed at the Synod of Bishops in Rome in 1985. The bishops desired, we are told, 'a catechism or compendium of all Catholic doctrine regarding both faith and morals [as] a point of reference for the catechisms or compendiums that are prepared in various regions. The presentation of doctrine must be biblical and liturgical. It must be sound doctrine suited to the present life of Christians.' The pope entrusted this task to a commission of cardinals and bishops over which Cardinal Joseph Ratzinger presided. Nine successive drafts were produced with comments from 'numerous theologians, exegetes and catechists, and, above all, of the Bishops of the whole world, in order to produce a better text'. Eventually a catechism was hammered out which could be commended by the pope to 'all the Church's Pastors and the Christian faithful' as 'a sure and authentic reference text for teaching Catholic doctrine and particularly for preparing local catechisms'. The catechism was also commended to everyone 'who wants to know what the Catholic Church believes' with the assurance that 'it is meant to support ecumenical efforts that are moved by the holy desire for the unity of all Christians, showing carefully the content and wondrous harmony of the catholic faith'.

This guide to orthodoxy which emerged after such careful preparation and with such an extensive purpose records many welcome developments in the official teaching of the Roman Catholic Church. Several million copies have been sold in English and other languages, demonstrating the size and seriousness of public interest. The project marked the thirtieth anniversary of the opening of the Second Vatican Council and many of the numerous quotations come from that council's documents. However, disquiet has also been quite widely expressed.

Vatican II was somewhat ambiguous. It opened windows to other churches, to the modern world and to the future; it resulted in many changes in church life and some new emphases in official teaching; it seemed to acknowledge, and even to bless, some pluralism in the Church's life; it raised many hopes or fears of more radical changes, leading to a period of considerable uncertainty. Yet (not surprisingly) it was often conservative and it took care to be loyal to the papacy and to previous councils. It is this conservative side that the new catechism proclaims, sometimes by changing the order in the subject matter, sometimes by selecting one quotation rather than another, sometimes by stressing how many old doctrines were left untouched, sometimes by reviving doctrines which the majority in the council left unmentioned. The mood is different from the confusing but creative 1960s. This catechism of 1992 is the manifesto of a period which has been called the Catholic Restoration, when strong leadership by John Paul II and Cardinal Ratzinger has been the focus of a determined effort to stabilize and unite the Roman Catholic Church in one theology and one discipline. One sign has been the character of the final version of the catechism in English. The translation refers to 'men' instead of 'people' or 'all', for the Vatican does not bless what has become current usage where the language reflects the challenge of feminism.

Vatican II wanted a 'directory' dealing with the 'fundamental principles' of 'the catechetical instruction of the Christian people', and that was issued in 1971, but it did not ask for a new and 'universal' catechism. In this it was unlike the Council of Trent, which resulted in the catechism of 1566. In *Catechesi Tradendae* (1979) John Paul II encouraged 'the Episcopal Conferences of the whole world . . . to prepare genuine catechisms which will be faithful to the essential content of Revelation and up to date in method'. There was no mention of a 'universal' catechism at that stage. Now there seems to be some danger that the detailed catechism which has been authorized so solemnly may be used in a way that would be alien to the spirit of the majority in the council, by not allowing enough local liberty. At least, many Roman Catholic commentators have expressed this fear. The catechism itself teaches that its 'adaptation' is 'indispensable'. This is 'required by differences of culture, age, spiritual maturity and social or ecclesial condition' (24). But such 'adaptation' might have been easier had the catechism included a fuller discussion of 'fundamental principles' together with a fuller expression of the questions of our time. As it is, interpretations enjoying local authority will have to be made in catechisms which will need the approval of the Vatican before they can be published. We shall have to see whether the next French catechism will be as lively as *Pierres Vivantes* (1981). Gone are the days when the Dutch bishops could take pride in their *New Catechism* (1967) and see it used widely before it was revised after criticism by a commission of cardinals. Any criticisms will have to be voiced either by Roman Catholics who may be accused of disloyalty, or by other commentators who may be dismissed as ignorant outsiders or prejudiced enemies.

I am myself not a Roman Catholic and I am aware that much of what I have to say will seem strange, even offensive, if any attention is paid to it in the Roman Catholic Church. But I do not offer my criticisms as a bigoted Protestant, as a very radical Modernist or even as an Anglican who pretends that everything in his own church is better. My Roman Catholic friends whom I love include members of my family. The Anglican scholars who have been so kind as to comment on this book in draft, but who might be embarrassed if I named them, have saved me from some errors of fact or manners (although no doubt some remain) because of their intimate knowledge of Roman Catholic theology and life. And I have not formulated my criticisms by frequent references to Anglican doctrines and customs. If I did so, I might be accused of believing that they have the same kind of authority as is claimed by the teachers of the Roman Catholic Church.

Chapter 6 includes some reference to the 1983 *Code of Canon Law*, since it seemed important to refer to the rule book. I offer some reasons why I am among those who do not wish to live under such a regime but I do not argue that the rules of any other church are altogether superior. Nor do I deny that this code is an improvement on the code of 1917, which in its turn improved the codes of 1500 and 1582 and the previous jumble of medieval laws added to Gratian's *Harmony of Discordant Canons*.

Why, then do I dare to dedicate this book to a pope, the venerated supreme pastor of what is by far the largest branch of the Christian Church? For one reason. Although I write in 1994, a year which to you, Holy Father, may seem far off, I think I can imagine something of your situation. You preside over a church which was transformed in the twentieth century. My own contemporaries who are Roman Catholics in Western Europe and North America may tend to think that the most significant event in church history during our century was the change from being the Church as a fortress repelling enemies by firing off dogmas to being the Church as the pilgrim People of God, loving God and God's world, moving into the future with a joyful faith. And that change, I profoundly agree, is a matter for great thanksgiving. But most Catholics who are in communion with Rome read 'the signs of the times' and give thanks in a different perspective. In 1900 almost two-thirds of the world's Roman Catholics lived in Europe and North America. As I write, almost three-quarters of the much larger numbers live in Latin America, Asia and Africa. The Church has become both more educated and more humble, as the Second Vatican Council registered. But that was probably the last council to be dominated by Europe, for the world-wide Church has also become less white, less rich and more distant from the Vatican. The consequences of both these revolutionary developments will set the agenda for your own years as pope. And some of the challenges which will confront you will be more or less the same throughout the Church, whatever the region.

You will have inherited a severe decline in the number of priests. The number leaving the priesthood in the period 1960–80 was large and many of those remaining are now elderly. In France, for example, or the USA the decline has been very serious, and in the Netherlands the year's crop of new priests fell between 1963 and 1983 from 302 to 32. There are compensations, for this decline has helped to make Roman Catholicism much more of a lay movement like the Church in the days of the apostles. But as an outstanding pastor yourself you will, I am sure, be deeply concerned that the priests, however dedicated, however young, are too few in relation to those who look to them to provide the sacraments, loving care and some teaching. Already in the 1990s there is only one priest to every ten thousand Brazilian Catholics. The Vatican estimates one to more than seven thousand in South America as a whole, and one to more than four thousand in Africa. It seems that the main cause of the numerical decline or restriction has been the wish of actual or potential priests to exercise their human right to marry (as St Peter certainly did). Therefore I hope that you are embarking, however hesitantly, on the policy of allowing this officially in the Latin Church, as it has always been allowed among the 'easterns' who accept papal authority. You face also the rising movement to release the talents of women in church and society. Therefore, for you the question whether women may be selected and ordained to be priests may be no longer closed, and the Anglican decisions about this may no longer be an obstacle on the road to unity.

An easier decision for you is whether women may be deacons, as Phoebe was when St Paul wrote to the church over which you now preside (Rom 16.1, 2). But another hard decision is demanded of you by the conviction of multitudes of the Roman Catholic married laity (not to speak of other Christians) that sexual intercourse which transmits love need not always be 'open to the transmission of life'. Will you allow artificial contraception? You will not if you agree with the teaching repeated in this catechism with all the weight of Roman authority. But may I say that you will if you are to comment convincingly on the expected doubling of the world's population in the twenty-first century (from about six to at least twelve billion) and if the clergy of the Roman Catholic Church are to regain the respect of the laity as teachers of sexual morality?

So I hope now that one day you will inherit the legacy of many centuries, yet your mind will be open to the possibility of substantial changes. When that day comes, there may be a hearing for the wide-ranging criticisms and suggestions which I try to sum up in this book, for the obviously urgent questions which I have just mentioned about gender and sexuality give rise to wider questions. What is the authority of the Bible and of the Church? What is the heart of Christian faith, and what diversity in its expressions is right? What is sex for and what is priesthood for? If we Christians disagree about many matters, what is a realistic hope for our unity? These, too, are 'questions of our time' which I try to ask in this book. In the sixteenth century, nationalist politics sharply increased the force of the Protestant question: what is the authority of the Bible? In the twenty-first century, the importance of sexuality in human life may give explosive power to the Catholic question: what is the authority of the Church?

If you should make any of the answers outlined here your own in your own words, and act on them in your own ways, that would be a major miracle. Under your primacy bishops appointed by the Vatican govern the Roman Catholic Church and most of these bishops are by nature and conviction conservative. This includes the cardinals who will have elected you. And many of the churchgoing laity – men, women and children for whom bishops have a pastoral responsibility felt keenly by the conscience – are more conservative than the bishops themselves. They could be alarmed or hurt even more deeply by proposals for change. Many voices will be raised, many of them coming from your own heart, warning you not to divide the Church whose unity has been so solemnly entrusted to you. You will be reminded about the innumerable divisions of the Protestants who have followed their private judgements in defiance of the mind of the Church. You will be warned against countenancing the 'chaos' which is said to paralyse the Anglican Church from which I come. You will also be warned against sacrificing the truths entrusted to your guardianship for the sake of conformity to liberalism, modernism, post-modernism, agnosticism, materialism and other passing fashions of a godless age. Every time you look at your surroundings in St Peter's basilica and the Vatican palace, every time you address an audience of pilgrims, you will see the triumph of conservative faith. So it may seem common sense to expect few changes in the positions authorised yet again and very confidently in this catechism and this canon law. It is far more likely that under you the 'deposit of faith' will be guarded conservatively, as it was under John Paul II or Paul VI or John XXIII as well as under Pius XII and his predecessors.

But there have been many marvellous and creative changes in the history of the Roman Catholic Church, including the papacy. It was a miracle when the church of Rome survived the might of the Roman empire's persecutions, and the corruption of its own wealth and power, to be the centre of the great civilization of medieval Europe. It was a miracle when the Council of Trent inaugurated a Catholic Reformation, pouring new energy into the life and mission of the Church in many countries and continents after a period when it had seemed that despite many scandals reform was impossible. It was a miracle when the Second Vatican Council again changed Catholic thought and life, after a period when it was widely assumed that no further council would be necessary and the only tendency would be an ever-increasing weight of hierarchy and dogma. With great respect I now submit that it will be your dangerous duty to convene the Third Vatican Council. The work of the Second included some theologians and lay people as advisers to the bishops, with observers from other churches. It seems to be the logic of our ecumenical movement, which Vatican II blessed, that in connection with the next council many uncomfortable voices should be heard. And that dialogue could be the beginning of the restoration of our full communion with each other and with the Christ who cannot be divided.

Whatever you or Vatican III may decide, I hope that in this life or the next I may be allowed to pray that God the life-giving Holy Spirit may guide you, as he guided so many of your predecessors, to teach truth and to practise love. If I humbly echo words spoken in Rome in 1967 by Athenagoras, Patriarch of Constantinople, I must do so knowing that the 1960s are over and that the 1990s have again brought out into the open difficulties about the papacy long felt by the Eastern Orthodox as well as by others. But I do echo that eastern patriarch's tribute, in that time of hope, that the Bishop of Rome is 'the bearer of apostolic grace and the successor to a shining company of holy and wise men who have shed lustre on this see which, by honour and rank, stands first in the living body of Christian churches dispersed throughout the world; and whose holiness, wisdom and valiant fight for the common faith of the undivided Church are a permanent asset and treasure for the entire Christian world'.

DAVID L. EDWARDS

1

The true glory of Catholicism

THE WORD 'CATHOLIC' is inclusive. As the new catechism says, 'it means "universal", in the sense of "according to the totality" or "in keeping with the whole"' (830). It derives from two Greek words – a reminder of Catholicism's history. Ideally, the Catholic Church is the Church of all. And the reality of the Roman Catholic Church is inclusive to a very large extent. Quite often when I have been an Anglican visitor to some country other than England I have had the thought-provoking experience of finding in the local Roman Catholic church an atmosphere both devout and local. More than any other Christian body in the world today, the Roman Catholic Church covers and includes the world. Had the apostle Paul, who was to die in Rome, been able to see this immense development, he might have greeted it with the ecstatic words he wrote to the Galatians: 'Baptized into union with him, you have all put on Christ like a garment. There is no such thing as Jew and Greek, slave and freeman, male and female; for you are all one in Christ Jesus' (3.27, 28). And very often when I have been studying the history or the current affairs of the Christian Church, I have been reminded that my own Church of England, or the Anglican Communion which has now spread (but often thinly) into many other nations, scarcely matters in comparison with the Catholicism which is in communion with the Bishop of Rome and which massively spans the continents and the centuries.

No vision of Christian unity is worth much which excludes this vast fellowship of Christians, by far the largest Christian body in history or in the world today. The World Council of Churches cannot fully live up to its title while the Roman Catholic Church does not belong to it.

'Ecumenical' is a word very close to 'Catholic' in its significance, for it means 'of the inhabited world'. The modern ecumenical movement for Christian unity is often said to have begun with the World Missionary Conference in Edinburgh in 1910, but its scope was limited until in 1964 the Second Vatican Council's decree on ecumenism encouraged Roman Catholic participation. And as I look back on my own long involvement in the ecumenical movement, I am astonished that we who are not Roman Catholics have been so slow to acknowledge how much we have missed by lack of contact with fellow-Christians who are. The World Council of Churches, I think, still has a Rome-shaped gap.

The glories of Catholic Rome are visible and humbling. Awestruck pilgrimages to the 'eternal city' were part of my preparation for this book. And the numbers are impressive, even if they cannot be calculated precisely. The Vatican's estimate is that in 1990 there were about 928,500,000 Roman Catholics in the world, with 4,210 bishops, 403,173 priests, 17,525 permanent deacons, 944,637 members of religious orders, 31,419 members of secular institutes, 2,765 lay missionaries and 378,504 catechists. But the true glory of Catholicism, as seen in the RC Church, does not depend on the visible splendours of Rome or on numbers. Even in countries where Roman Catholics are a small minority they have many attitudes which speak of spiritual largeness, and the constant emphasis that to be a Catholic means to be 'according to the whole' explains why so many Christians who are not in communion with the Bishop of Rome have claimed to be Catholics according to their own consciences. That is, for example, the claim of the ancient Orthodox churches of the east which have rejected the developing claims of the papacy. It is also a claim made by churches which rejected papal jurisdiction during the Reformation of the sixteenth century or later – including my own Anglicanism. Here, the Anglo-Catholic movement which specially stresses this claim has been strong but every other Anglican has affirmed belief in the One, Holy, Catholic and Apostolic Church.

This very widespread celebration of the Catholicity (universality) of the Church is connected with the belief that the continuing existence of the Church is part of the will of God. As John Wesley observed, the New Testament knows no such thing as a solitary Christian. What the New Testament does know is Jesus Christ taking great care over the selection and training of his disciples, eating meals with them which culminated in his last supper, commanding them to eat the bread and drink the wine in remembrance of him after his death, appearing to them in power, promising them that they would be led by the Holy Spirit and sending them out as missionaries on fire. And the New Testament is a library of books written about Jesus Christ by early members of the Church – a library gradually selected from other books by the Church. Without the Church's witness, we should know nothing of Jesus Christ. Without its life which keeps his message alive, we could not meet him for ourselves, even if our meeting takes place outside the Church's structures. Christians who are Catholic are also sinners, but it should never be forgotten that, having castigated them for immorality, Paul could tell the Christians in Corinth that 'you are Christ's body, and each of you a limb or organ of it' (1 Cor 12.27). Many find such claims about the Church difficult to believe, but an invitation may be extended to anyone who, with whatever doubts, wants to meet Jesus Christ. It is an invitation to meet Christians: 'Reach your finger here; look at my hands. Reach your hand here and put it in my side' (John 20.27).

This sense of largeness, of universality, is safeguarded by a visible structure, since Catholicism properly results in an organization which is, although inspired, human. A group of Christians is not left on its own. It is served by a priest who is commissioned and cared for by the wider Church. It belongs to a diocese whose chief pastor is a bishop. The bishop is also part of a wider fellowship whose faith he teaches. He is ordained by other bishops and consults with them ('collegiality'). And the bishops of a region gather under an archbishop ('primacy'). Should all the bishops of the world have a leader? All that I need say now is that this is obviously desirable – and obviously difficult.

The People of God on earth

It is part of the true glory of Catholicism that it is not elitist. As this catechism teaches, 'from the beginning this one Church has been marked by a great diversity which comes from both the variety of God's gifts and the diversity of those who receive them' (814). This brings problems. One is that in order to be Catholic the Church must include people who are not holy. Indeed, as this catechism teaches, 'all members of the Church, including ministers, must acknowledge that they are sinners. In everyone, the weeds of sin will be mixed with the good wheat of the Gospel until the end of time' (827). Because of this it will always be necessary to protest against – or at least, to be silently sceptical about – some compliments to the Church which seem exaggerated. We may blink when we read quotations from saints in this catechism (795) to the effect that 'we have become not only Christians, but Christ himself' (Augustine) or 'Jesus Christ and the Church are just one and we shouldn't complicate the matter' (Joan of Arc). But in many of its attitudes and actions the Catholic Church is 'pastoral', which means that it includes in its embrace those who are impure. Recently it has been a model to other churches in its generosity to members of faith-communities which are not Christian.

In the new catechism we are told that

> throughout history down to the present day, men have given expression to their quest for God in their religious beliefs and behaviour: their prayers, sacrifices, rituals, meditations and so forth. These forms of religious expression, despite the ambiguities they often bring with them, are so universal that the human person can be called a religious being. (28)

Quoting the Second Vatican Council, the catechism says that 'the Church considers all goodness and truth found in these religions as a preparation for the Gospel, a gift from him who enlightens all men that they may at length have life' (843). Elsewhere it says bluntly that 'faith in Jesus Christ and in the one who sent him for our salvation is necessary for obtaining that salvation' (161). But in another passage quoted in this catechism, Vatican II seemed to say that God welcomes non-Christians into heaven – an idea which has distressed a considerable number of Christians. Of course the council was not sentimentally universalist. We are reminded that it taught that 'they could not be saved who, knowing that the Catholic Church was founded as necessary by God, would refuse either to enter it, or to remain in it' (846). But the council did not predict that there would be many people so foolish as to reject an invitation which they understood to be an invitation to heaven, and it did promise that 'those who, through no fault of their own, do not know the Gospel of Christ and his Church, but who nevertheless seek God with a sincere heart, and, moved by grace, try in their actions to do his will as they know it through the dictates of their conscience – those, too, may obtain eternal salvation' (847).

Elsewhere the catechism repeats that 'the Church does not know of any means other than Baptism that assures entrance into eternal beatitude', but it adds that 'God is not bound by his sacraments', so that 'it may be supposed' that 'every man who is ignorant of the Gospel of Christ and his Church, but seeks the truth and does the will of God according to his understanding of it . . . would have desired Baptism if he had known of its necessity'. Therefore such non-Christians 'can be saved' (1257, 1260).

The basic attitude of the Catholic Church to baptized Christians is also humane, because it takes human nature into account. One of the earliest theologians, Irenaeus, taught that 'the glory of God is a human being come alive' and one of the greatest, Thomas Aquinas, endorsed the maxim that in the process the grace of God builds on nature. In its Part Two

('The Celebration of the Christian Mystery') the new catechism, like the slightly earlier codification of canon law, repeats the pattern with which Roman Catholics are happily familiar. In recognition of the fact that children are shaped by their families in all parts of their beings, infants born into Christian families are also baptized as members of a larger family, the Church. They do not have to wait until they are no longer able to be fully Christian children. And because growing human beings are touched by God in many ways which are neither coldly intellectual nor dramatically emotional, a rich pattern is provided of aids to the communication between God and humanity. Children, adolescents and adults are invited to experience the mystery of the Creator through created people and things. People who have lived specially close to God, the saints, are pictured and talked about so that they may become the encouraging friends of today's Christians. People who have dedicated their lives to God with a special commitment, the pastors and teachers ordained and lay, are provided so that Christians may learn that it is possible to become holy without ceasing to be human. Many communities or associations are encouraged for the strengthening of spiritual life. Buildings are provided which demonstrate the truth of the saying that 'we make our architecture and then our architecture makes us'. In those buildings (and sometimes outside them) the sacraments are provided, and in these little dramas other material, everyday things, are used so that human beings may be reached without ceasing to be physical. Water is used in Baptism. Bread and wine are used in the Eucharist or Mass. Other physical realities are used. Hands are laid on heads at Confirmation and Ordination, as a sign of prayer for the gift of the Holy Spirit. Sexual intercourse is used as the completion of the process of holy marriage. Oil is used as a sign of prayers for the Spirit's strengthening, for the healing of the sick and for the peace of the dying. Incense is used as an uplift to the sight and to the sense of smell. And many other symbols are used as help to Christians who remain creatures in space and time. Art is used: because of Catholicism, Christian images have inspired great, as well as more easily popular, art. Music is used, gloriously or catchingly. The Church's year is used: the changing seasons of Advent, Christmas, Epiphany, Lent, Easter and Pentecost help Christians to enter step by step into the story of salvation and many other festivals are aids to understanding and celebrating salvation's results. Pilgrimages are encouraged to places where holiness has been lived. In brief, Catholicism is a religion for human beings who need down-to-earth help.

But the Catholic Church is more than a theatre where what is seen arouses the emotions. The symbols and signs which the Church uses, and specially the sacraments, are used by God to communicate gracious power, so that the new catechism teaches that 'celebrated worthily in faith, the sacraments confer the grace that they signify' (1127). Faith is needed but 'the Church's faith precedes the faith of the believer, who is invited to adhere to it' (1124).

In communities or as individuals, many Catholics have given their whole lives to prayer and one of the most valuable features of the new catechism is its teaching about prayer, gathered into Part Four. Specially valuable is its collection of jewels out of the treasury of Catholic prayer. This rightly reaches its climax in an exposition of the Lord's Prayer; it is beautifully well said that 'we pray first for the Kingdom, then for what is necessary to accept it and co-operate with its coming' (2632). But the catechism includes saints' prayers, and it quotes the words of Teresa of Avila (227):

> Let nothing trouble you, let nothing frighten you.
> Everything passes, God never changes.
> Patience obtains all.
> Whoever has God wants for nothing.
> God alone is enough.

From prayer comes the morality of Christians. For all the sins of its members, the Catholic Church has embodied and encouraged sincere, authentic and often heroic morality in innumerable ways.

Part Three of the new catechism ('Life in Christ') teaches a morality which in many parts would be shared by almost all Christians and admired by many others. The emphasis is often on happiness in a catechism which begins: 'God, infinitely perfect and blessed in himself, in a plan of sheer goodness freely created man to share his own blessed life'. There is warm praise for human virtues such as prudence, justice, fortitude and temperance. The whole range of personal and family life is covered – although, as many think, not always persuasively. Since Leo XIII issued *Rerum Novarum* in 1891, upholding private property but also the right of workers to combine in order to secure just wages, the Social Encyclicals of the popes have constituted the most comprehensive and influential teaching about the foundations of politics and economics to be found anywhere in the Christian world. Here the applause has been accompanied by fewer reservations about current teaching, whatever may be thought about the past.

What stands out from the modern Social Encyclicals is the combination of 'solidarity' with 'subsidiarity'. The first key word recognizes the fact that human nature is social, needing for its fulfilment the State, the family, voluntary associations and many other institutions. That involves a Christian concern for the 'distribution of goods and remuneration for work', indeed 'a more just social order' (1940). The second key word recognizes the fact that human nature also needs the neighbourhood, the association of human beings on a human scale, so that 'a community of a higher order should not interfere with the internal life of a community of a lower order, depriving the latter of its functions, but rather should support it in case of need and help to co-ordinate its activity with the activities of the rest of society, always with a view to the common good' (1883). This is wise teaching, even if the Vatican has not always been a model of the support of Christian communities lower than itself. Such teaching has assisted in the downfall of totalitarian ideologies which have tormented the twentieth century – much as in previous centuries the persecuted Body of Christ defied and outlived previous tyrannies. The Roman Catholic Church is fully entitled to claim a share in the credit for the Christian victory over the diabolical evil of Hitler and Stalin.

And the teaching about solidarity has led in recent times to a strong plea for solidarity among nations. In this catechism war is attacked (although absolute pacifism is not defended) and it is said that 'perverse mechanisms', 'abusive financial systems' and 'iniquitous commercial relations' which 'obstruct the development of less advanced nations must be curbed', particularly since the prosperity of the rich nations is based on resources for which they did not pay a fair price (2438–2439). 'The efforts of poor countries working for growth and liberation must be sustained' (2440). 'Those who are oppressed by poverty are the object of a preferential love on the part of the Church' (2448). Such teachings have inspired many local statements and actions. They will deserve to be remembered if the human race survives its persistent follies.

Conscience, love and truth

Bishops and priests are for Catholics the authorized carriers of the divine forgiveness. Therefore provision is made for the public or private confession of sins against God and the neighbour, leading to liberation from the burden of guilt – a burden which may otherwise deeply damage humanity. Yet this new catechism repeats the insistence that in the last analysis the individual's conscience is to be followed. We read that 'God created man a rational being, conferring on him the dignity of a person who can initiate and control his own actions. God willed that man should be "left in the hand of his own counsel", that he might of his own accord seek the Creator and freely attain full and blessed perfection by cleaving to him' (1730). The Second Vatican Council is quoted as teaching that 'nobody may be forced to act against his convictions, nor is anyone to be restrained from acting in accord with his conscience in religious matters, in private or public, alone or in association with others' – and it is clearly added that this right persists even among 'those who do not live up to their obligation of seeking the truth and adhering to it' (2106). The contrast between those words and the persecutions of the past, initiated or commended by the Roman Catholic Church among other bodies claiming to be Christian (including Anglicans), could not be greater.

Catholicism acknowledges that real love has roots in human nature as well as in God's grace. 'The practice of all the virtues is animated and inspired by charity, which upholds and purifies our human ability to love, and raises it to the supernatural perfection of divine love' (1827). Therefore love is at the heart of Catholicism, whatever may be thought about unloving acts by Catholics in common with Protestants. This catechism (2298) regrets that in the past 'pastors of the Church' often failed to protest against 'cruel practices to maintain law and order' and 'adopted in their own tribunals the prescriptions of Roman law concerning torture'. (It is a diplomatically phrased apology for the Inquisition.) But the Council of Trent is quoted approvingly: 'The whole concern or doctrine and its teaching must be directed to the love that never ends. Whether something is proposed for belief, for hope or for action, the love of our Lord must always be made accessible, so that anyone can see that all the works of perfect Christian virtue spring from love and have no other objective than to arrive at love' (25).

This new catechism also reminds us, in equally striking terms, of the importance of truth. In what I have written or quoted so far, Catholicism is praised as being humane, down-to-earth and loving. So it is, essentially. But that is not all there is to Catholicism. In this catechism the Old Testament is cited as attesting that 'God is the source of all truth' and it said that 'to his disciples Jesus teaches the unconditional love of truth'. Vatican II is quoted as teaching that 'it is in accordance with their dignity that all men, because they are persons . . . are both impelled by their nature and bound by a moral obligation to seek the truth, especially religious truth. They are also bound to adhere to the truth once they come to know it and to direct their whole lives in accordance with the demands of truth' (2465–2467).

It should come as no surprise that the present claims of what has become known as the *magisterium* (the papacy, the considerable bureaucracy which acts on behalf of the papacy, and the councils of bishops), and the lesser claims made by individual bishops and priests, are all claims to teach not opinion but truth, based on beliefs that such authorities are inspired by 'the Spirit of Truth' (John 14.17), the Spirit guiding 'into all the truth' (John 16.13), the Spirit making 'the Church of the living God the pillar and bulwark of the truth' (1 Tim 3.15). Every one of the 2,865 paragraphs of this new *Catechism of the Catholic Church* states the truth as its authors, or the other authorities quoted, understand the truth. As one who doubts or denies the truth of many statements made in this long document, I have to insist to myself and to any reader that the positions taken are sincerely believed to be true. The comprehensive extent of this catechism, the great care taken in its preparation, the long history of systematic study and teaching which lies behind it, the confidence that it will lead to further study and teaching around the world – all these are features of Roman Catholicism as service to the truth. Those of us who are not Roman Catholics should not pretend that any of us have records which match this record of continuous, deeply serious, officially sponsored and officially publicized rational thinking about God ('theology'). In this respect at least, Roman Catholicism is a model deserving imitation everywhere.

It is therefore the duty of many of us who care seriously about the truth in Christianity to study this catechism, testing its truthfulness as best we may. We are 'impelled' and 'bound' to do so. It is very difficult, and therefore rare, to be rigorous without being uncharitable, and to speak the truth in love; but nothing less than that must be our aim as we respond to this catechism, which is nothing less than a summary of the Roman Catholic Church's official teaching in the 1990s.

Before the final revision of the chapters which follow, I have therefore taken advice and I have asked myself whether it is right to include so much criticism. At three points in particular it may be felt that I have failed to preserve that spirit of love which is the soul of the ecumenical movement bringing Christians together. I criticize this catechism for being too conservative in some of its teachings, and it may seem that I have forgotten that many Christians who are not Roman Catholics, as well as many who are, would prefer a tradition which has such immense authority to my own views, which are modernizing if not 'Modernist'. I criticize incidents in the history of the papacy and it may seem that I am an old-fashioned Protestant controversialist. And at the end I am unable to be very positive about the future shape of the 'Petrine ministry' of the 'universal pastor', the Bishop of Rome. In these matters the reader will have to judge, but I submit brief explanations of my motives.

I have tried to express not merely my own opinions but positions which are shared by many Roman Catholics who like me have been influenced by modern critical scholarship and by the modern feeling that one ought not to claim too much dogmatic certainty about religion. The positions which I defend against the conservatism of this catechism will, I hope, be seen even more widely in the future to reflect (not completely!) the unromantic splendour of truth; or at least they will, I hope, be seen to be positions which a Christian may hold as alternatives to what has been orthodoxy and to be motivated by the love of Jesus who taught 'the unconditional love of truth'.

I have had to go into the history of the papacy in some detail. This is because it is still claimed that the Roman Catholic Church is, and always has been, so closely connected with Jesus Christ himself that its leadership is entitled to the 'assent' of all Christians even when it does not claim to be stating an infallible dogma. But in common with many others I hold that history shows that the official position has in fact changed quite often – and also that the Church's leadership, being human, has been prone to theological, moral or political errors, so that it has been, and is, not always entitled to 'assent' or obedience. Many Roman Catholics have reached the same sad conclusion. And of course I do not claim that the leadership of any other church has been any different. As Paul observed, we Christians all have the glory – in pots made of earth. I beg readers not to think that my critical treatment of the history of the popes, which in some respects contrasts sadly with their developing claims, is my idea of a balanced, fair summary of the whole history of Roman Catholicism. It is my ambition to include such a summary in a book still to be written, and to be called with a mixture of thanksgiving and penitence *The First Two Thousand Years*.

In my last chapter I am hesitant about the functions of the popes of the coming centuries in the service of the truth which is the Gospel, Christ's news about God. This is because it is not for me to say what will prove possible and acceptable as unifying institutions after changes which I cannot foresee. Nor can I predict what personalities will take the lead. (Those who elect popes tend to want a fresh personality.) After pleading for greater modesty, it would not be fitting to attempt to pontificate about what is at present unknowable: the future. But I am convinced that Catholicism has a very long and a very great future, with the Bishop of Rome as its most influential unifier, teacher and pastor. Otherwise I should not have troubled to work on this troublesome book.

CHAPTER

2

The truth
about the Bible

THE NEW CATECHISM often teaches that the Bible provides the most
important message which Catholic faith hears. The leadership or
magisterium of the Church 'is not superior to the Word of God, but is its
servant' (86). 'Through all the words of Sacred Scripture, God speaks a
single Word, his one utterance in whom he expresses himself completely.
For this reason, the Church has always venerated the Scriptures as she
venerates the Lord's Body' (102, 103). That priority is very welcome, for
in earlier times the lack of reliable and officially encouraged translations
from Hebrew and Greek into the living languages of the peoples was a gap
in Catholicism. One problem was that unofficial translations contained
notes contradicting Catholic teachings, but it was a tragedy that in late
medieval England (for example) the bishops prohibited any translation at
all. When the English Bible began to shape the language and life of the
nation, it could not be forgotten that in 1536 William Tyndale, a
translator often echoed in the new versions, had been burned for heresy.
Filling another gap, Luther's Bible in German was mightily influential
and the next century virtually identified international Protestantism with
Bible-preaching, Bible-reading and Bible-quoting. The impact of the
Bible on the consciences and the imaginations, the emotions and the
actions, of countless Christians was the greatest achievement of the
Reformation and did much to compensate for the tragic loss of so much
beauty, piety and settled happiness in the Catholic centuries.

Roman Catholic translations did appear in response to these challenges,
but none had the circulation of the Protestant versions, which the papacy
was still denouncing vigorously in the nineteenth century. There were for

long no RC equivalents to the Bible societies which distributed these Protestant versions far and wide. Many signals were given that the laity needed to study the Bible less than they needed instruction by the clergy, for the doctrinal confusion in Protestantism seemed to show that without interpretation by the Church's tradition lay use of the Bible could disturb and mislead. When the laity were given authorized translations, the superiority of the Latin Vulgate (mainly the work of Jerome in the fourth century) was still indicated. Its Latin terms influenced even scholars who sought to be Bible-based. In 1546 the Council of Trent pronounced this the only 'authentic' translation: 'let no one dare or presume to reject it on any grounds'. Modern scholarship has often vindicated Jerome's use of ancient manuscripts but his work, like every other scholar's, was not perfect and it was not progress that no authorized revision was published between 1592 and 1926. When Ronald Knox published a new English translation of the Bible at the request of the Roman Catholic bishops of England and Wales in the 1940s, it was still based on the Vulgate, not on the original texts (which were, however, consulted). But in the 1960s Pope Paul VI encouraged new, including 'common', or ecumenical translations of the Bible, and in this book I have used one such, the Revised English Bible (1989).

This catechism of 1992 clearly teaches that 'the study of the sacred page should be the very soul of sacred theology' and that all the faithful should read 'the divine Scriptures' frequently. 'Ignorance of the Scriptures is ignorance of Christ' (a quotation from Jerome also used by Vatican II), so that 'access to the sacred Scriptures ought to be opened wide to the Christian faithful' (131–133). And because of its reverence for the Bible, confirmed by innumerable quotations from it, many of the teachings in this catechism will command the assent of almost all believing and practising Christians.

Because the Bible is thus opened to all, many modern Christians are, however, able to question whether the catechism uses the Bible satisfactorily. Nowadays the exposition of the Bible by high ecclesiastical authority can be challenged by a person whose relevant knowledge is confined to a reading of the plain words of Scripture. But sometimes a question may be asked by a person who, without necessarily being an expert, has access not only to the Bible itself but also to some part of the immense volume of modern scholarly study of it, including a very large number of Roman Catholic contributions. When Richard Simon pioneered modern, 'critical' biblical scholarship among Roman Catholics, he was attacked on all sides before his death in 1712; and when another Frenchman, M. J. Lagrange, took up the task at the École Biblique in Jerusalem in the 1890s, he had his wings clipped by the Pontifical Biblical

Commission established in 1902. However, as we can see immediately by looking into such a work as the *New Jerome Biblical Commentary* edited by Raymond Brown and others in 1989, a firm grasp of the Bible is no longer out of the ordinary Roman Catholic's reach, and RC biblical scholarship is no longer confined to a few harassed specialists. In his foreword to that commentary, Cardinal Carlo Martini wrote that 'the concentration on problems of historical and literary criticism springs from serious attention to the "marvellous condescension" of God in transmitting his word in human language. It is precisely this route that leads us more deeply into an understanding of the message.'

In this situation, when there is so much to celebrate, it is disappointing that biblical texts which begin the prologue to this new catechism come from sources which are widely known to be vulnerable in the light of biblical scholarship.

One text is John 17.3: 'Father . . . this is eternal life, that they may know you, the only true God, and Jesus Christ whom you have sent'. These words come strangely in the midst of a prayer offered by Jesus and today almost all scholars would agree that they are the words not of Jesus but of the author of the gospel. Other words to express this truth might have been chosen.

Another text is Acts 4.12: 'There is no other name under heaven given among mortals by which we must be saved'. These words ascribed to Peter have been made controversial by being held to deny the hope of heaven to all adherents of non-Christian religions (as this catechism does not). They can be quoted in a way that suggests that Peter was making a totally damning judgement about all the founders and teachers who are venerated in these religions although it is probable that he was unaware of the existence of India (for example). But it is most unlikely that these words are entirely accurate records of what was said. Luke, the author of Acts, did not claim to have been present on this occasion and it is generally thought that he wrote some fifty years after the event. The speeches in the Acts of the Apostles appear to be his compositions. The claim that Jesus is the unique 'saviour' is gloriously true and vitally important. It refers to the experienced fact that Jesus saves people from sins and fears, and from other entanglement in evil, with a power which no other founder or teacher of a religion has exercised. It seems a pity not to express this truth by some other reference to the New Testament. We may also regret the teaching (183) that 'the Lord himself affirms: "The one who believes and is baptized will be saved; the one who does not believe will be condemned" '. This is a quotation of Mark 16.16, generally regarded as an addition to Mark's authentic gospel, which ends at 16.8. The catechism itself is far more cautious in its attitude to non-Christians.

A similarly critical question arises about Matthew 28.18–20, quoted in the second paragraph of the catechism. This 'great commission' has been an inspiration to many heroic lives but it seems to almost all scholars highly improbable that before his ascension into heaven Jesus Christ urged his apostles to 'make disciples in all nations and to baptize them in the name of the Father and of the Son and of the Holy Spirit'. It is far more likely that this formula reflects the practice of the church known to Matthew, having been developed from the earlier practice of baptizing 'in the name of Jesus Christ' (referred to in 1 Cor 1.13 and Acts 2.38; 10.48). And the surprise that Gentiles could be baptized, emphasized in the Acts of the Apostles, would not have been so great had the Lord of the Church clearly commanded this inclusiveness.

The prominence given to these texts as a prologue to the whole catechism seems to be open to question because if we are to hear 'the single Word' which God 'speaks' in the Scriptures, we need to try to distinguish between the transmission of that Word and interference which echoes voices which, however worthy of our attention, are not divine. Therefore many of us who are (for better or for worse) modern have to ask questions which include this one: what is the true relationship between the Word of God and words in the Bible which witnessed to that Word? In our time the Word may need to be translated from the expressions used in a vanished age, as the words in Hebrew, Greek or Latin once needed to be translated into the languages of many peoples.

The real authority of myths

The catechism which begins with these less than central texts pays too little serious attention to other questions raised by modern critical study of the Bible.

The Hebrew Scriptures seem to be usually quoted as if they related actual events; for example, we are told that 'the covenant with Noah after the flood' was an event in 'the divine economy towards the nations' (56). It may seem pedantic to make such criticisms, for the catechism does sometimes reflect knowledge of the work of the scholars; for example, although we are told that King David was 'the first prophet of Jewish and Christian prayer' in the psalms 'which bear his name' (2579), we can also find a reference to the fact that 'the psalms arose from the communities of the Holy Land and the Diaspora' (2586). More important is a failure which matters to prayer itself – the failure to respond to the questions of our time about the Old Testament. For example, the story of Abraham is told as if he really was 'asked to sacrifice the son God had given him' – asked by God 'as a final stage in the purification of his faith' (2572). Many now ask: what kind of God was that? Quite often the catechism shows that the absence of full attention to modern biblical scholarship can lead to some highly questionable theology which is inferior to the theology now being taught by individual Roman Catholics at academic and popular levels.

We are told that 'God fashioned man with his own hands' (704). That is a quotation from Irenaeus in the second century and the catechism adds that the hands were 'the Son and the Holy Spirit'. A recognition of a metaphor may well be implied, but the catechism goes on to repeat from Irenaeus that this creation meant that 'even what was visible would bear the divine form', which may leave the untutored thinking that the invisible God really has a 'form' (whatever is meant by that) like a human being's – and no attention is paid to the truly marvellous story of the actual emergence of *homo sapiens* in evolution. We are also told that 'the account of the Fall in Genesis 3 uses figurative language, but affirms a primeval event, a deed that took place at the beginning of the history of man. Revelation gives us certainty of faith that the whole of human history is marked by the original fault freely committed by our first parents' (390).

These parents, Adam and Eve, were, we are taught, created 'in a state that would be surpassed only by the glory of the new creation in Christ' (374). It was a state of 'holiness' – not of innocence, before moral decisions can, or need, be made – and it was 'intended to be fully "divinized" by God in glory'. There is no mention of the various ancient speculations about what would have been the lives of Adam and Eve had they not sinned, but we are told that by their 'first disobedience' they 'immediately lost the grace of original holiness', 'death makes its entrance into human history' and the whole of creation became 'alien and hostile to humanity' and 'subject to decay' (398–400).

This section of the catechism, which virtually repeats the Council of Trent's decree (1546), will seem to most readers to imply an acceptance of the literal truth of the Adam and Eve story, and as such it will seem to contradict scientific knowledge. There are many gaps and uncertainties in science as it exists in the 1990s, but it is known that *homo sapiens* evolved from less developed animals through many stages between ape and man. Early members of this species must have been much closer in their behaviour to less developed animals than to the saints who define 'holiness'. Everything that is material decays, however slowly, and everything that lives dies, usually quite quickly; at no stage could a human being have been immortal physically. But species which survive and flourish do so because their environment favours their equipment and their needs; it is not 'alien and hostile'. All that we know. We do not live in the pre-scientific age when the Roman Catechism of 1566 could advise: 'By referring to the sacred history of Genesis the pastor will easily make himself familiar with these things for the instruction of the faithful'.

This catechism of 1992 shows, however, that the progress made in the official RC use of this part of Genesis has been limited despite the welcome given here to 'many scientific studies which have greatly enriched our knowledge of the age and dimensions of the cosmos, the development of life forms and the appearance of man' (283). As late as the 1890s scholars who accepted that Adam's body was a transformation of previous existing bodies were being forced by the Vatican to withdraw their publications, but in 1950 Pius XII allowed this as a 'speculation'. That pope still insisted on 'monogenism' (the belief that the whole species of *homo sapiens* is descended from one father). Such a belief about early man cannot be disproved because the evidence provided by a few scattered fossils is so uncertain, but monogenism is a belief not commonly held about any other species. It has been argued by some RC theologians that the 'death' resulting from Adam's fall has been spiritual disaster, not biological death – an idea which reflects the truth that we die physically not because we are sinners but because we are animals. However, this 1992 catechism tells us firmly that 'the Church's *magisterium*, as authentic interpreter of the affirmations of Scripture and Tradition, teaches that death entered the world through sin' (1008).

The catechism adds an account of 'original sin' which is inferior to the account given by many RC theologians nowadays.

We are told that

following St Paul, the Church has always taught that the overwhelming misery which oppresses men and their inclination towards evil and death cannot be understood apart from their connection with Adam's sin and the fact that he has transmitted to us a sin with which we are all born afflicted, a sin which is the 'death of the soul'. Because of this certainty of faith, the Church baptizes, for the remission of sins, even tiny infants who have not committed personal sin. (403)

This teaching said to be both the only way of understanding and a 'certainty' asks us to believe in a God who allows or orders 'the overwhelming misery that oppresses people and their inclination towards evil and death' because one man, the first to be created, was disobedient to him and because the sin of Adam has been transmitted to every other human being before that human being is born. An individual is not guilty, we are told, merely because he or she has sinned; he or she is guilty (and therefore liable to be excluded from heaven) because another individual, Adam, sinned many thousands of years ago. A tiny infant who is innocent because incapable of moral decisions still needs to be baptized 'for the remission of sins'.

Among the great teachers of the Catholic Church, Augustine held that unbaptized babies who die go to a mild version of hell, while Thomas Aquinas held that in 'limbo' they are merely deprived forever of the beatific vision of God. In 1439 the Council of Florence taught that unbaptized adults have inherited Adam's 'original' sin, although they may not have committed their own unrepented 'mortal' sins. Therefore they must go straight to hell. This tradition was little changed by the Protestant Reformers, as the Book of Common Prayer of the Church of England (1662) bears witness when it gives its reasons for baptizing infants. To many Christians in our time, however, a God who deals in any such way with humanity, including innocent infants, does not seem to be a just judge, let alone the loving Father of whom Jesus spoke.

It comes as a relief to know that, despite its claim to the authority of Genesis as interpreted by Paul to the Romans (in chapter 5), this explanation of human sinfulness and mortality is not taught elsewhere in the Hebrew or Christian Scriptures except in the Wisdom of Solomon (2.24), which blames the devil, and Ecclesiasticus (25.24), which blames Eve. It is also a relief to see that the catechism does not require us to believe that this story explains why the Middle East is fertile in parts ('a garden in Eden away to the east'); why men and women have the same flesh ('the rib he had taken out of the man the Lord God built into a woman'); why snakes crawl in the ground, seem to eat dust and can be poisonous; why women have sexual appetites and pains in labour; and why agriculture can be a sweaty business. In this ancient Hebrew myth all those explanations are as prominent as is the explanation of sin and death, yet modern people are not asked to treat them with complete solemnity – any more than we are asked to take the story of the Tower of Babel in Genesis 11 literally as the explanation of the existence of many languages.

It is sad that this should be the catechism's teaching about sin, evil and death, for it suggests that if we are to take Christian doctrine seriously we must take literally the myth of a golden age in the remote past. A far more illuminating interpretation of the great story of Adam and Eve has been offered by many modern teachers of Christianity including Roman Catholics. It is fully compatible with scientific knowledge and fully authoritative for modern consciences. In Hebrew 'Adam' means 'Man' and 'Eve' means 'life'. Putting things very simply, the myth dramatizes several facts about our human condition. None of us lives in Paradise. All of us inherit a partly evil legacy from the sins of the past before we were born. Men and women (not infants) have the 'knowledge of good and evil' but do not make the moral decisions which are wanted by the God revealed in the Bible. Often our inclination is towards evil. Some of our wrong decisions put us out of harmony with our Creator. Some put us out of harmony with our environment which is his creation, for we damage nature by wanton misuse. Some wreck the dignified harmony between the sexes. Some cause human deaths through violence, the unjust distribution of resources, or the neglect of health. Another terrible reminder of human feebleness is provided by the fact that everyone dies, whether or not that is anyone's fault. So the myth is a very powerful picture of the evil and misery known in human existence in every generation. It portrays the Living Man as in need of salvation and it teaches that the Living God comes to the rescue when it says that 'the man and his wife heard the sound of the Lord God walking about in the garden at the time of the evening breeze'.

The story of Adam and Eve does not explain why, amid all the glories of the garden of Eden, the serpent was so wickedly 'cunning' that he caused their downfall. In other words, it does not discuss the ultimate origins of evil in a creation which often seems, on the whole, good. But this catechism tells us that

> Scripture and the Church's tradition see in this being [the serpent] a fallen angel, called 'Satan' or 'the devil' . . . The Church teaches that Satan was at first a good angel, created by God . . . Scripture speaks of a sin of these angels. This 'fall' consists in the free choice of these created spirits, who radically and irrevocably rejected God and his reign . . . It is the irrevocable character of their choice, and not a defect in God's infinite mercy, that makes the angels' sin unforgivable.

John of Damascus, who died before 750, is then quoted as teaching: 'There is no repentance for angels after their fall, just as there is no repentance for men after death' (391–393). Many modern Christians are, however, likely to ask: what are we to make of that myth, which admittedly inspired Dante and Milton? How can we know about this fall of the angels, as momentous as it is mysterious?

The existence of the 'spiritual, non-corporeal beings that the sacred Scriptures usually call "angels" ' is, this catechism tells us, a 'truth of faith' since 'the witness of Scripture is as clear as the unanimity of Tradition' (328). And the stories about angels in the Hebrew Bible seem to be taken literally (332). However, the story of the rebellion against God by Satan and other bad angels was told in the first book of Enoch (written in the second century before Christ and preserved in Ethiopic). It is not in the Hebrew Bible. (There, the prologue to the story of Noah in Genesis

6. 1–8, when 'the Lord saw how great was the wickedness of human beings on earth', tells of the 'sons of the gods' having 'intercourse with mortals' and producing giants, and the prologue to the book of Job suggests that Satan remained on speaking, even familiar, terms with God long after the Fall: these are different myths.) The story is referred to briefly in the New Testament, but not in places which are sufficiently central to justify its key position in this catechism. It is mentioned in the Letter of Jude (6) immediately before references to angels committing fornication and indulging in unnatural lusts, and the archangel Michael disputing with the devil for the possession of Moses' body. A similar reference to the story is made (not by Peter) in the Second Letter of Peter (2.4).

Detailed beliefs about angels became prominent late in the history and scriptures of ancient Israel and further details were developed for Christians mainly by the visionary last book of the Bible and by a mystical theologian who wrote about 500 and was called Dionysius. The mission of angels is mentioned without argument or elaboration in many passages of Scripture, including the teaching of Jesus and reports about his life and resurrection, but in modern times it has often been thought that this is an example of the use of popular imagery which had the additional merit of preserving a reverent reticence about the direct activity of God. 'Satan' or 'the devil' is often referred to in the New Testament, but in modern times the difficulty of attributing personality to negative evil has often been appreciated, and again it has been suggested that conventional language was being used. In this connection it was used to express by personal imagery the abiding truth of the infectious power of evil, strengthened by more-than-personal organizations, customs and atmospheres – the 'principalities and powers' which the letters to the Ephesians and Colossians say have been defeated by Christ.

Many modern Christians, including Roman Catholics, do not put the existence of angels close to the heart of their faith. Many interpret the old stories as imaginative attempts to picture the facts that evil is Man's adversary (in Hebrew *satan*), and that God's will to save us from evil uses many messengers (in Greek *angeloi*). There is no strong movement to remove references to angels from Christian worship, one reason being that modern Christians are often inclined to think it probable that non-human life exists on other planets in our mysteriously immense universe. And who are we to exclude non-humans from 'the whole company of heaven'? But to many Christians in our time, it is not clear that anything of spiritual value would be lost if all the references in the Bible or Christian history to the work of bad angels were translated into references to the power of evil, and if all references to good angels were held to be expressions referring to the work of God.

The basic argument against the literal truth of the myth of the fall of the angels is, however, similar to the argument about blaming sin, evil and death on Adam's fall. If taken literally, the story asks us to believe in a God who created a being (now Satan, not Adam) who could never be forgiven for one act of disobedience, yet who was given the power to corrupt for ever both humanity and the rest of the visible creation. As this catechism recognizes, when fallen angels are believed to have such power it becomes a 'great mystery' that divine providence, which 'with strength and gentleness guides human and cosmic history' should 'permit diabolical activity' (395).

It seems a pity that the extensive Christian discussion about the mystery of evil in relation to the mystery of God ('theodicy') should be trivialized by this reliance on the obscure myth of the angels' fall. It seems wiser to conclude that we cannot understand why such dismaying quantities of the human inclination to folly and wickedness, and of other features of existence which are usually reckoned evil, should have been permitted by a loving and powerful Creator to exist. The book of Job demonstrates for ever that these things should not be blamed entirely on the individual who commits a sin. Any creation must be imperfect; otherwise it too would be divine. But is this creation really 'the best of all possible worlds'? (Was Voltaire wrong to ridicule Leibniz?) Is it a sufficient consolation to say that 'all shall be well' in the end? (Was Ivan Karamazov wrong?) Is life in the end meaningless? (Was Macbeth or Lear wrong?) Yet in the midst of our asking or our agnosticism, perhaps our anguish, we can continue to believe in that Creator if we also believe that the good in the creation outweighs the evil, or in the end conquers or transforms it. A bold saying of Thomas Aquinas is quoted: 'God permits evil in order to draw forth some greater good' (412). Such a faith can be held in a manner that is not complacent. It could have been stated persuasively in this catechism, as light in our human darkness.

Given the human inclination to sin, what is good behaviour? The use of the Ten Commandments to answer that question is a very old custom. The Roman Catechism of 1566 adhered to the early, medieval and Protestant practice of basing Christian teaching about morality on the famous ten and there is a modern way of continuing this tradition, expanding them so that they 'state what is required in the love of God and love of neighbour' (2067). Much in the teaching about 'the life of faith' in Part Three, based on these commandments, is both careful and convincing. But it is nowadays inevitable that many should ask what authority these 'commandments' retain.

A convincing answer is not helped when this catechism repeats from Scripture, without explanation, that God 'spoke with a loud voice' and 'wrote with his finger' (2056–2058). This apparently literal acceptance of the myth that the Law of Moses was directly revealed by God to Israel in the wilderness is immediately qualified by the reminder that the Ten Commandments are given in two versions, in Exodus (20.1–17) and Deuteronomy (5.6–22). It may be asked whether it would not have been wiser to state explicitly that in the form which is in the Scriptures, the Law of Moses was not entirely the work of God's voice or finger, or of the inspired mind of Moses. It was the result of the development of legislation (which Jews and Christians are entitled to think inspired) arising in a number of different situations in Israel's history.

The historical development of the Hebrew Scriptures has been explored in many scholarly studies, including distinguished contributions by Roman Catholics. After those studies, it still seems truthful to say positively that the authority of the Law of Moses is the authority possessed by the beginnings of a process of ethical and social teaching which covered many years and which eventually included 613 commandments in Scripture according to the standard rabbinic calculation. This great moral tradition has never ceased in the history of Judaism; yet Christians believe that it was radically and rightly changed by the revolutionary impact of Jesus. Many Christians, including Roman Catholics, also think that the Christian part of this tradition ought to continue to be creative, age after age, under continuing inspiration by God as times change. That is an authority to which modern consciences can submit and on which modern behaviour can be based. And this is not a merely academic point. Among the duties of Christians in such a time as this, none can be more important than the proclamation of a basis for the difference between right and wrong which can be recognized as belonging to the real world.

The New Testament

As the new catechism expounds the New Testament, the question about the relationship between the words of the Bible and the realities of life (past, present and future) intensifies.

We find here, as we found in the treatment of the Hebrew Scriptures, welcome words which imply a blessing, not only on the faithful laity's more intimate knowledge of the Bible, but also on the labours of honest scholars in collaboration with their non-RC colleagues. But this catechism comes very near to an untrue fundamentalism in its introductory, general statements about the inspiration and truth of Sacred Scripture, quoting the teaching of Vatican II that 'all the books of the Old and the New Testaments, whole and entire, in all their parts . . . have God for their author'. (Since the fifth century the Latin word *auctor* has been used in this connection, but it is better translated as Originator.) God 'employed' the human authors of the sacred books so that they 'should consign to writing all that he wanted written, and no more. Since all that the inspired authors or sacred writers affirm should be regarded as affirmed by the Holy Spirit, we must acknowledge that the books of Scripture firmly, faithfully and without error teach that truth which God, *for the sake of our salvation*, wished to see confided to the Sacred Scriptures' (105–107).

The words which I have put into italics can be used as a charter for truthful biblical studies. In *Divino Afflante Spiritu* (1945), Pius XII quoted the teaching of Leo XIII: 'there is no error whatsoever if the sacred writer, speaking of things of the physical order, used terms which were commonly used at the time to speak of things in no way profitable to salvation'. Pope Pius himself taught that 'in order to determine what the authors of the ancient Near East intended to signify by their words and what literary forms they intended to use', it was necessary 'to make proper use of the aids afforded by history, archaeology, ethnology and other sciences'. Such a blessing on biblical studies permitted loyal Roman Catholic scholars to agree with non-RC colleagues that, for example, the story of Jonah and the whale need not be taken literally. Even parts of the Scriptures which are apparently historical may be taken as examples of a 'literary form' which is not strictly factual, such as the accounts given in Chronicles of events narrated somewhat more factually in the books of Samuel and Kings. Indeed, in 1975 a distinguished American scholar, Raymond Brown, whose writings display a full acceptance of historical criticism of the New Testament, rejoiced that Vatican II 'made it possible to restrict inerrancy to the essential religious affirmations of a biblical book made for the sake of our salvation' (*Crises Facing the Church*, p. 115). Aidan Nichols, a prominent English theologian, holds that 'it is the entire Bible as a self-correcting whole that enables us to identify the inerrant aspect of any one text' (*The Shape of Catholic Theology*, 1991, p. 154).

In this catechism of 1992 some flexibility in interpreting the Bible is recommended. There is approving reference to 'an ancient tradition' which teaches that in addition to the literal sense of a passage, there may be an allegorical sense ('we can acquire a more profound understanding of historical events by recognizing their significance in Christ'), a moral sense ('the events reported in Scripture can lead us to act justly') and an anagogical sense ('we can view realities and events in terms of their eternal significance'). But no clear reference is made to more modern ways of interpreting the Bible, which start from the belief that what is authoritative for the Christian is not any particular text read out of context but the message which is proclaimed by the authors of the Bible taken as a whole, with the story of Jesus at its centre.

The reference to the 'ancient tradition' insists, as Thomas Aquinas did, that 'all other senses of Scripture are based on the literal', defined here as 'the meaning conveyed by the words of Scripture and discovered by exegesis, following the rules of sound interpretation' (116). But if we ask what these rules are, we are firmly reminded that Vatican II decreed that

it is the task of exegetes to work toward a better understanding and explanation of the meaning of Sacred Scripture, in order that their research may help the Church to form a firmer judgement. For, of course, everything that has been said about the manner of interpreting Scripture is ultimately subject to the judgement of the Church which exercises the divinely conferred commission and ministry of watching over and interpreting the Word of God. (119)

Although the rules of good scholarship are not excluded, it is clear that in the last resort the decisive rules, and therefore interpretations, are made by the bishops headed by the pope, to be accepted by scholars along with everyone else.

The Second Vatican Council, as quoted here, also declared that the Church holds firmly that the four gospels, 'whose historicity she unhesitatingly affirms, faithfully hand on what Jesus, the Son of God, while he lived among men, really did and taught for their eternal salvation'. In some recognition of modern scholarship which has shown the extent to which the history in the gospels has been edited and preached before being written, it was added that the apostles handed on to their hearers after Christ's ascension a 'fuller understanding' of what he had said and done and that the authors of the gospels 'chose certain of the many elements which had been handed down, either orally or already in written form; others they synthesized or explained with an eye to the situation of the churches'. But this cautious acknowledgement of editorial elements in the gospels was checked by the statement that 'always they have told us the honest truth about Jesus' (126).

Christians who have accepted the solid results of modern scholarship would not dispute that the intention of the gospel writers was to tell the truth about their Lord. But innumerable studies have shown that the final writers of the gospels differed in their perceptions of it. Many of the differences were minor, but these include different versions of the material common to Luke and Matthew, so that not all the sayings of Jesus in the gospels can be reported with complete accuracy. There are substantial differences between the editorial tendencies of Mark, Luke and Matthew and there are irreconcilable differences between the account of the life of

Jesus which emerges from these three 'synoptic' gospels and John's gospel. In the former, Jesus cleanses the Temple near the end; in the latter, near the beginning. In the former, the Last Supper is the Passover meal; in the latter it takes place a day earlier. The Jesus who is portrayed by John often rebukes 'the Jews' for not recognizing that he is the Messiah and the 'only Son of God', and this catechism quotes such sayings along with sayings from the other three gospels (444). Yet in the other gospels Jesus is in public reticent about himself to the point of secrecy. Another serious example of differences may be found in any study of the accounts of the Resurrection in the four gospels, comparing them with the earlier teaching recorded by Paul (1 Cor 15.3–7). Even the Lord's Prayer and the Beatitudes come to us in slightly different versions.

Fortunately, however, the reader will not be burdened here by one more summary of the conclusions of modern study of the gospels. I attempted to provide such a summary in *The Real Jesus* (1992), emphasizing that although many differences between the gospels can be proved to exist by a careful reading, substantial information about the truly historical Jesus is conveyed by them, and is reliable either certainly or with a high probability. The gospels are painted portraits, not photographs, but they tell us much about the man from Nazareth – and about the 'Living One' (Rev 1.18).

Many of these detailed differences do not matter much if we are concerned, as this catechism rightly says we should be, 'for our eternal salvation'. But if we are also concerned for truth, as this catechism memorably tells us to be, we may blink when we are told that the historicity of all four gospels must be affirmed without hesitation. It is erroneous to claim that the gospels are completely 'without error', for they disagree with each other at points small or large. And for honest students of the Scriptures, this matters in practice. The Congregation for the Doctrine of the Faith subjected Edward Schillebeeckx, the most eminent New Testament scholar among Roman Catholics, to a humiliating interrogation during the 1970s, because his laboriously set-out researches had led him to some conclusions thought to be heretical. This investigation was dropped, but it inspired Peter Hebblethwaite, who was to be the sympathetic biographer of Paul VI, to protest in *The New Inquisition?* (1980). It also matters that when considering theological or ethical problems Christians need not think that the problems are entirely solved by quotations of texts taken out of the context provided by the whole Bible.

One illustration may be given here of the difficulties which arise when Christians are taught in a style which first treats the New Testament as if its message were more systematic than it is, and then makes doctrine more systematic still on the basis of the Church's tradition. This example does not refer to a trivial matter.

After death

In the synoptic gospels the impression is often given that Jesus hoped that the End (the end of human life lived in the conditions of 'this age') would come within the lifetimes of his first hearers. It would be accompanied by terrible suffering – which seems to be the time of trial referred to in the Lord's Prayer, although this catechism feels obliged to wrestle with the translation 'lead us not into temptation' (2846). But it would end in the coming of God's 'reign on earth as in heaven'. In the surviving literature of early Christianity the impression is often given that this hope burned brightly for the first generation. The hope was disappointed: that is the subject of, for example, the Second Letter of Peter. But the New Testament also records a tradition, beginning with the teaching of Jesus himself, that the exact date of the coming 'Kingdom of God' or 'Day of the Lord' was not known. The Lord would come in glory and judgement 'like a thief in the night'. This element of agnosticism enabled Christianity to survive when it turned out that the End would not come quickly. However, the expectation or urgent hope that the government of God was about to be set up on earth provided the original context for the New Testament's teachings about life in eternity.

References need not be given now to the biblical texts cited in the voluminous scholarly discussion of that expectation or hope of the imminent End, partly because the new catechism takes no account of that discussion. Nor does it dwell on the answer often given in the Johannine gospel and letters, that 'eternal life' has already begun for the Christian believer. Instead it interprets the New Testament as a fairly systematic source of information about the prospects in life after death. It tells us that

the New Testament speaks of judgement primarily in its aspect of the final encounter with Christ in his second coming, but also repeatedly affirms that immediately after death each will be rewarded in accordance with his works and faith . . . Each man receives his eternal retribution in his immortal soul at the very moment of his death, in a particular judgement that refers his life to Christ: either entrance into the blessedness of heaven – through a purification or immediately – or immediate and everlasting damnation. (1021–1022)

The catechism tells us what is meant by purgatory, heaven and hell, drawing on Scripture and the Church's elaborated tradition but exposing itself to some questions often asked in our time.

The Councils of Florence and Trent formulated the doctrine concerning purgatory in 1439 and 1563, using the image of a cleansing fire to express the 'final purification of the elect' (1031). The basic idea is that the dead will need to be purified before entering heaven (understood as life 'with' or even 'in' the all-holy God) and that idea is probably acceptable to most Christians in our time. It certainly is acceptable to me, for it expresses my hope for myself – the hope that knowing God's love more fully will make even me clean. A lot that I hope is true is packed into a few words in the First Letter of John: 'Dear Friends, we are now God's children; what we shall be has not yet been disclosed, but we know that when Christ appears we shall be like him, for we shall see him as he is. As he is pure, everyone who has grasped this hope makes himself pure' (3.2, 3). But the more detailed teaching about purgatory formulated by those councils has been widely rejected, by Eastern Orthodox as well as by Anglicans and Protestants. This is partly because the teaching includes the idea of purgatory as 'punishment' as well as purification, an idea which had led to notorious claims and practices in the name of the Roman Catholic Church. Even in this catechism of 1992 the Church is said to have authority to secure the release of the dead from the pains of purgatory. Paul VI discouraged crude references to remission of periods in purgatory secured by specified prayers or pilgrimages, but his still-conservative teaching is endorsed in this catechism:

> An indulgence is the remission before God of the temporal punishment due to sins whose guilt has already been forgiven, which the faithful Christian who is duly disposed gains under certain prescribed conditions through the help of the Church which, as minister of redemption, dispenses and applies with authority the treasury of the satisfactions of Christ and the saints. An indulgence is either plenary or partial, according as it removes either part or all of the temporal punishment due to sin. (1471)

It is added in this catechism, repeating the teaching of Sixtus IV in 1476: 'Indulgence may be applied to the living or the dead'. But such teaching is indeed hard to reconcile with the accounts in the gospels of what Jesus said to his contemporaries about God the holy Father's forgiveness; and it goes beyond anything taught elsewhere in the New Testament, as the footnotes in this part of the catechism show by being both sparse and irrelevant. One reference is to a metaphor used by Paul:

'If anyone's building burns down, he will have to bear the loss; yet he will escape with his life, though only by passing through the fire' (1 Cor 3.15). But the metaphor is used about 'God's building', the Church to which individual Christians contribute materials which may be destroyed: it is not used about an individual's punishment by fire after death. Another text, about 'faith which stands the test' as 'gold passes through the assayer's fire' (1 Pet 1.7) is also about life before death. The third text refers to Judas Maccabeus who paid for a sacrifice in order that some Jews guilty of idolatry might be freed from their sin after death – scarcely a decisive act instructing Christians to pay for Masses for the dead (2 Macc 12.45).

The doctrine which the catechism endorses includes the teaching that even when guilt has been forgiven punishment is exacted by God – as if the father welcomed the prodigal son back to a term in prison. It also teaches that God has entrusted 'the treasury of the satisfactions of Christ' to the Church, to be distributed by it, as if the divine Judge has abdicated. It associates the 'satisfactions' of the saints with Christ's own work of at-one-ment between the Father and humanity, in a link which at least obscures the New Testament's constant emphasis that Christ is the one 'mediator' and the one perfect 'sacrifice'. And even if its references to fire are not intended to be taken literally, it appears to commit the philosophical howler of saying that in eternity there can be periods of time ('temporal punishment'). That leads to the actual dating of the 'indulgences' still to be seen in some churches as promises to remit years, months or days in purgatory despite Paul VI's care. In Luther's time the doctrine of purgatory led to what was effectively the sale of indulgences on behalf of the papacy and to what was heard as the announcement that a soul escaped purgatory's pains through a benefactor's payment to the Church. That claim was never taught formally by the Church, and was denounced by some of the faithful, but another late medieval practice was encouraged by popes and bishops – the multiplication of Masses praying for the dead in purgatory, again with payments to the clergy. Such practices, now generally regarded as abuses, aroused the Protestant attacks on 'sacrifices of Masses'.

Purgatory is different from the endless punishment in hell. But 'the Church', we are warned, 'affirms the existence of hell and its eternity'. Immediately after death the souls of those who die in a state of mortal sin descend into hell, where they suffer the punishments of hell, with 'eternal fire' (1035).

The reticence of this catechism about the nature of hell's endless punishment is in notable contrast with much teaching in the past. The Roman Catechism of 1566 spoke of 'inextinguishable fire...with every kind of suffering'. In the English and Welsh catechism of 1889 it was taught that 'those who die in mortal sin will go to hell for all eternity' and will be 'punished for ever in the fire of hell' (125, 134). It was then explained that 'mortal sin is a serious offence against God' and that 'by the "forgiveness of sins" I mean that Christ has left the power of forgiving sins to the pastors of his Church' (111, 121). It is easy to understand the popular belief that anyone who had committed a serious sin and had not confessed it to a priest before dying was doomed to hell – a belief which brought terror to the laity as well as status to the clergy. In contrast, in the 1992 catechism it is stressed that hell's chief punishment is 'eternal separation from God, in whom alone man can possess the life and happiness for which he was created and for which he longs' (1035). 'God predestines no one to go to hell'; anyone in hell would be guilty of 'a wilful turning away from God and persistence in it to the end' (1037). Hell is 'self-exclusion from communion with God' (1033). Moreover, the teaching of Vatican II is quoted that 'for a sin to be mortal, three conditions must be met': 'Mortal sin is sin whose object is grave matter and which is also committed with full knowledge and deliberate consent' (1857). These careful words suggest that if anyone goes to hell, it is because, by a choice persisted in to the end, that person deliberately consents to sin mortally, knowing that the inevitable consequence is the rejection of God, life and happiness.

One of the biggest changes in Christianity since the seventeenth century has been the decline of the vivid fear of hell. Passionately serious 'hell-fire' preaching (an example is given in James Joyce's *Portrait of the Artist as a Young Man*) is much rarer than joking about the traditional imagery of hell, which is derived from the fires and the worms which consumed the rubbish dumps in the valley of Gehenna outside Jerusalem. The belief that God has so arranged matters that most of humanity will end up in hell since they have not confessed their serious sins to priests before their deaths is now widely seen as incompatible with the revelation of God as supremely loving. That is also nowadays a general reaction to the belief that hell involves excruciating and endless torments of a physical or semi-physical kind. Mercifully, the catechism avoids such teaching which was given by multitudes of preachers and even theologians in past ages. It also avoids the mistake (nowadays much more popular) of failing to see that if human beings have been given free will by their Creator they must always be free to refuse to accept his love. Many, probably most, serious modern Christians therefore find it necessary to believe that hell as self-inflicted separation from God is a possible development of the evil in human hearts.

But I am among those Christians who would say that this catechism's handling of this profoundly solemn subject may still be questioned on two points. Would it not be more in keeping with the New Testament's teaching taken as a whole to emphasize that the revelation of God's holy love after death will be infinitely clearer than most people's comprehension of it before death, so that many may be expected to 'repent' then by turning in love to this God – and the God who is Love may be expected to act like the father in the parable of the prodigal son? It seems wrong to teach that no repentance is possible after death, as this catechism still does in places – although it also says that 'certain offences can be forgiven in the age to come' (1031). That stern teaching suggests that the Father leaves most of his children to be doomed by circumstances which have made it virtually impossible for them to understand his love at all fully: their heritage has been too crippling, this life has been too grim, the Gospel has been too hidden. Like the soldiers who crucified Jesus, many people who do wrong 'do not know what they are doing' before they die. But death must be an education, and it was the hope of Paul that when 'the Gentiles have been admitted in full strength . . . the whole of Israel will be saved . . . for in shutting all mankind in the prison of their disobedience, God's purpose was to show mercy to all mankind' (Rom 11.25–32).

Secondly, would it not be more in keeping with the revealed mercy of God to believe and teach that the alternative to eternal life 'with' and 'in him', were anyone to choose that alternative, would be not endless suffering but destruction as if by fire, the annihilation of 'the second death' (Rev 20.14)?

There is a similar, and similarly welcome, reticence in this catechism about heaven. In some contrast with the catechism of 1566 (which endorsed Augustine's belief that if troubled by excessive weight on earth the righteous would be less fat in heaven), we are wisely told that 'this mystery of blessed communion with God and all who are in Christ is beyond all understanding and description' although 'Scripture speaks of it in images: life, light, peace, wedding feast, wine of the kingdom, the Father's house, the heavenly Jerusalem, paradise' (1027). But even here a question may be asked. The teaching of Benedict XII in 1336 is endorsed that the blessed dead 'already before they take up their bodies again . . . have been, are and will be in heaven in the heavenly kingdom and celestial paradise with Christ, joined to the company of the holy angels' (1023). We may ask: if all that glory may be enjoyed for ever immediately after death or purification, what further important joy could be provided by a physical resurrection?

In support of the teaching of two councils in the thirteenth century that at the last judgement all of the dead 'will rise again with their own bodies which they now bear' (999, 1059), this catechism reminds us about Christ's risen body. But it also teaches that 'in his risen body he passes from the state of death to another life beyond time and space' (646). It quotes Paul's vision of the 'spiritual body' in 1 Corinthians 15. But it does not quote his statement that 'flesh and blood can never possess the kingdom of God, the perishable cannot possess the imperishable' (15.44, 50). The catechism also quotes part of Paul's vision of a transformed universe in Romans 8, in support of the teaching of Irenaeus that the world will be 'restored to its original state' and 'be at the service of the just' (1047). But Paul's vision was not intended as a contradiction of modern scientific knowledge. It did not explore the origins and probable future of our universe and of our planet in it. It did not discuss the Big Bang when the kind of matter which we know began, or the separation of Earth from the sun, or its very slow development before it could support human life, or its future return to its parent having become uninhabitable, or the fate of the rest of the universe in terms of physics. With no down-to-earth explanation, and of course with no reference to the prediction of the Big Crunch found in much modern astronomy, Paul allowed us to glimpse a mystical vision of a glory beyond dimensions and changes because beyond space and time. Somehow all creation is 'to be freed from the shackles of mortality and is to enter upon the glorious liberty of the children of God' (8.21).

Scripture and Tradition

I have not argued (as many Protestant Christians have done) that the Bible speaks for itself and does not need to be interpreted. The Bible has human authors who differ in their dates, convictions and styles. It was written not by people like us but by Hebrews or Jews (with a very few Gentiles) living thousands of years ago. It is not a book but a sizeable library. Particular texts need to be understood in the light of the message of the Bible, taken as a whole. Their literal sense needs to be studied, but we need also to study their significance 'in Christ', their significance for our conduct and their significance for our eternal life.

We have to decide what this message carrying this significance is by selecting what seems to us most important in the Bible. Who, then, are the 'we' who must decide? We are not at all likely to be spiritually or intellectually equipped to give a wise answer if we rely exclusively on our own resources. We need a community around us and that community needs its living tradition, the 'handing on' of a belief or practice from person to person and generation to generation. In the history of Christianity, the words 'tradition' and 'traditions' occur as early as the

Second Letter to the Thessalonians (2.15; 3.6). Naturally and properly, a tradition about traditions arose: 'Timothy, keep safe what has been entrusted to you' (1 Tim 6.20). And rightly, most Christians have believed that the God revealed in Scripture has also used tradition to reveal his nature and his wishes. Scripture was written when tradition already existed; the books constituting Scripture were authorized by tradition; and God has used tradition since Scripture. The Council of Trent declared that divine revelation is handed on in 'traditions written in books and without writing'. That shocked Protestants whose motto has been 'Scripture alone', but it seems acceptable to most Christians, specially with the cautious amendment of Vatican II which quietly substituted 'Holy Tradition' for Trent's 'traditions'. It is also good to know that Trent changed an earlier draft which had said that divine revelation was handed on *'partly* in books and *partly* without writing' – which would have hindered Vatican II's insistence on the priority of Holy Scripture as the fountain or seed of all Holy Tradition.

However, we must use the minds given to us to make our own judgements about the truth. We do so even if we decide that the Bible or our community's whole tradition is bound to be completely correct. And we must use our consciences to separate the good and the evil in what is proposed to us, even if our moral decision is that the Bible or our community commands nothing but the good. So by the guidance of the Holy Spirit working through a joint operation between our community, our reason based on our knowledge and our conscience based on our experience, we have to say what Scripture or Tradition means to us in life and death. To say this is not 'Liberal Protestantism' or 'Modernism'. It is said, in a simple or sophisticated manner, by countless Christians who connect Christianity with truth and goodness, within as well as outside the Roman Catholic Church.

Unfortunately, Christians have often disagreed when reporting the results for them of weighing these authorities in the balance. In the fifth century Vincent of Lérins taught that what should be believed is 'what has been believed always, everywhere, by everyone'. That is of course a very attractive idea. But insistence on full agreement of that kind would not produce a very extensive Gospel, and Christians with different versions of the Gospel have disagreed substantially – in New Testament times as well as later. Nowadays most Christians would accordingly agree that much diversity of beliefs is legitimate or at any rate inevitable. Most Christians would also agree that much development in their different beliefs is also acceptable; that there is no need to pretend that what is believed now is precisely what was believed 'always, everywhere, by everyone'. But if Christianity is basically defined by Christ himself, there must be limits to the legitimate developments. And there disputes arise. To many Christians the *magisterium* (leadership) of the Roman Catholic Church seems right to rebuke some Protestant developments. But to many Christians it seems sad that, as this catechism demonstrates, 'tradition' has developed in such a way that the *magisterium* demands the assent of reason and conscience by everyone, everywhere, to doctrines which may be questioned within the family of the faithful.

I now briefly consider some questions which are simpler to answer, since they concern the facts of history. This catechism repeats the claims of the *magisterium* that certain events must be believed by all Christians as having occurred in New Testament times. It does so without being able to produce any sound evidence that the events did occur. It relies on the authority of 'tradition'. But a tradition cannot reliably vouch for truths about history unless the witnesses who started the tradition were in a position to know about the events. A tradition which develops an understanding of the significance of past events may well be wiser than the first reactions of those who stood closest to the events. But a tradition cannot develop a reliable claim that events actually occurred if there is no surviving evidence about them that is reliable. Tradition is not, in Austin Farrer's phrase, a 'fact factory'.

Mary

The Roman Catholic Church has made itself different from all other Christian bodies by officially insisting that all Christians must believe the historical truth of certain events said to have taken place in the life of Mary the mother of Jesus. The truth of these events is believed to have been affirmed conclusively by the papacy and – amid widely venerated appearances of Mary herself, including those at Lourdes (1858), Knock (1879) and Fatima (1917) – these definitions of doctrine have been the background to hundreds of Marian congresses, thousands of Marian books and millions of prayers before candlelit statues, the medieval icon in Czestochowa in Poland or the portrait believed to have been imprinted miraculously on an Aztec Indian's poncho in Guadalupe, Mexico, in 1531. She has often been addressed as 'Queen of Heaven' and 'Help of Christians'. In 1891 Leo XIII proclaimed that 'nobody can approach Christ except through the Mother' and in 1933 Pius XI termed her 'Co-Redemptrix'. In 1942 Pius XII, who called her '*Mediatrix* of all the graces', consecrated the world to the 'Immaculate Heart of Mary'. Since the 1960s, although these titles have to a large extent fallen out of use, there has been no official revision of the doctrines out of which they sprang. But since the New Testament is silent about the events announced in these doctrines, and since there is no reliable evidence from any other source, many Christians think it right to deny that belief in them should be included among essential Christian beliefs. It is not enough to refer to the mysterious appearance in the Revelation of John of 'a woman robed with the sun, beneath her feet the moon, and on her head a crown of twelve stars' who gives birth to a boy 'destined to rule all nations with a rod of iron' and then flees into the wilderness for 1,260 days (12.1–6). This figure of the imagination was probably never intended to be Mary. Before the fifth century it was usually interpreted as a symbol of the Church and many modern scholars treat it as a symbol of Israel.

This catechism repeats the dogma of the Immaculate Conception proclaimed by Pius IX in 1854. It is the teaching that 'the most Blessed Virgin Mary was, from the moment of her conception, by the singular grace and privilege of Almighty God and in view of the merits of Jesus Christ, the Saviour of the human race, preserved immune from all stain of original sin' (491). Without quoting any authority, the catechism adds that 'by the grace of God, Mary remained free of every personal sin her whole life long' (493).

We have no cause to doubt that God's grace gave Jesus a holy mother. But the writers of the New Testament do not seem to have believed that she was so 'singular' as to be completely sinless. Without naming her, Paul reminded the Galatians that 'God sent his Son, born of a woman, born under the law, to buy freedom for those who were under the law' (4.4). In Luke's gospel the angel's salutation is best translated not 'full of grace' but 'most favoured one!' (1.28). In the same gospel Mary is astonished to find the young Jesus in the Temple and asks him: 'My son, why have you treated us like this?' It is a very human scene of misunderstanding (2.41–52). In the same gospel a woman calls out to the adult Jesus: 'Happy the womb that carried you and the breasts that suckled you!' He rejoins: 'No, happy are those who hear the word of God and keep it' (11.27, 28).

There is a similar response in Mark's gospel when his mother and brothers have asked Jesus to come out to them. Jesus prefers to stay with the circle about him, saying 'Here are my mother and my brothers. Whoever does the will of God is my brother and sister and mother' (3.31–35). Earlier in the same passage we are told: 'When his family heard about it they set out to take charge of him. "He is out of his mind," they said' (3.21). In the same passage people who say that Jesus is possessed by a demon are warned that 'whoever slanders the Holy Spirit can never be forgiven' (3.29). Later in his gospel Mark includes as a saying of Jesus: 'A prophet never lacks honour except in his home town, among his relations and his own family' (6.4). It seems that Mark would not have shared the opinion of this catechism that 'throughout her life . . . Mary's faith never wavered' (149). Instead he lets us glimpse a thoroughly human woman in a thoroughly human family and suggests that through this material came salvation.

The legend that Mary was conceived miraculously when her parents Joachim and Anne were childless first appeared in the second century, but it is not known when the belief that she was sinless originated. In the second century two theologians, Irenaeus and Justin, thought of her as the new Eve because she accepted the Incarnation in contrast with the first Eve's disobedience. In the next century, another, Origen, used the title 'God-bearer' (*Theotokos*) which was formally upheld by the Council of Ephesus (431) in the course of its emphasis that Christ was one person, the Son of Mary and God the Son. This title was translated into Latin as *Mater Dei*, 'Mother of God'. The belief that Mary was 'all holy' seems to have been widespread in the churches of the east by about 750. It took another three hundred years for it to be celebrated in English monasteries (for example), but in the western Church it was gradually linked with Augustine's teaching about 'original' sin, so that it was made more precise by saying that Mary was free of 'original' sin from the moment of her conception. However, Augustine himself did not teach this doctrine, which has been rejected by almost all the teachers of orthodoxy in the east. Western theologians who criticized the developed belief included Ambrose, Anselm, Bernard, Albert, Bonaventure and Thomas Aquinas, who wrote that had she been so conceived 'she would not have needed to be redeemed by Christ' (an objection not completely answered in the definition of 1854). In 1439 the Council of Basle formally commended the belief as a 'pious doctrine' but in 1570 Pius V was still teaching that to deny it was not heresy. In 1476 Sixtus IV authorized an optional 'feast' celebrating the Immaculate Conception in the Church's year and this was made a 'day of obligation' in 1708, but in 1840 Gregory XVI was still refusing a dogmatic definition of the compulsory belief because many bishops and theologians still opposed that degree of precision.

It is easy to understand why devotion to Mary developed as it did, so that the catechism of 1566 taught that Jesus was formed 'of the pure blood of the immaculate Virgin'. But history provides no evidence that she actually was sinless from her conception or her birth. It provides something more encouraging to us: evidence that she was human.

This catechism reaffirms belief in Mary's 'real and perpetual virginity, even while giving birth to the Son of God made man' (499). This belief is indeed hard to fit into the far more important belief that Jesus was truly 'born'. Irenaeus, Origen and later theologians held that the birth of Jesus did not end the virginity of his mother. So did a synod of bishops in 694.

But if we seek historical evidence, we have to turn to the New Testament, where we find none at all. Belief in the 'Virgin Birth' is different from the more restricted belief embodied in the gospels of Luke and Matthew that Jesus was conceived 'without human seed' (496). The 'Virginal Conception' has been accepted by most Christians (including Anglicans) but a brief reference to some difficulties which arise when it is taken literally will be offered later in this book, for this belief, too, is not easy for those who learn from science that being human starts with the fertilization of an egg and thus with a genetic inheritance. If Jesus was conceived and born in the usual way, it was still a 'miracle' in the sense of being a marvel – and it affirmed the glory of motherhood.

The catechism grants that 'brothers' of Jesus are mentioned by Paul and by Mark (3.31–35, with 'sisters' in 6.3). It abandons the suggestion that these words often mean 'cousins' in Greek (and Jerome, who at one time thought this, abandoned the idea before his death in 420), merely referring to passages in Genesis where in the Hebrew 'brothers' can mean 'close kinsmen'. Instead we are asked to believe that 'James and Joseph are the sons of another Mary', said to be a 'close relation' mentioned as 'the mother of James and Joseph' in Matthew 27.56 (500). But Mary, James and Joseph were common names, and the other gospels do not suggest that the identification of this 'other Mary' at the foot of the cross was vitally important, although according to this catechism she was the mother of the James who played a very important part in the early Church because he was the 'brother' of the Lord. In Mark's gospel (15.47) she is 'Mary the mother of Joseph'; in Luke's she is not named (23.49); in John's (19.25) she is 'Mary wife of Clopas' and the 'sister' of Mary the mother of Jesus. The fourth-century historian Eusebius emphasized that James was the 'brother' of Jesus and reported that his successor on the 'throne' of the Church in Jerusalem, Simon son of Clopas, 'who was a cousin – at any rate, so it is said – of the Saviour'. Eusebius also reported that one of the Saviour's brothers, Judas, had descendants who were church leaders.

In Matthew's gospel (13.55–56) the people of Nazareth ask about Jesus: 'Is he not the carpenter's son? Is not his mother called Mary, his brothers James, Joseph, Simon and Judas? Are not all his sisters here with us?' The catechism does not explain why all these young people were treated by neighbours as the children of Mary the mother of Jesus when their own mother was alive and a 'close relation' of hers. Nor does it explain why in the Acts of the Apostles we are told that after the Resurrection the apostles were joined in prayer by 'a group of women and Mary the mother of Jesus, and his brothers' (1.14). Nor does it explain why Matthew believed that Joseph 'had no intercourse with her until her son was born' (1.25) – nor why Luke referred to Jesus as the 'first born' son of Mary (2.7). But the even more serious objection to the insistence on Mary's perpetual virginity is, of course, that it may encourage the dirty-minded, and to women oppressive, attitude that the normal processes of conception and birth are unclean. And it suggests that if true marriage requires 'consummation' (as the RC Church teaches), then Mary and Joseph were not really married and she is no example to those who are.

This catechism quotes the Second Vatican Council as teaching that 'the Immaculate Virgin . . . when the course of her earthly life was finished, was taken up *body and soul* into the glory of heaven and exalted by the Lord as Queen over all things, so that she might be more fully conformed to her Son, the Lord of Lords and the conqueror of sin and death' (966). The words which I have italicized repeat the 'infallible' proclamation of the dogma of the Assumption by Pius XII in 1950. The pope claimed that 'this truth is based on Sacred Scripture', and added that 'if anyone should dare wilfully to deny or call into doubt that which we have defined, let him know that he has fallen away completely from the divine and Catholic faith'.

The catechism refers to the celebration of Mary's 'falling asleep' in a Byzantine liturgy which not only avoids saying that she died but also shows that it is being poetic rather than precise when it says: 'you did not leave the world, O Mother of God'. But the earliest surviving evidence for the belief that there was something physically extraordinary about the end of Mary's earthly life is found in the second half of the fourth century. It is found in legends that appear to have been influenced by the 'Gnostic' contempt for the body which was judged heretical by most Christians. These documents usually say that she died in Jerusalem but that her body was either taken into heaven on its way to burial or raised after three days, although one may imply that she was 'assumed' before death. In one or other of these forms the story seems to have been accepted more widely in the fifth and sixth centuries by those 'Monophysites' who had abandoned the belief that Christ had a human nature and who in compensation stressed Mary's glorified humanity. It was also now celebrated by the Orthodox in Jerusalem. The story was accepted by a western bishop, Gregory of Tours, who died in 594, and the acceptance seems to have become general in the churches of the east at about, or not long after, that date. In Rome Pope Sergius I seems to have introduced the 'feast' celebrating the physical 'assumption' before his death in 701 and within the next hundred years that celebration became general in the west. In the thirteenth century, theologians such as Albert, Bonaventure and Thomas Aquinas defended the belief, which, however, did not necessarily involve believing that Mary did not die – a belief first mentioned by Epiphanius in the fourth century. This was not explicitly taught in the papal dogma of

1950, but it certainly has been suggested by all the pictures of the body rising into the sky.

Unless one accepts the authority claimed by Pius XII, it seems reasonable to conclude that there is no reliable evidence about Mary's later life. It seems suspicious that this later life was by tradition located in Ephesus, a centre of worship of the pagan mother-goddess, as an alternative to Jerusalem. But this does not mean that Christians who need historical evidence have to maintain a complete silence about the mother of the Saviour. The Anglican–Roman Catholic International Commission of theologians published in 1981 an agreement that

> Christian understanding of Mary is inseparably linked with the doctrines of Christ and the Church. We agree and recognize the grace and unique vocation of Mary, Mother of God Incarnate (*Theotokos*), in observing her festivals, and in according her honour in the communion of saints. We agree that she was prepared by divine grace to be the mother of our Redeemer, by whom she was herself redeemed and received into glory. We further agree in recognizing in Mary a model of holiness, obedience and faith for all Christians.

In his contribution to *Mary's Place in Christian Dialogue* (1982), a Jesuit scholar, Edward Yarnold, proposed this as a theological interpretation:

> The Immaculate Conception means that it is of faith that God's grace requires human co-operation, provides the conditions which make the response possible and fruitful, and results in sanctification, so that the holiness of the Church will be verifiable in the life of its members, and will overflow from member to member; the Assumption means that all that is truly of value in human existence continues after death, when it is transformed in heaven. (p. 130)

It seems a pity when some such words are not thought to be sufficient to avoid a complete falling away from the Catholic faith. This is specially sad when the truth of the Gospel proclaimed in the New Testament has to be communicated to a modern age which is sceptical about the truthfulness of many traditional expressions of Christian faith but which does strongly believe in that dignity of women which has been affirmed so gloriously by the images of Mary in Catholic devotion and art. How moving is the international collection of modern images of Mary in the basilica of Nazareth, near the village well where she unquestionably drew water! How thought-provoking is the sight of churches dedicated to Mary of Nazareth as a conspicuous feature of the Kremlin in Moscow! In such an age as ours it is important that Christians are able to say together that the mother of Jesus, linked with her son as only a mother can be linked with her child, was 'the Lord's servant' (Luke 1.38) who obeyed God 'my Saviour' (1.47) in a way that led her to the spiritual glory of heaven. For any human being other than the Son of Mary, there can be no glory higher than that. All mothers, all women, everyone can take heart.

However, it is claimed that the Roman Catholic Church, and in particular the papacy, has been given by Christ such an authority that the criticisms of the use of the Bible outlined in this chapter matter little or nothing. The Church, it is said, listens to the Bible – but the Church also interprets it. The *magisterium* is the servant of the Word of God – but the *magisterium* also decides what that Word is. It is therefore necessary to explore the truth about the Church, which is no light task.

3

The truth
about the Church

THE CATECHISM repeats claims which every Christian ought to ponder about the Roman Catholic Church's official leadership, the *magisterium*. There are, it is claimed, occasions when this leadership is incapable of making a mistake. It is also claimed that even on lesser occasions, the teaching of a pope, or the united teaching of the bishops, is always entitled to 'assent'.

In response I want to argue that the leadership has a record of teaching with so much truth and good in it that it does not need to applaud itself quite so loudly. The criticisms which it also deserves on its mixed record would be less severe had it been able to admit with the rest of us that to be human is to be liable to error. All Christians, their leaders included, have made grievous errors. I could write a history of Anglicanism which would be a catalogue of intellectual and moral errors, and I could write an autobiography which would be a shameful confession. If a human being or a human group wishes to leave an impression of infallibility, or of a right to automatic assent, the only wise strategy is silence. Moreover, the early Christians seem to have known they were only human. There is no evidence in the New Testament that Peter exercised the kind of authority which was to be claimed, step by step, in the history of the papacy. When we study the period when the intentions of Jesus, or of his apostles, might have been remembered by being transmitted by word of mouth although not written down in any document which has survived, we do not find a pope, or even bishops, of the sort which we see in this catechism.

If this lack of evidence supporting the catechism's claims from the 'apostolic' and 'sub-apostolic' ages is acknowledged – as it recently has been by many Roman Catholic scholars – it ought to be asked why, if God intended later generations to accept the developed powers of the pope and the bishops, he did not supply clearer evidence about their links with Christ and the apostles. And if it is claimed that all the doctrines expounded by the *magisterium* ought to be believed as divinely revealed propositions despite any personal defects in popes or bishops, it still ought to be asked whether the actual performance of this official leadership has justified the claims it has made for its authority. Are these leaders, said to be sometimes infallible and always entitled to assent, 'known by their fruits' (Matt 7.20) to deserve to be treated as representatives of Christ? If it is said that their personal failings or mistakes do not diminish the authority which they exercise when they teach officially on behalf of Christ, how are such teachings which deserve assent to be distinguished from their errors? And if it is thought that history shows them to be liable to moral or intellectual error, is it safe to exempt them from criticism by the faithful while they are still in office? If they were wrong then, are they always right now? These questions have to be asked – and they cannot be answered without considering historical facts which are sometimes difficult to recall, and sometimes painful.

Before we plunge into the details of history, however, it is right that we should have before our eyes details of the claims repeated in this catechism, since the meaning of the term *infallibilitas* can so easily be misunderstood. The word seems to have been coined in 1342. It means the inability to make a mistake, but its use in official Roman Catholic theology has been special. Quotations within these quotations are from the Second Vatican Council.

Infallibility and the right to assent by the faithful

This catechism teaches that 'in order to preserve the Church in the purity of the faith handed on by the apostles, Christ who is the Truth willed on her a share in his own infallibility' (889). And it explains how his wish is carried out:

The Roman Pontiff, head of the college of bishops, enjoys this infallibility in virtue of his office when as the supreme pastor and teacher of all the faithful – who confirms his brethren in the faith – he proclaims by a definitive act a doctrine pertaining to faith or morals . . . The infallibility promised to the Church is also present in the body of bishops when, together with Peter's successor, they exercise the supreme *magisterium*, above all in an ecumenical council. When the Church, through its supreme *magisterium*, proposes a doctrine 'for belief as being divinely revealed', and as the teaching of Christ, the definitions 'must be adhered to with the obedience of faith'. This infallibility extends as far as the deposit of divine Revelation itself. (891)

The Pope, Bishop of Rome and Peter's successor, 'is the perpetual and visible source and foundation of the unity both of the bishops and of the whole company of the faithful.' 'For the Roman Pontiff, by reason of his office as Vicar of Christ and pastor of the whole Church, has full, supreme and universal power over the whole Church, a power which he can always exercise unhindered.' 'The college or body of bishops' . . . has 'supreme and full authority over the universal Church, but this power cannot be exercised without the agreement of the Roman Pontiff.' (882–883)

The infallibility which is claimed has some limits. It applies only to a 'definitive act' by which the pope 'proclaims a doctrine pertaining to faith or morals': it does not apply to other papal teaching. It also applies to an ecumenical council of bishops when it 'proposes' a belief 'divinely revealed' and 'taught by Christ' in the 'deposit of revelation'. Infallibility is not claimed for teaching by individual bishops or by councils which do not repeat what has been divinely revealed and what Christ taught. Moreover this catechism does not explicitly teach that God may have revealed to the bishops a truth not contained in Christ's teaching. Nor does it explicitly claim infallibility for teachings agreed by all the bishops which have not been formulated by an ecumenical council. Certainly an Anglican must be grateful for the clarification of these limits to a far simpler and wider claim repeated in the 'penny' catechism of 1889 for the instruction of generations of Roman Catholics in England and Wales: 'The Church cannot err in what she teaches as to faith or morals, for she is our infallible guide in both' (100). And certainly an Anglican must be grateful that no pope has formally claimed to be teaching infallibly since the definitions of the dogmas of the Immaculate Conception and the Physical Assumption which we have already considered. Moreover, as Pope Paul VI observed in 1965, Vatican II did not formally claim that any of its teachings was infallible.

However, the First Vatican Council's definition of papal infallibility, endorsed and strongly encouraged (indeed, prompted) by Pius IX in 1870, was clearly presented as a dogma which was itself infallible. It explicitly rejected the idea that the Church as a whole has the right to question 'infallible' papal teaching:

The Roman Pontiff when he speaks *ex cathedra*, that is, when exercising the office of pastor and teacher of all Christians, he defines with his supreme apostolic authority a doctrine concerning faith or morals to be held by the universal Church, through the divine assistance promised to him in blessed Peter, is possessed of that infallibility with which the divine Redeemer willed his Church to be endowed in defining faith and morals: and therefore such definitions of the Roman Pontiff are irreformable of themselves and not from the consent of the Church.

If we ask what is the extent of the 'deposit of divine Revelation' taught by Christ, which must provide the material for such infallible doctrines, we are told by this catechism: 'This infallibility extends as far as does the deposit of divine Revelation; it also extends to those elements of doctrine, including morals, without which the saving truths of the faith cannot be preserved, explained or observed' (2035). That definition extends the potential scope of 'infallibility' over a wide area. Many fears have been voiced that the papal condemnation of artificial contraception (for example) may be declared infallible. Plainly, the claim to infallibility does not mean that the pope and the bishops must be ruled by, or confined to, 'revelation' understood as the words of Christ in Scripture. The catechism understands Christ's own infallibility in these terms which seem to be more cautious than those used about the Church: 'Christ enjoyed in his human knowledge the fullness of understanding of the eternal plans he had come to reveal. What he admitted to not knowing in this area, he elsewhere declared himself not sent to reveal' (474).

The claim to obedience made in this catechism also covers teachings which are not stated to be infallible. We are told:

Divine assistance is also given to the successors of the apostles, teaching in communion with the successor of Peter, and, in a particular way to the Bishop of Rome, pastor of the whole Church, when, without arriving at an infallible definition and without pronouncing in a 'definitive manner', they propose in the exercise of the ordinary *magisterium* a doctrine that leads to a better understanding of Revelation in matters of faith and morals. To this ordinary teaching the faithful are to adhere with a 'religious assent' which, though distinct from the obedience of faith, is nonetheless an extension of it. (892)

Some RC theologians have argued that this 'religious assent' (a phrase quoted from Vatican II) means no more than that non-infallible teachings should be studied as carefully as possible before making up one's mind. This is said to be the logic of Vatican II's insistence on religious liberty, including in the decree on ecumenism 'a proper freedom even in the theological elaborations of revealed truth' and resulting in the new canon law's recognition that theologians 'enjoy a lawful freedom of enquiry and of prudently expressing their opinions on matters in which they have expertise' (218). However, it seems far-fetched to interpret this catechism as a licence to disagree. The word may sometimes imply a degree of non-commitment, but it does not in this case. The catechism clearly teaches that all Roman Catholics ought to agree with their bishops about these doctrines, since these lead to a 'better understanding' of what has been divinely revealed. Indeed, the new canon law (1371) provides that a person who persists in rejecting a doctrine in this category is to be 'punished'. Accordingly in 1986 Professor Charles Curran was deprived of his post in the Catholic University of America by the Sacred Congregation for the Doctrine of the Faith for refusing to teach that there were no circumstances in which a good Catholic could use artificial contraception within marriage. And six years later one of Latin America's leading theologians, Leonardo Boff, left the priesthood after 28 years in disgust at the Vatican's censorship of his work. Even archbishops have recently been punished for failure to conform to the Vatican's instructions, from Hunthausen in Seattle to Milingo in Zambia.

It has also been argued that the Second Vatican Council gave a wide liberty to make certain doctrines optional. This suggestion has been based particularly on a passage in the decree on ecumenism, encouraging experts to take part in dialogues with Christians who are not Roman Catholics. The council taught: 'When comparing doctrines with one another, they should remember that in Catholic doctrine there exists an order or "hierarchy" of truths, since they vary in their relation to the foundation of the Christian faith'. These words have been quoted as if they endorsed the beliefs of many Protestants that some doctrines are optional, with the implication that some faithful Christians are entitled to think them certainly or probably untrue or comparatively unimportant (*adiaphora* or 'things indifferent'). But Vatican II was careful to speak of 'Catholic doctrine' in the singular and of all its parts as 'truths', adding: 'All truths must be believed with the same faith'. The one point made by the council – and by innumerable other people in history – was that some truths are more important than others.

These far-reaching claims for, and by, the RC Church's leadership are defended by the new catechism's emphasis (repeated from Vatican II) that the contents of Catholic doctrine are not confined to the Bible. 'Both Scripture and Tradition must be accepted and honoured with equal sentiments of devotion and reverence', we are told, since 'the Tradition in question comes from the apostles and hands on what they received from

Jesus' teaching and example and what they learned from the Holy Spirit' (82–83). And if we ask what this Tradition says, we are clearly told: 'The task of giving an authentic interpretation of the Word of God, whether in its written form or in the form of Tradition, has been entrusted to the living teaching office of the Church alone. Its authority in this matter is exercised in the name of Jesus Christ' (85). Who, then, are the bishops who are the pope's junior partners? The catechism also makes this clear. They are bishops appointed after his 'special intervention' (1559).

In this catechism historical grounds are given for these very high claims to authority. The catechism of 1566 taught that bishops and priests constitute one 'sacerdotal order' while differing in power and dignity. But here there is a change. Vatican II is quoted as teaching that Christ constituted the twelve apostles 'in the form of a college or permanent assembly, at the head of which he placed Peter' (880) and that 'the apostles left bishops as their successors. They gave them their own position of teaching authority' (77). 'The office which the Lord confided to Peter, as first of the apostles, destined to be transmitted to his successors, is a permanent one . . . The bishops have by divine institution taken the place of the apostles as pastors of the Church, in such wise that whoever listens to them is listening to Christ and whoever despises them despises Christ and him who sent Christ' (862).

These claims are therefore based on a definite interpretation of the Church's history. It is not suggested that infallibility or the right to assent has been granted only to recent popes or to the three most recent Roman Catholic bishops' councils (Trent, Vatican I and Vatican II). The claims refer mainly to a much earlier period, for they depend on the transmission of such authority by Christ to Peter and by Peter to all Bishops of Rome, or by Christ to the apostles and by them to other bishops. It is claimed that the chain of transmitted authority begins in New Testament times and has never been broken. If this interpretation of history cannot be sustained by a study of the evidence, the claims themselves must either fall to the ground or else be supported only by sheer faith. But the new catechism has repeated the traditional appeal to the facts of history. To history, therefore, we must go. I have to rake over old ground because these momentous claims are based on that ground.

Matthew's account of Peter

Reference is made in the catechism to biblical texts which have often been held to justify papal claims. The First Vatican Council, for example, expounded 'this very clear teaching of the Holy Scriptures'. The most important of these texts is Matthew 16.13–20. Part of it is to be seen in letters five feet high running round the inside of the sixteenth-century dome of St Peter's basilica in Rome. In Caesarea Philippi, Peter has said to Jesus: 'You are the Messiah, the Son of the living God'. Jesus then says:

> Simon son of Jonah, you are favoured indeed! You did not learn that from any human being; it was revealed to you by my heavenly Father. And I say to you: You are Peter, the Rock: and on this rock I will build my Church, and the powers of death shall never conquer it. I will give you the keys of the Kingdom of Heaven; what you forbid on earth shall be forbidden in heaven, and what you allow on earth shall be allowed in heaven.

The words here translated as 'forbid' and 'allow' are literally 'bind' and 'loose'.

Over the centuries there has been an immense debate about the meaning of this passage in relation to the bishopric of Rome. The debate began when Tertullian in *De Pudicitia* (about 220) protested against the current bishop's willingness to preside over the forgiveness of sexual sins. 'Who are you', he wrote scornfully, 'to subvert the plain intention of the Lord, who conferred this power on Peter personally?' In particular the nature of the 'rock' has been discussed. Paul told the Corinthians that 'there can be no other foundation than the one already laid: I mean Jesus Christ himself' (1 Cor 3.11). Since *kepha* was the Aramaic original of the word translated into Greek as *petros*, Paul seems to have in mind here a reference to the group in the Corinthian Church which claimed 'I am for Cephas', quarrelling with those whose heroes were Paul himself or Apollos (1 Cor 1.12). He rejects all this cult of personality producing a division into parties. However, Matthew's plain meaning is that Peter was called 'Rock' by Jesus, and the nickname is applied to Simon, son of Jonah, so often in the New Testament that it is obviously right to accept his statement. Does he, then, mean that the rock on which the Church is to be built is Peter's faith rather than Peter's personality, as has been suggested (almost two hundred years after Tertullian) by Augustine among others? As Augustine came to recognize, the question is not answered by Matthew. The distinction between Peter as a believing disciple and Peter as a faltering man is not on view in this comparatively simple passage. Some modern scholars have suggested that this promise to Peter as 'Rock' may have been spoken by Jesus at the Last Supper or after the Resurrection. In contrast, John's gospel says that Jesus called Simon 'Rock' right at the beginning of their association (1.42). However, such questions do not arise if we concentrate on Matthew's gospel, where the context of this saying, Peter's 'confession' at Caesarea Philippi, is a turning point.

It is more relevant to our present inquiry if we consider whether this saying arose not from words spoken by Jesus (at some time) but from the early Church, from the teaching of some prophet in the name of Jesus; the Revelation of John includes powerful examples of such teaching. It is suspicious that the saying does not appear in the gospels of Mark and Luke when they tell of Peter's 'confession'. It is also suspicious that the Greek word *ekklēsia* ('Church') is used here, with only one other instance in all four gospels. This may translate the Aramaic or Hebrew word meaning 'people', *qahal*. It does in the Septuagint (the Greek version of the Hebrew Scriptures). In that case it may belong to an authentic saying of Jesus; other sayings speak of a community of disciples which he gathered as their 'shepherd'. But since Jesus made so few arrangements providing for a new people after his death, many scholars think it possible or probable that the saying comes from the Christian community behind Matthew's gospel, which may be the church in Antioch where Peter was, we know, based for a time. Fortunately it is not necessary to reach a definite opinion about this possibility for our present purpose. What we can know is that Matthew believed that these great words applied to Peter.

What did he understand them as implying? Experts in the Judaism of the time tell us that rabbis expounding the 'Law of Moses' were, if sufficiently authoritative, expected to 'bind' and 'loose' in the sense of saying in general terms what behaviour was, or was not, in keeping with the Law. If Peter exercised this authority in the Church of his day, or in part of it, the most significant questions settled by him would have been about the lawfulness of baptizing Gentiles and eating food regarded by Jews as unclean. In Acts 10.1 – 11.18 we read that after a revelation in a dream Peter did in fact lead the Church into accepting that 'God has granted life-giving repentance to the Gentiles also'. To the Gentiles, then, Peter unlocked the Kingdom of God. He had the vision (in more than one sense) that persuaded the Church to 'make all nations my disciples', its duty which was clear to Matthew (28.19). But Peter was not the only missionary to the Gentiles. Among the bishops who were leading theologians in the early Christian centuries, Cyprian is to be found writing that although Christ 'builds the Church upon one man . . . in order to signify unity, . . . the rest of the apostles were the same as Peter was, endowed with an equal share of honour and power' – while Augustine agreed that 'Peter, when he received the keys, was the symbol of the whole Church'. It seems probable that Matthew would have agreed with them. His gospel includes this saying about the twelve apostles as the judges of the Jews at the end of time: 'In the world that is to be, when the Son of

Man is seated on his glorious throne, you also will sit on twelve thrones, judging the twelve tribes of Israel' (19.28). It is, however, not said that Peter is to have the only, or the most, honourable throne on that Judgement Day. On the contrary, the ambitious mother of Zebedee's children is told: 'to sit on my right or on my left is not for me to appoint; that honour is for those to whom it has already been assigned by my father' (20.20–23).

Matthew's reference to the sins of Christians, including his second use of the word *ekklēsia*, is in a passage which almost certainly comes from the Church, not from Jesus. In 18.15–19 the instruction is given that 'if your brother does wrong' he is to be talked to first privately and then, if he will not listen, in the presence of witnesses. If he still refuses to listen, 'report the matter to the *ekklēsia*; and if he will not listen even to the *ekklēsia*, then treat him as you would a pagan or a tax-collector'. This passage is thought not to come from Jesus because it is incompatible with the generous treatment of pagans and tax-collectors often recorded in the gospels. But it is also incompatible with any idea that all problems would be referred to a strong leader. The whole *ekklēsia*, which here must mean the local Christian congregation, has the authority to 'bind' and 'loose' individuals.

In Paul's letters to the church in Corinth we have glimpses of the corporate exercise of the kind of authority which is envisaged in Matthew's gospel. In the first letter we find Paul condemning with an apostle's authority 'the union of a man with his stepmother' and ordering that he 'should be turned out of your community . . . When you are all assembled in the name of our Lord Jesus, and I am with you in spirit, through the power of our Lord Jesus you are to consign this man to Satan for the destruction of his body, so that his spirit may be saved on the day of the Lord' (5.1–5). Paul expects the excommunication to be so terrifying that unless the man repents he will somehow die. But in the second letter to the Christians in Corinth we find that 'something very different is called for now: you must forgive the offender and put heart into him; the man's distress must not be made so severe as to overwhelm him . . . Anyone who has your forgiveness has mine too: and when I speak of forgiving . . . I mean that as the representative of Christ I have forgiven him for your sake' (2.7–10). Here both the excommunication and the forgiveness of a sinful Christian are conveyed by the apostle and the congregation jointly.

What are we to make of words which may seem to guarantee that God will endorse all decisions about sinners made by Peter, or by Paul, or by the other apostles, or by the local congregation? We read in the new catechism that 'the words "bind" and "loose" mean: whomever you exclude from your communion will be excluded from communion with God; whomever you receive anew into your communion, God will welcome back into his' (1445). But that interpretation, which appears to claim for the Church's leadership the unconditional power to send people to heaven or hell, is questionable.

It is not Matthew's habit to provide a smooth synthesis of the various sayings which he reports; he is not drawing up a code of law. For example, in chapter 5 he records the saying that anyone who sets aside the least demand of the Jewish religious law 'will have the lowest place in the Kingdom of Heaven' alongside contradictions of that law concerning divorce, oath-taking and revenge. But the overwhelming impression left by his gospel is that God the Father or Jesus is the final judge, not Peter or the other apostles or the local *ekklēsia*. Many who have prophesied, driven out demons and performed miracles in the name of Jesus will be told at the End: 'I never knew you. Out of my sight; your deeds are evil!' (7.21–24). And the behaviour which Jesus judges to be Christian is humble. Those who are humble like children will be the greatest in the Kingdom of Heaven (18.4). 'Among you, whoever wants to be great must be your servant, and whoever wants to be first must be the slave of all' (20.26, 27). 'Do not call any man on earth "father", for you have one Father, and he is in heaven. Nor must you be called "teacher", you have one Teacher, the Messiah' (23.9, 10). And when Peter is not humble enough to accept the teaching of Jesus that the Messiah must suffer, he is told: 'Out of my sight, Satan; you are a stumbling block to me. You think as men think, not as God thinks' (16.23). Read in this context, the guarantee of divine endorsement appears to be limited to decisions or petitions which are truly made in the spirit of Jesus – not merely in his 'name' when the name is used lightly, but in what Paul calls 'the power of our Lord Jesus'.

How, then, was Peter's leadership viewed in the rest of the early Church? Did those Christians who were close to the life of Jesus of Nazareth in time agree with the First Vatican Council that Jesus had given Peter a 'primacy of jurisdiction' – the primacy of 'full and supreme jurisdiction over the whole Church', which 'the Roman Pontiff' now exercises as Peter's successor 'according to the institution of Christ our Lord himself' and therefore 'by divine law'?

Peter in the New Testament

Certainly Peter was prominent during the period after the Resurrection, as he had often been the spokesman of the disciples before it. Indeed, both Paul and Luke record the tradition that he was the first to encounter the risen Lord (1 Cor 15.5; Luke 24.34), a tradition which this catechism abandons in favour of Mary of Magdala (641). Luke depicts Peter as the leader of the church in Jerusalem until the time when, after his escape from prison, 'he left the house and went off elsewhere' (Acts 12.17). In Acts 15 Luke also describes the council which discussed the missionary work of Barnabas and Paul. Peter then spoke about the experience that 'from my lips Gentiles were to hear and believe the message of the gospel'. The discussion continued until James summed it up. It seems that for Luke this leadership in the early years in Jerusalem and in the beginnings of the Gentile mission was the answer to the prayer of Jesus that when Peter was restored to faith after being 'sifted like wheat' by Satan he would 'give strength' to his brother disciples (Luke 22.31–34). But Luke's gospel (22.24) also says that at the last supper the apostles could still have a dispute 'as to which of them should be considered the greatest', and after chapter 15 we learn nothing at all about Peter from the Acts of the Apostles. There, the climax is the arrival in Rome of Paul.

Paul's letter to the Galatians is one of the oldest surviving documents of Christianity and is often thought to be more historically accurate than Acts. It records that three years after Paul's conversion 'I did go up to Jerusalem to get to know Cephas, and I stayed two weeks with him'. That is a significant tribute to Peter's position, although Paul also met James the Lord's brother, who later seems to have taken over the leadership of the Jerusalem Christians from Peter. Fourteen years later Paul again visited Jerusalem, it seems for the council described in Acts. He had been nervous about the attitude of the 'men of repute' although now he added to the Galatians: 'not that their importance matters to me: God does not recognize these personal distinctions'. In the end, when 'they saw that I had been entrusted to take the gospel to the Gentiles as surely as Peter had been entrusted to take it to the Jews . . . Recognizing therefore the privilege bestowed on me, those who are reputed to be pillars of the community, James, Cephas and John, accepted Barnabas and me as partners and shook hands on it: the agreement was that we should go to the Gentiles, while they went to the Jews' (Gal 1.18 – 2.9).

It seems that Peter left Jerusalem to become an itinerant missionary, but Paul's letter goes on to show that the proposed division between the Jewish and Gentile missions ran up against the problem that the membership of many congregations was mixed. In Antioch this problem exploded. Peter took his meals with Gentiles 'until some messengers came from James'. But Paul tells the Galatians: 'I opposed him to his face, because he was clearly in the wrong . . . When I saw that their conduct did not square with the truth of the gospel, I said to Cephas in front of the whole congregation, "If you, a Jew born and bred, live like a Gentile, and not like a Jew, how can you insist that Gentiles must live like Jews?"' (2.11–14). This letter shows that Paul still acknowledged Peter's special position but did not treat him as an infallible teacher and ruler whom he must obey. The letter also suggests that Peter did not treat James as a subordinate: he changed his position when rebuked by that leader who now presided over the church in Jerusalem.

In contrast with the survival of some of Paul's letters, the New Testament contains no document which is indisputably the authentic work of Peter. The Second Letter ascribed to him and addressed 'to those who share equally with us in the privileges of faith' is thought by many scholars to have been written long after his death, in the second century. The First Letter – which may be connected with him more closely, whether or not he dictated it to Silvanus (5.12) – is a call to holiness, to the domestic virtues, and to humility in accepting suffering. The emphasis is on the 'people of God' as 'a chosen race, a royal priesthood' (2.9). In the appeal to 'the elders of your community', Peter is presented merely as a 'fellow-elder and a witness to Christ's suffering, and as one who has shared the glory to be revealed' (5.1). No human bishops are mentioned, the emphasis being on 'the Shepherd and Guardian of your souls' (2.25). The elders are 'to look after the flock of God whose shepherds you are', but not 'lording it over your charges' because the Lord is the only 'chief shepherd' (5.2, 4). Nor is Rome mentioned explicitly, although the letter ends with 'greetings from your sister church in Babylon', which is probably a reference to Rome.

In the second century two bishops outside Rome, Papias and Irenaeus, accepted the belief that Mark's gospel had been written by Peter's assistant on the basis of the great apostle's memories and this gospel (the earliest of the New Testament's four) adds to the evidence that Peter was special, as in the instruction: 'go and say to his disciples and Peter' (16.7). But whoever supplied Mark with his material had no wish to idealize Peter. Mark gives no reason for calling Simon 'Rock' (3.16); the shattering rebuke to Peter as 'Satan' is included, but not any transfer of the keys to the Kingdom of God (8.32); at the Transfiguration Peter 'did not know what to say, they were so terrified' (9.6); he is warned that 'many who are first will be last and the last first' (10.31); his boast that 'everyone else may lose faith, but I will not' is soon followed by sleep, denials and tears (chapter 14). It may be that the Resurrection appearance to Peter mentioned by Paul was described in a lost ending to Mark's gospel, but it seems more likely that this gospel was brought to a close at 16.8, without boasting about any restoration of Peter as an apostle. If so, Mark ends in an atmosphere of humble awe at the mystery of the empty tomb which women, not apostles, had discovered.

Beginning with Ambrose (Bishop of Milan 364–397), Catholics who wish to link Peter with the Bishops of Rome have often quoted from John's gospel the words of the Risen Lord: 'Feed my lambs, tend my sheep, feed my sheep' (21.15–17). It seems likely that the epilogue to which this passage belongs was added partly in order to pay tribute to Peter's pastoral work with feelings of gratitude intensified by the vivid memory of his crucifixion (21.18, 19). But this passage does not say that Peter is to be the only, or even the chief, shepherd of the flock. Three times it says that he will be a shepherd again because he loves Jesus, although three times during the trial of his Master he denied knowing him (18.12–27). It would be out of keeping with this gospel if this commission were thought to encourage power or pride in Peter. On the contrary, John (18.10, 11) tells us that when Jesus was arrested it was Peter who used a sword and it was Peter who was rebuked; the other gospels do not name Peter here. John (13.2–7) also tells us that when Jesus washed his disciples' feet it was Peter who protested and it was Peter who was warned that 'you have no part with me' if he did not accept and practise that example of humility. The other gospels do not mention this incident, but John thinks it so significant that he relates it in preference to reporting the institution of the Eucharist.

It seems that all references to Peter in this gospel should be read in the light of the fact that it was based on a tradition going back to an anonymous disciple (21.20–24) – 'the disciple he loved', who at the Last Supper was 'reclining close beside Jesus', so that Peter had to ask Jesus a question through him (13.21–25). In the empty tomb this disciple, who had 'run faster than Peter', also believed the Resurrection before him (20.1–9). Peter's brother, Andrew, was the first to call Jesus 'Messiah' (1.41). Mary of Magdala, not Peter, was the first to see the risen Lord (20.10–18). Like the other gospels, John's is not an unqualified advertisement for Peter's authority.

In this gospel Peter has a share in the awesome power which has been communicated by the risen Lord to all 'the disciples' (whose number is not mentioned and who are not here given the title 'apostle'): 'Receive the Holy Spirit! If you forgive anyone's sins, they are forgiven; if you pronounce them unforgiven, unforgiven they remain' (20.21, 22). It is, however, far from certain that these words were spoken by the historical Jesus, for they come in a gospel which is usually dated at about AD 100 and which (it is widely agreed) is more interested in the disciples' spiritual union with their risen Lord than in accurate reporting. It is also far from certain that they imply that the disciples' verdicts would always be vindicated by the Lord, for the gospel contains many warnings about spiritual dangers. And the Letters of John give no sign that the leaders of the community behind this gospel believed that they had the authority to forgive serious sins committed after Baptism. This community seems to be different from the congregation in Corinth addressed by Paul. It is said to need no teacher apart from 'the Holy One' and to include no one who sins – which seems to mean, no one whose sins are major (1 John 2.20, 27; 3.6–9). No prayer should be offered for a 'deadly' sin, but if a 'brother' sees another sinning in a way which is not deadly he should pray for that sinner with the assurance that God will still 'grant life' (5.16). It therefore seems probable that what this gospel's promise means is that the disciples when baptizing penitents in complete obedience to their Lord will be endorsed by that Lord. It seems clear that the Church took many centuries to develop a comprehensive penitential system for the baptized, operated by the clergy. The development brought great blessings, but the historical evidence raises a problem when this catechism teaches that 'Christ instituted the sacrament of Penance for all sinful members of his Church, above all for those who, since Baptism, have fallen into grave sin . . . and wounded ecclesial communion' (1446).

The Letter to the Hebrews contained this warning: 'If we deliberately persist in sin after receiving the knowledge of the truth, there can be no further sacrifice for sins; there remains only a terrifying expectation of judgement, of a fierce fire which will consume God's enemies' (10.26). In the early centuries it was thought that only Baptism could wash away sin completely, so that if one had to pursue an occupation which was likely to lead into serious sin it was safest to postpone Baptism until death was near. We do not know how many acted in this belief, but the Christian emperors did from Constantine who died in 337 to Theodosius I who was baptized in 379. We also know that during the persecutions before Constantine's reign it was disputed who, if anyone, in the Church had authority to forgive apostasy (the renunciation of Christian faith). We also know that the system which emerged was as this catechism describes (1447). 'Rarely', and at least in some regions 'only once in a lifetime', Christians who had committed specially serious sins such as adultery could be admitted to 'a very rigorous discipline, by which penitents had to do public penance for their sins, often for years'. The catechism candidly refers to the origins of the present, very different, system:

> During the seventh century Irish missionaries, inspired by the eastern monastic tradition, took to continental Europe the private practice of penance . . . This new practice envisioned the possibility of repetition and so opened the way to a regular frequenting of this sacrament and allowed the forgiveness of serious sins and venial sins to be integrated into one sacramental celebration.

The private and detailed confession of sins to a priest at least once a year was made compulsory for Catholics by the Lateran Council in 1215. That history deserves to be remembered when we read the claim that 'Christ instituted the sacrament of Penance'.

The position of the historical Peter in the first generation of Christians, as revealed by this fragmentary evidence in the New Testament, seems to have been this: the spokesman became first the leader and then the missionary. There is no reason to doubt the tradition that he concluded his mission by being martyred in Rome. The simple shrine built in his honour probably in the 160s was uncovered during excavations in the 1940s beneath the present great basilica of St Peter in Rome. However, no reliable evidence survives about any other connection between Peter and Rome. Not many years after the building of that shrine Irenaeus, Bishop of Lyons, was writing that Peter and Paul had 'founded and established' the Roman church, but Paul's letter to Rome contradicts that claim. It was the letter of a stranger, and while stressing that in his missionary work he made it a firm principle 'not to build on another man's foundation' (15.20) he made no mention of Peter and expressed his 'longing' to visit Rome (1.11). It was to be for 'a time of rest' on his way to Spain (15.28, 32).

Rome's only 'eminent apostles' mentioned in Paul's letter (16.7) are the otherwise unknown Andronicus and Junia (a woman's name) or Junias (a man's). Although the apostles were the Church's 'foundation' in some sense (Eph 2.20; Rev 21.14) we know little about them. Despite the title given to Luke's second volume by later tradition, almost all the acts of the apostles went unrecorded. A comparison of Mark 3.13–19 with other gospels reveals some uncertainty about the names of the Twelve. Paul seems to say that it was a necessary qualification for an apostle to have seen the risen Lord (1 Cor 9.1), but more than five hundred Christians are reported to have been so qualified and in the list of witnesses 'the apostles' seem to be a wider group than the Twelve (1 Cor 15.6–8). When writing to Corinth he refers with pride to the sufferings of 'apostles' who seem to be numerous missionaries and also with contempt to 'super-apostles' who have stirred up trouble during a visit. In his First Letter to the Thessalonians he calls Silvanus and Timothy 'apostles of Christ' (2.6). In one passage of Acts (14.4, 14) Luke calls Barnabas and Paul 'apostles' but otherwise he seems to confine the title to the Twelve. He says that when the apostle James was martyred (12.2) he was not replaced, in contrast with the earlier choice of Matthias in place of Judas (1.26). This seems to imply that the Twelve had discharged their task as witnesses to the Resurrection and, under Christ, founders of the community which fulfilled the mission of the twelve tribes of Israel. But some of this flexibility or confusion in the use of the term *apostolos* arises because it could mean no more than ambassador, representative or messenger (as in 2 Cor 8.23).

The New Testament therefore provides no evidence establishing the existence of 'the apostles' as a 'college' which under Peter corporately instructed and governed the whole Church and then transmitted its authority to another college, this time composed of 'bishops'. On the contrary, the letters and gospels collected in the New Testament reflect various personal or local ways of proclaiming the Gospel. Personal leadership seems to have passed from Peter to James in Jerusalem and to Paul in much of the Gentile mission. Pre-eminence seems to have migrated from Jerusalem to other cities around the eastern Mediterranean and, in the west, to Rome.

Bishops at the beginning

Do the Bishops of Rome inherit the promises to Peter in Matthew 16.13–20? The only certain evidence which we have about the Roman church during the first period after the martyrdoms of Peter and Paul comes from the letters which have survived. One is often dated to the 90s, but may come from the second century. It was written by Ignatius on his way to martyrdom, begging the Christians in Rome not to attempt to stop that glorious end to his earthly life. Ignatius was himself Bishop of Antioch, and he told the Christians in Smyrna: 'Nobody should do anything that has to do with the Church without the bishop's approval. You should regard as valid a Eucharist celebrated by the bishop or by someone he authorises. Where the bishop is present there let the congregation gather, just as where Jesus Christ is there is the Catholic Church' (8.2). That is the first mention of *katholikos* in Christian literature, and the letters of Ignatius leave a vivid impression of the unity of spirit between the scattered and harassed congregations. But Ignatius never says that the apostles transmitted to the college of bishops the authority of which this catechism speaks, and his letter to Rome makes no mention of such a bishop there. The Roman church is told that it deserves its fame because 'you rank first in love', which seems to refer to its financial gifts to other congregations. Instead of saying that he will not interfere in a church which has its own bishop who is Peter's successor and therefore supreme over all other bishops, Ignatius writes: 'I do not give you orders like Peter and Paul. They were apostles: I am a convict' (4.3). He does not even claim to be Peter's successor as Bishop of Antioch. In this catechism his letter to the Christians in Tralles, praising their bishop Polybius, is quoted (1593). What is not quoted is his teaching that while the bishop 'has the role of the Father and the presbyters are like God's council and an apostolic band', it is the deacons who 'represent Jesus Christ'.

The document called the First Letter of Clement was written about 96. The original title is probably preserved in the Coptic version: 'The Letter of the Romans to the Corinthians'. This long – indeed, verbose – letter shows that the Roman church exercised the right to rebuke the church in Corinth, defending some clergy described both as 'bishops' (*episkopoi*, meaning 'overseers') and as 'presbyters' (*presbyteroi*, meaning 'elders'). They had been deprived of their leadership by 'impetuous' younger men. Quoting many examples of the importance of obedience to seniors in the Old Testament (and also in the Roman army and the universe), the writer urges the restoration of order. No bishop who has a position similar to that of Ignatius, either in Corinth or in Rome, is mentioned. There is no reason to doubt that the writer was the Clement who appears as the third of the 'Bishops of Rome' in lists recorded by Hegesippus and Irenaeus between 160 and 180 (approximately). He was, it seems, the presbyter-bishop who handled the Roman church's official correspondence. He probably also often presided over the congregation, since it is difficult to imagine that another had the ability and assurance shown in this letter. But the new catechism goes beyond this evidence when it calls Clement 'Pope' (1900).

The letter hints that Peter and Paul had been betrayed into the hands of the police, or at least had been vigorously attacked, by some members of the Roman church:

> By reason of rivalry and envy the greatest and most righteous pillars were persecuted and done to death. Let us set before our eyes the noble apostles. Peter, who because of wicked jealousy endured suffering not once or twice but often, bore his witness and went to the glorious place which he deserved. Because of rivalry and contention Paul showed how to win the prize for patient endurance . . . (5.2–5)

But nowhere does the writer claim to be Peter's successor. The link with the apostles is through leaders (in the plural) who lead worship:

> The apostles preached in country and city and appointed their first converts, after testing them by the Spirit, to be the bishops and deacons of future believers . . . They later added a rule to the effect that, should these die, other approved men should succeed to their ministry. In the light of this, we reckon it a breach of justice to remove from their ministry men appointed either by them (the apostles) or, later on and with the whole church's consent, by others of proper standing – men who, enjoying everybody's approval, have ministered to Christ's flock faultlessly, humbly, quietly and unassumingly. (42.4; 44.2–3)

This passage does not prove that the apostles founded a college of bishops as distinct from presbyters. Paul's surviving letters to Corinth do not mention presbyter-bishops or deacons. This silence seems significant because he makes practical arrangements about the ordering of worship, moral discipline and an important collection for the church in Jerusalem and he says that 'within our community God has appointed in the first place apostles, in the second place prophets, thirdly teachers; then miracle-workers, then those who have gifts of healing, or ability to help others or power to guide them, or the gift of tongues of various kinds' (1 Cor 12.28). However, it is possible that he agreed to the appointment of presbyter-bishops in a letter which has not survived. He certainly urged congregations to obey their leaders; he did so in the earliest of his surviving letters (1 Thess 5.12–13). Timothy and Titus were his agents and in the post-Pauline Letter to Titus (1.5–9) the appointment of suitable 'elders' in each town, including at least one bishop, to be 'God's steward' and a sound teacher, is said to be in accordance with his principles. But 'a curious fact about the New Testament', writes one Roman Catholic scholar, Avery Dulles, 'is the absence of any precise indication as to whether there were officers specially designated by cultic functions' (*Models of the Church*, 1976, p. 152). Another, Edward Schillebeeckx, notes that in the New Testament 'there is certainly still no formal procedure, not even a special liturgical framework, for the selection and appointment of specific leaders, prophets or teachers in the communities' (*The Church with a Human Face*, 1985, p. 60). And this letter of Clement says that if presbyters appointed 'with the whole church's consent by men of proper standing' are to be deposed, it must be by the church as a whole, no mention being made of the powers of a bishop or other successor to the apostles. The apostles are invoked by Clement as having set the example of appointing leaders in an orderly manner.

The evidence that has survived indicates a considerable variety in the general leadership of the congregations. Paul's letter to another church, in Philippi, is addressed to 'bishops and deacons' as well as to 'all God's people'. The words *episkopoi* and *diakonoi* may have meant simply superintendents and servants, or leaders and helpers, and may have been derived from the titles of the honorary officers of the religious and other clubs flourishing in the Gentile world at the time. The later First Letter to Timothy (3.1–13) lists moral qualifications for being a bishop or deacon, but like the Letter to Titus it provides no job description. We learn only that 'elders who give good service as leaders should be reckoned worthy of a double stipend, in particular those who work hard at preaching and teaching' (5.17). Schillebeeckx concludes that in these Pastoral Epistles 'the *episkopos* is one of the presbyters, but evidently not all presbyters can be called *episkopos*' (p. 67).

Although Paul never uses the term 'elders' in his surviving letters, Luke believed that there were in his day, at least in Jerusalem and Ephesus, 'elders' given charge over the congregation by the Spirit (Acts 11.30; 15.4; 20.17–38). The word 'elders' seems to have been taken from the senior men who led the Jewish synagogues. But titles do not seem to have been uniform. Other documents speak merely of 'leaders' (e.g. Heb 13.7), and the Letter to the Ephesians mentions 'apostles, prophets, evangelists, pastors and teachers' (4.11). In the messages to the seven churches in the Revelation of John no church leaders are mentioned, although the congregation in Ephesus is congratulated: 'you have put to the test those who claim to be apostles but are not, and you have found them to be false' (2.2). The letters are addressed not explicitly to the bishops of these churches but to their 'angels', whatever may be meant by that term. Here we seem to be given glimpses of congregations which would need firm leadership once prophetic messages of this calibre were no longer available as unifying guidance. Such leadership is called *episkopē* by Luke (Acts 1.20; 20.28), but he hints broadly that after Paul's last visit there was a struggle for it between rival elders in Ephesus (20.30). The Third Letter of John, itself written by an 'elder', praises Demetrius in contrast with Diotrephes 'who enjoys taking the lead'.

It seems highly probable that the speed of the process by which one of the presbyter-bishops took the lead over the others differed from church to church. It was rapid in Jerusalem under James and in some other churches whose life we can still glimpse, but the evidence suggests that in the whole of Egypt (for example) there was only one bishop until after the death of Demetrius, Bishop of Alexandria, in 231. The catechism goes far beyond the evidence when it asserts that 'the apostles left bishops as their successors and gave them their own position of teaching authority' (77) and that 'since the beginning the ordained ministry has been conferred and exercised in three degrees: bishops, presbyters and deacons' (1593). A similar claim made in the Book of Common Prayer of the Church of England (1662) is similarly unsustainable and has not been repeated in later Anglican documents.

It seems that the Roman church remained conservative, and therefore presbyterian, for longer than most. As the Roman Catholic scholar J. M. R. Tillard notes, 'we have no serious proof that there was a single bishop at Rome, other than a college of presbyters or bishops, before the middle of the second century' (*The Bishop of Rome*, 1983, p. 83). Documents surviving from Christian Rome towards the middle of that century do not mention any monarchical bishop. The books of the martyred theologian Justin do not, although he refers to deacons and to a 'president' (*proestōs*) at the Eucharist. *The Shepherd of Hermas* mentions bishops, presbyters and deacons, all in the plural. It includes a request for copies to be sent to other churches by 'Clement' – which may refer to a new church secretary of that name, or may suggest that the author was placing his story in a Rome which had existed some forty years before he wrote. *The Muratorian Canon*, which was compiled in Rome about 175, says that Hermas wrote 'while his brother Pius, the bishop, was filling the chair of the church of the city of Rome'. This is one of the surviving fragments of evidence which suggest that the first monarchical 'Bishop of Rome' emerged in the 140s or thereabouts.

The development of the papacy

In the lists compiled to demonstrate (it seems, not reliably) the succession of the Bishops of Rome, Anicetus is the tenth name. Soon after 155 Polycarp, the aged Bishop of Smyrna, visited him and tried to persuade him to begin the celebration of Easter, already traditional in Asia Minor. He refused. However, his successor, Soter, did adopt this Easter tradition and a letter from Dionysius, president of the church in Corinth, survives in fragments, fulsomely acknowledging gifts and a letter in which Soter had given his advice. Early in his onslaught *Against the Heresies* (about 180) Irenaeus recorded a list tracing the succession of twelve bishops of Rome back to the appointment of Linus by Peter and Paul. 'In this very order and succession', he wrote, 'the apostolic tradition in the Church and the preaching of the truth have come down even to us.' He referred to 'this very great, oldest and well-known church' and taught that 'every church – that is, the faithful from everywhere – must be in harmony with this church because of its more powerful pre-eminence'. But confusingly he added that this respect for Rome was due to it not only because its own bishops conveyed the apostles' teaching but also because 'the apostolic tradition is preserved in it by people from everywhere' – in other words, by Christians visiting or settling in the capital from all over the empire. And far from acknowledging the universal jurisdiction of the Bishop of Rome as the inheritor of Peter's universal authority, Irenaeus protested successfully when Bishop Victor tried to excommunicate the bishops of Asia Minor for celebrating Easter on 14 Nisan in the Jewish calendar instead of on the Sunday after it.

In the next century the Roman bishop could expect not only persecution and even execution by the State but also opposition from rivals within the Church. Hippolytus, a disciple of Irenaeus, taught that 'the Holy Spirit bestows the fullness of grace on those who believe rightly that they may know how those who are at the head of the Church should teach the tradition and maintain it in all things'. But he agreed to be set up as a rival bishop ('antipope' would be the later term) to Callistus, who was theologically less able and ethically less rigorist. His *Apostolic Tradition* shows that by now the Roman bishop was expected to preside over the Eucharist as a 'high priest' and to 'forgive sins', but the dispute between Hippolytus and Callistus was about the limits of forgiveness in the system for public penance if the sins were serious. Hippolytus believed that the discretionary power of the bishop as he presided over this public system ought to be strictly limited. Strict rigorism had been defended against an earlier pope by the theologian Tertullian (who died about 225), and the dispute continued when a later pope, Cornelius, had a rival in Novatian.

In Carthage the influential Bishop Cyprian (who was martyred in 258) valued the example given by Rome of willingness to admit as penitents Christians who had lapsed either during persecution or through sexual sins. Cyprian denied that 'confessors' (Christians who had defied persecutors more heroically but had survived) could declare the forgiveness of sins. This power belonged, he maintained, to the bishops in solidarity with the senior bishop, the Bishop of Rome. He then referred 'to the chair of Peter and to the original (*principalem*) church, whence the unity of the bishops (*sacerdotum*) took its rise', and to 'the fact that these are the Romans whose faith was praised by the apostle's proclamation, to whom false faith can have no access'. However, when a later Bishop of Rome, Stephen, taught that baptisms by schismatics or heretics were to be treated by Catholics as valid – another sign of the Roman church's generosity to people repenting after human weakness – Cyprian led the North African bishops in the rejection of this doctrine. There is some uncertainty because there were two editions of his treatise on *The Unity of the Catholic Church*, only one of which taught the unity of believers around the 'chair of Peter', but it seems clear that his basic position was that the Bishop of Rome had precedence but not jurisdiction, being among bishops the first among equals. He often called bishops 'priests', comparing them with the Jewish high priests as he emphasized their presidency at the Eucharist in Jesus' place.

In the fourth Christian century the 'conversion' of the emperor Constantine, although probably shallow, soon brought peace and prosperity to the Roman church, and it proved to be momentous because its consequences eventually made the Christianity of the whole of western Europe Roman. But for a time it did not greatly magnify Rome's religious position.

As the leadership of the Church turned its attention to theological disputes the action involved eastern bishops equipped with philosophical skills and emperors based on the new capital, Constantinople, and possessed both of political power and of their own opinions about which form of the Christian religion would best serve their empire's unity. Bishop Silvester sent envoys from Rome to the Council of Nicaea (325), but that gathering of bishops indicated its idea of his proper authority by deciding that the church of Alexandria should have a jurisdiction like his, but in its case over Egypt, Libya and the 'Pentapolis'. Clearly he was regarded as the senior bishop in the west. Rome continued to have a reputation for orthodoxy. The outline of its teaching of candidates for baptism in this period was almost exactly the same as the 'Apostles' Creed' which was first so called about 380. (Its present form is first found about 725.) Its bishops usually defended Bishop Athanasius of Alexandria when bitter doctrinal disputes continued after the Council of Nicaea, although one (Liberius) temporarily altered this position. About 340 Bishop Julius wrote from Rome to the eastern bishops: 'Why was nothing written to us about the church of Alexandria? Are you ignorant that the custom has been for word to be written first to us, and then for a just sentence to be passed from this place?' The eastern bishops rejected this claim, but not long afterwards the bishops of the leading churches of the west agreed that in certain circumstances bishops could appeal to Rome if threatened with deposition.

In the next century the great bishop and theologian Augustine was happy to regard his controversy with Pelagius as having been settled when the Bishop of Rome, 'president of the Church in the west', had spoken. In 451 the bishops' council in Chalcedon hailed a 'tome' in which Bishop Leo had summed up orthodoxy as 'the voice of Peter'. But in neither case was the Bishop of Rome treated as later popes were to be. For Augustine, authority over the Church was exercised by its one Lord, who acted partly through the Scriptures, partly through synods of bishops and partly through the Spirit touching the individual's heart. For the Council of Chalcedon, the Bishop of Rome was to be honoured mainly because Rome had been 'the imperial city'. Now that Constantinople had become the capital of the eastern half of the empire, it seemed proper that its church should be 'magnified like Rome in ecclesiastical matters'. So the decision of the council of 381 that the Bishop of Constantinople should have 'the privileges of honour after the Bishop of Rome' was endorsed, much to the Roman bishop's disapproval.

During the fifth century the position of the Bishop of Rome was strengthened. The main cause was not his defence of the orthodox faith. Orthodoxy was decided by councils meeting in the east at the command of the emperor and under his presidency or his nominee's. In 451, for the first time, this nominee was also Rome's representative. In the crucial

Council of Constantinople in 381 there seems to have been no western participation at all. In between councils, theological creativity centred on the rival bishops and churches of Alexandria, Antioch and Constantinople. The chief factor in the ecclesiastical progress of Rome was now the decline of the authority of emperors in the west, accompanied by the fear of anarchy. The empire's capital was moved to Constantinople in 330. The empire was divided into east and west in 395, with the dividing lines between Greece and Italy and between Greek and Latin as the official languages. The western capital was moved first to Milan and then to Ravenna, and after 476 there was no western emperor. Barbarians swept over western Europe and North Africa. If Christians, they were often unorthodox. The Bishop of Rome now became not only that poverty-stricken but still historic and prestigious city's principal figure, and not only Italy's largest landowner, but also the west's chief reminder of Christian stability, classical civilization and administrative efficiency. No other bishop in the west could be a rival, for the Bishop of Rome was 'Patriarch of the West'. Amid stormy waters, here was a rock on which the house of Europe might one day be rebuilt. And the belief was beginning to spread that because of the great promise to Peter, the Bishop of Rome could lock anyone who defied him in the everlasting torments of hell.

Even in the Greek-speaking east, which usually reckoned itself superior to the west, no Christian centre had this prestige. Long ago Jerusalem had been destroyed by Rome's secular power. Now Constantinople, claiming to be the 'new Rome', had the disadvantage of novelty. Its bishops also had the handicap of proximity to the eastern (Byzantine) emperors, for these inherited Constantine's own attitude that he had the right to control religion as well as politics – and the emperors' religious opinions might not coincide with the 'orthodoxy' of most of the bishops. Between 726 and 842 emperors were among the 'iconoclasts' who attacked all religious pictures and statues as idols, and many churchmen who defended their traditional images were imprisoned or executed. Byzantine emperors continued to be powerful in ecclesiastical affairs until the last of the line fell during the fall of Constantinople in 1453. Many Christians in the east were motivated by anti-imperialism when they rebelled against the decisions of bishops' councils which were always convened, and often controlled, by these emperors who claimed to be God's representatives on earth. The 'patriarchs' (as they came to be called) of the three leading sees were often at loggerheads in the doctrinal disputes which the emperors tried to control, and the history of these bishops was too often a history of alleged heresies which laid them open to rebukes. In contrast, Rome could seem as independent, stable and reliable as granite.

In Rome the bishop claiming to be the successor of a martyred fisherman was not always aloof from the violence of these times. In 366 Damasus hired thugs to massacre his opponents as part of his election to what he (for the first time) called the 'apostolic see'. But churches in Italy, Gaul (later France) and Spain (not North Africa) accepted a further development when Siricius, elected in 384, called himself 'pope' or 'father' and began to issue 'decretals' in the same style as the edicts of the emperors. Men who in an earlier period might have been civil servants or ministers in the empire were now serving the Church, and Rome's ecclesiastical authority was expanded by some imperious bishops including Innocent I (elected in 401) and Leo I (elected in 440), men of a stature thought to deserve the old title of the pagan emperors, *pontifex maximus* ('the greatest priest'). In 495 the pre-eminent use of the title 'Vicar (deputy) of Christ' was claimed by another pope, Gelasius I. It was no longer enough to be Peter's voice or vicar. The title 'Vicar of Christ' had been applied regularly to bishops elsewhere before this, however, and this practice continued for another five hundred years. In the 290s Diocletian had divided his empire into twelve 'dioceses' and had placed a 'Vicar of the Emperor' at the head of each. Now in the west many Christians came to accept the Bishop of Rome as the paternal pope, the supreme priest, Christ's emperor-like deputy, the guide of the bishops of other dioceses.

There was an inevitable backlash from eastern bishops. As early as 343 most of them boycotted the Council of Sardica and held a rival council of their own. Ecclesiastical relations between Rome and Constantinople broke down between 484 and 519 – an omen of things to come. For a time the eastern emperor recovered control of Italy and therefore of Rome. But in 590 a really great leader, Gregory I, who had previously been 'prefect' (civil governor) of Rome, was elected pope. Aristocrat and monk, writer and ruler, he tirelessly organized an Italy now devastated by barbarians. He made peace with the invading Lombards without consulting the emperor, in a move which signalled the split between the west and the Byzantine empire. He sent missionaries to the barbarians' northern neighbours, the English, in a move which was to lead to the expansion of papal authority over northern Europe when the English in their turn sent missionaries there. Gregory was personally humble, calling himself 'servant of the servants of God'. He ordered that in the west he alone should be called 'pope' but when the Patriarch of Alexandria addressed him as 'universal bishop' that courtesy was rebuked: 'Away with those words which inflate vanity and wound charity!' 'I know what I am and what you are', Gregory told the eastern bishops. 'In rank you are my brothers, in manner of life my fathers. I have therefore not given orders but have simply done my best to indicate what I think useful.' In the same spirit, however, he strongly objected to the Bishop of Constantinople calling himself 'Ecumenical Patriarch'. What he did in the sphere where he thought he could give orders, western Europe, was to act as the tactful, uniquely able and energetic pastor and leader of grateful churches. Anglicans have always had a special reason to be grateful to him, for he sent the mission which began the conversion of those of the English (the majority) who were not being reached by the Celtic missionaries originating in Ireland. Although he discouraged any idea that this mission should insist on exclusively Roman customs in the new churches, Christian England's link with Rome was to have central significance in the religion and civilization of the Middle Ages.

The record of the papacy

If today many Christians including Anglicans criticize the record of the papacy, the complaint is not about Gregory the Great. It is about many of his successors – and he had many, for his belief that the end of the world was about to occur was premature. The record illustrates the truth of the well-known saying of Lord Acton, a great Roman Catholic historian who was stern in his verdicts on popes, that all power tends to corrupt.

The 'temporal power' of the popes was traditionally justified by the argument that they needed to be independent and, looking back, most Christians would agree that the popes needed their own economic base. But it would also be very widely agreed that too much of their energy was spent on the acquisition and defence of the papal states which covered the middle of Italy, and on the administrative problems, shifting alliances and military campaigns which resulted from the possession of this large earthly kingdom. This helped to make sure that all popes between 1523 and 1978 were Italians, yet the papacy hindered the political unity of the Italian people, with effects still felt in Italian politics at the end of the twentieth century.

The consolidation and expansion of these territorial possessions were based on two deals. Charlemagne was crowned as the first 'Holy Roman' emperor by Pope Leo III in 800. Charlemagne claimed that he had been taken by surprise and Leo did him homage, but an alliance was struck. An earlier agreement had been reached between Charlemagne's father Pepin and Pope Stephen II, in 754. In exchange for support which he needed Pepin then promised the papacy a large slice of Italy controlled by his rival, the King of the Lombards. It was probably on this occasion that the 'Donation of Constantine' was produced by the pope. This was a forged document, purporting to show that the emperor Constantine had offered the imperial crown to Pope Silvester, had recognized him as the ruler of 'all the churches of God in the world' and had conferred on him dominion over Rome, Italy and 'the provinces, places and cities of the western regions'. This edict was generally accepted as authentic in western Europe until scholars (beginning with Lorenzo Valla) exposed the fraud in the fifteenth century.

So for more than twelve hundred years all popes became politicians in competition or conflict with emperors, kings, princes or city states. The last armed conflict between a pope and an emperor was in 1708. Several popes commanded their own armies in the field. More used the spiritual weapon of excommunication in their political struggles. The scandal would have been less had the papal states become a model of good government, but for many periods including the nineteenth century (when Italy was becoming a more or less modern nation in the teeth of papal opposition) the evidence points in the opposite direction. Few popes enjoyed a reign long enough to establish a continuous policy and few had been prepared for this role in secular government by their previous experience. They had to rule through agents – their own relatives, local aristocrats, humbler laity or clergy – who were often unsuitable. Although participating in violence, in intrigues, in the oppression of taxpayers, in the censorship or punishment of any criticism, or in sheer corruption or incompetence, the popes consistently claimed that their lordship over the papal states was necessary if they were to be spiritual leaders. Gregory XVI restated that claim eloquently in *Mirari Vos* (1832) and it seemed to be an integral part of the Roman Catholic Church's doctrine until the treaty between Pius XI and Mussolini in 1929 established the Vatican as a state inside Italy. This entanglement in devilry seemed essential to the fulfilment of the duties entrusted to Peter and his successors by the Christ depicted in St Matthew's gospel as rejecting an offer of 'all the kingdoms of the world in their glory' and as promising a better kingdom to the poor in the spirit, the sorrowful, the gentle, the hungry for righteousness, the merciful, the pure and the peacemakers.

Their role as militant monarchs was developed when successive popes, beginning with Urban VI in 1096, sponsored armed crusades against the Muslims. Most of the papal eloquence in this cause produced nothing but humiliating rebuffs from fellow-rulers who refused to get involved (the last instance was in 1517) or disastrous defeats for the crusaders including misled children. But the damage done to the relations between Christianity and Islam lasted much longer than these farces or tragedies. The crusades are still remembered by Muslims – more than the words of Vatican II that the Church looks on them 'with esteem' since they too 'adore one God' and 'revere' Jesus. And the crusades further embittered relations between Catholics and Orthodox, as 'Latin' patriarchs were established first in Antioch and Jerusalem and then in Constantinople itself after massacres of the Orthodox and sacrilege in their churches committed as part of a crusade. To the north the Teutonic Knights waged a kind of crusade with papal blessing, acquiring large lands to the east of Germany which in 1234 were placed under the pope as overlord.

The wealth of the papacy meant that it was often coveted by men grossly unsuitable for a position of spiritual leadership. These could be the nominees of families already wealthy in Rome or in the rest of Italy, or of monarchs outside that turbulent country. The results were sometimes spectacular, as will be agreed even if we dismiss some of the stories about sexual irregularities. Almost a century and a half of what has been called 'pornocracy' in the papacy was inaugurated when in 897 the body of Pope Formosus was dug up by a successor who in local politics belonged to a rival faction. The decaying corpse was clothed in papal robes, tried, condemned, deprived of the fingers which had bestowed the apostolic blessing and thrown into the Tiber. Two other popes were teenagers when elected. Essentially political rivalries meant that another pope, Benedict IX, a man of violent and scandalous life, was deposed three times between 1032 and 1048.

From 1309 to 1377 the papacy was dominated by Frenchmen influenced by the French monarchy and was based not on Rome but on Avignon in the south of France. There Clement VI in particular lived in a luxury which was notorious (and thus the food of legends) partly because of its extravagance, partly because those sharing the pope's pleasures conspicuously included both relatives and mistresses, and partly because some of the expense was funded by the profits of a trade in 'indulgences'. These, His Holiness explained in *Unigenitus* (1343), could draw on the 'treasury of merits' accumulated by the Church.

Back in Rome, the papacy's corruption became infamous when a Franciscan friar, Sixtus IV (elected in 1471), consented to crimes including murder by his enriched nephews. Alexander VI (elected in 1492) made his family name, Borgia, stink for the next five centuries. The ruthless warrior Julius II (elected in 1503) had about him, as was said, nothing of the priest except the name and the dress. His more pacific successor, Leo X, spent with such reckless extravagance on his pleasures, as well as on his patronage of the arts, that he authorized the sale of the 'indulgences' which aroused the entirely justified indignation of Martin Luther in 1517. Fifty years passed before a pope prohibited such commerce. Later popes of the Renaissance appointed as cardinals two grandsons aged fourteen and sixteen (in 1534) and a youth named Innocenzo with whom Julius III had become infatuated.

In the long period which we are here covering very briefly, there were many popes who were not flagrantly immoral princes, but it was a further tragedy that the cause of reform was often associated with personally moral popes who led the Church to moral or political disaster. In reaction against the disturbing power of the sexual instinct, and also against the involvement of the clergy in family life which would distract them from putting the interests of the Church first, many popes after Leo IX (elected in 1049) did their utmost to end the practice of allowing clergy to be married. Abundant evidence suggests that even when celibacy had become the universal law of the western Church (in 1123) many medieval clergy, including some of the popes, found the imposition a burden too heavy to bear. The results were much scandal (the city of Rome being most notorious for prostitution) and some guilt.

In reaction against the influence of monarchs and landowners on the appointments of bishops and lesser clergy (and of popes), many popes were involved in fierce struggles against 'lay investiture'. If fellow-rulers defended their hereditary rights to make appointments in the Church, or at least to 'invest' ceremonially men appointed by the Church, whole countries could find themselves placed under a papal 'interdict' prohibiting most acts of Catholic worship. That was the experience of England in 1208–14, to give only one example. Pope Innocent III claimed the right to choose an emperor, as when he preferred Otto to a rival also 'elected' in 1198 although he later deposed him. His claim to choose an Archbishop of Canterbury was in comparison trivial, although his consequent dispute with King John led to the interdict. When the king surrendered to him as overlord and promised a large annual tax, he vetoed concessions made to mere barons such as those in Magna Carta (1215). He also became feudal overlord of the kingdoms of Aragon (in Spain), Portugal and Poland. When the crusade which he had sponsored was diverted to conquer and sack Constantinople in 1204 his reaction was mild, but when some heretical Christians in the south of France, the Albigenses, killed one of his agents he ordered another massacre called a crusade in 1208. Under his pontificate all Jews and Muslims were ordered to wear a distinctive dress exposing them to the prejudices of 'Christians'.

The pope's dispute with the emperor over 'lay investiture' was settled when it was agreed that bishops and abbots should be freely elected (but at first in the emperor's presence) and 'invested' with the symbols of their spiritual authority while the emperor retained the right to invest them with the sceptres symbolizing their worldly wealth. But free elections did not survive for ever. From the 1310s, instead of insisting on free elections the papacy claimed the right to 'provide' appointments to bishoprics and other wealthy posts in the Church. Normally these appointments would be of men acceptable to the local rulers, but opportunities were taken to 'provide' (for example) non-resident Italians to English bishoprics.

Armed, as was thought, with supernatural as well as political power, a pope who asserted himself against other rulers could win some dramatic victories. The most famous was the abject humiliation of King Henry IV by Pope Gregory VII at Canossa in 1077. Gregory seemed to have vindicated the right to depose all princes in Church or State which he had asserted in his *Dictatus Papae* (together with the doctrine, which his successors did not reaffirm, that 'a rightly elected pope is, without question, a saint, made so by the merits of Peter'). But such victories seldom lasted. In this instance, King Henry soon rallied his forces, set up his own pope, seized Rome and caused Gregory to die broken-hearted. Almost a thousand years later popes were still claiming to be among the rulers of this world, but in fact they relied on the protection of foreign troops and when the French emperor withdrew his troops from Rome in 1870 the story of the Vicar of Christ as the successor of Caesar ended.

It was inevitable that a papacy so immersed in local or international politics should be surrounded by controversies about elections. These were frequent because usually the pope was well on in years when elected. In 1059 it was settled that the election (not necessarily of a Roman) should be made by cardinals who were nominally the clergy of churches in Rome, the laity merely adding their assent, but that very practice caused unsettlement. The cardinals' conclave was a small meeting, often riven by personal jealousies. Cardinals often tried to impose conditions on candidates and when a newly elected pope disappointed those who had voted for him – as he often did – or when a Roman mob or a more distant emperor brought pressure to bear – as also happened – an 'antipope' could be elected as a rival. There were almost forty such antipopes before the line ended in 1449, and between 1378 and 1417 the whole of Christendom was divided into two allegiances. That Great Schism was ended when the Council of Pisa deposed Gregory XII and Benedict XIII, and when the Council of Constance deposed a third 'pope', having convicted him of a list of sins which have delighted anti-papal historians.

Nor was the papacy thought to be so firmly exalted above controversy that a charge of heresy was inconceivable. The Council of Pisa declared both Gregory XII and Benedict XIII heretical. A pope might correct his predecessor, as when in 1336 Benedict XII corrected the teaching of John XXII that the beatific vision of God could not be enjoyed by the saints before the final judgement of all humanity. In 553 Pope Vigilius was judged heretical by the Second Council of Constantinople until he agreed with the council's theology, and in 680 another pope, Honorius, was censured by the Third Council of Constantinople.

Much has been made controversially of the last mentioned lapse from orthodoxy, but it amounted merely to agreeing with some eastern churchmen that Christ had 'two distinct natures and one operation', even 'one will'. Honorius agreed because the eastern emperor was at that stage trying to placate, and recover control over, Christians who had broken away affirming that Christ had only one 'nature', and it seemed a shrewd compromise to say that he had only one will. The emperor certainly had.

Many modern Christians who are not deeply impressed by such disputes are likely to be more concerned about what passed for orthodoxy during the Middle Ages – the assertion of the pope's will as the will of Christ. And among eastern Christians with a far deeper respect for the teachings about the natures and wills of Christ agreed by the ecumenical councils, indignation about the developing claims of the papacy has been great. In 863 Nicholas I deposed and excommunicated Photius, who had become Patriarch of Constantinople after his predecessor's abdication – and Photius replied by holding a synod which deposed and excommunicated Nicholas. That schism lasted until 879, but it turned out to be the forerunner of mutual excommunications between the pope's envoy and the patriarch in 1054, not lifted in theory until 1965 (when the situation remained much the same on the ground). Councils held in Lyons in 1274 and in Florence in 1439 failed to heal the breach because neither side was in the end willing to compromise after claims such as those made in the 1260s by no less a theologian than Thomas Aquinas. In his treatise *Against the Errors of the Greeks* he insisted that the pope had plenitude of power over the whole Church in succession to Peter: he 'decides what is part of faith' – the faith necessary to salvation. The churches in the east passionately rejected such claims as heretical novelties. The people in those churches repudiated the concessions which bishops had made in the hope of getting help from the west against the Muslims. When Eastern Orthodox and Roman Catholics did share a Eucharist, it was the last act of Christian worship in the church of the Holy Wisdom in a doomed Constantinople.

The assertion of papal power reached its medieval climax as the thirteenth became the fourteenth century. Boniface VIII seems to have been hated by almost everyone apart from his relatives whom he enriched, but he was never abashed. In *Clericis Laicos* (1296) he denounced the taxation of the French clergy by their king without his consent. 'The laity', he announced, 'have always felt hostile to the clergy', forgetting that 'all power over the clergy, over the persons and property of the Church, is denied to them.' So all involved in such taxation 'automatically incur excommunication'. Six years later he issued *Unam Sanctam*. There he appealed to a text spoken by Jesus on his way to Gethsemane: 'Enough!' This was in reply to the disciples' 'Lord, we have two swords here'. The pope did not dwell on the question which the Lord had asked: 'When I sent you out barefoot without purse or pack, were you ever short of anything?' (Luke 22.35–38). Instead this was his bizarre interpretation:

> Both swords, the spiritual and the material, are in the power of the Church, the one, indeed, to be wielded for the Church, the other by the Church; the one by the hand of the priest, the other by the hands of kings and knights, but by the priest's will and permission . . . We declare, announce and define that it is altogether necessary to salvation for every human creature to be subject to the Roman pontiff.

To many it must seem that this version of the Gospel is heretical. The only reason for not so describing it is, it seems, that it had somewhat more modest precedents in the teaching of some previous popes. Eight hundred years previously Gelasius I had taught that it was 'impossible for the apostolic see to be stained by any false doctrine or to be contaminated by error'. Particularly was teaching about papal supremacy found in the False Decretals, a collection of papal letters down to the 720s mostly forged in France and invoked by Nicholas I in 865.

Boniface VIII has sometimes been defended as a churchman who made extravagant propaganda when under pressure because he was obsessed by his ultimately unsuccessful struggle with King Philip of France. But the claims of popes to the right to allocate the kingdoms of this world continued. Most spectacularly, in 1493 the Borgia pope, Alexander VI, 'by the authority of Almighty God bestowed on blessed Peter', bestowed on the Spanish monarchs 'all the islands and mainlands, found or to be found' lying to the west of a line drawn across the Atlantic, the lands of the east (including Brazil) having been given to Portugal. In 1570 a far more austere pope, Pius V, deposed the 'heretical' Elizabeth as Queen of England and authorized other nations to overthrow her government by force. This was, he explained, an exercise of the 'plenitude of power' entrusted by Christ 'to Peter's successor, the Roman pontiff' in order that he might 'govern' the Church 'outside which there is no salvation'. By this act he made every faithful Roman Catholic in England a potential traitor, so that he unintentionally contributed to the cruel deaths of many martyrs while Elizabeth continued to reign.

That was the last exercise of the papal power to depose a ruler, however, and it may be thought more significant that Pope Pius, who had been Inquisitor General in Rome, directly secured the deaths of many non-royal heretics. The Jews whom he denounced while pope, banishing them to a ghetto as Christ-killers, were lucky to escape with their lives. The Roman ghetto lasted until popes no longer ruled Rome.

In 1231 Gregory IX made obstinate heretics condemned by special courts liable to execution by secular rulers. In 1252 Innocent IV (who described himself as 'the bodily presence of Christ') allowed the torture of suspects – a decision not reversed by the papacy before 1816. Other customs commended by popes to inquisitors showed neither mercy nor justice during the proceedings. The Spanish Inquisition was established in 1478 by Sixtus IV (who also drew satisfaction from his profitable licensing of brothels in Rome). It rapidly ordered the burning of about two thousand people who had not sufficiently converted from Judaism or Islam. Six years later Innocent VIII, the father of several illegitimate children, called for the severest punishments, meaning torture and death, for heretical witches who, he alleged, had among other terrible deeds hindered men from performing the sexual act. Thus he blessed a long campaign of witch-hunting. The involvement of the papacy in such iniquities was defended over many centuries by the argument that without it many more people would have become heretics and so been sentenced by God to the greater agonies of hell. A more modern, and more valid, defence has been that popes shared the cruel and ignorant prejudices of their times. They were no worse than contemporary rulers.

Recently many Roman Catholics, including popes and expert historians, have expressed a profound regret about the failure or slowness of the papacy, and of the Church in general, to undertake serious reforms in response to the deeply religious protests which exploded in the Reformation of the sixteenth century. These protests got sadly entangled in the political causes of national or civic independence, in greed for the Church's wealth, in cruelty towards continuing Catholics and in sheer vandalism destroying beauty built up by the Catholic centuries. Many aspects of the Reformation were shameful. But it has become generally acknowledged that for many believing Christians – as many of the Protestants were, passionately – the driving force behind the Reformation was the conviction that the medieval Church, in obedience to the papacy, had become entangled in many doctrines and practices which were incompatible with the New Testament. Many Catholics who were not willing to break with Rome agreed that the Church needed to be reformed 'in head and members'. Some popes also agreed, the short-lived Hadrian VI (1522–23) being the first example. But far too little was done, leaving a vacuum in the leadership of reform which during some crucial years was filled by some lay rulers anxious to extend their power and by some prophetic preachers who, in exasperation at the behaviour of the papacy, preferred the belief that these rulers had been raised up by God to lead the cause of reform.

Luther's visit to Rome left him scandalized by the spectacle of the Renaissance papacy's luxury and corruption, but his outrage had parallels all over Europe. Back in Germany, his encounter with the sale of indulgences shocked him further, but that difficulty could be matched by countless examples of the laity unable to defend the positions of the clergy although they were often themselves happily devout. Long before Luther's time the Orthodox churches of the east had protested against the western doctrines surrounding the idea of purgatory. In the west many of the laity resented the formal, and apparently final although unbiblical, decision of Pius II in 1462 that they should not receive the wine in Holy Communion. The restriction had become general in the west by about 1200 despite strenuous papal condemnations of it in earlier years. It led on to the doctrine of 'concomitance', for as the Council of Constance reminded the faithful in 1415 'it can in no way be doubted that the body and the blood of Christ are truly and integrally contained under the species of bread as well as under that of wine'.

Luther's religious experience was profoundly personal but also, in less intense forms, widespread. He met the God of love in the Bible. Mercy reaching Christians through their faith in Christ was 'the righteousness of God' – and he had not found that God amid all the busy 'works' and real strengths of late medieval piety. As Protestantism spread, countless Christians met that God as they met the message of the Scriptures in their own language. The Augsburg Confession drawn up by Lutheran theologians for their dialogue with Catholics in 1530 showed that, given good will on both sides, the gap between them could have been narrowed at many points and might perhaps have ceased to be a division. But that 'confession' avoided the all-important subject of the papacy – a silence which was a sign of the suspicion reigning on both sides.

The division of western Christianity was not ended by the fairly small number of mostly Italian bishops who attended the sessions of the Council of Trent (1545, 1551–52, 1562–63). That council began the moral reform of bishops and priests: they were to be trained in seminaries, they were to reside in their places of duty, they were to be pastors and preachers. It encouraged the laity to be regular at confession and Mass and it stressed the sacredness of marriage and the family. It inaugurated the more intense spirituality which became the soul of the 'Counter-Reformation'. This spirituality burned within a fireplace created by a new sense of order and discipline, for the effects of the council included the reformulated catechism of 1566, the rephrased Mass of 1570 and a reformed code of canon law in 1580 – all destined to be authoritative into the twentieth century. It also formulated some doctrines in ways which often avoided the crudities of late medieval popular Catholicism. But its teachings about penance, purgatory and indulgences could not be expected to satisfy Protestant consciences. Against the evidence of the Bibles which were now being printed extensively, it claimed that the seven sacraments of the medieval Church had all been instituted by Christ. It did not restore the right to receive the consecrated wine to the laity or the right to marry to the clergy. And, like the two Vatican Councils which were to follow it after long intervals, it failed to establish any authority which could continue the process of reform and renewal if the papacy were to fail.

The modern papacy

The papal power which had been exerted in the Middle Ages to rule much of Italy, to topple monarchs, to allocate continents to colonizers, and to send heretics and witches to preliminary tortures and the stake, is clearly not the power which this catechism defends. Many Roman Catholics have denounced it as eloquently as any Protestant. Indeed, many Roman Catholics have been among those protesting that since the age of the Reformation the papacy has sometimes been too weak, rather than too strong, in relation to secular rulers.

For example, under pressure from them Clement XIV reluctantly agreed to the suppression of the Jesuit order which had served the papacy with heroic obedience. It was 'perpetually broken up and dissolved' in 1773 – until 1814. More damaging to the papacy's good name were the success of Pius XI in concluding a concordat (treaty) with the new Nazi government in 1933 and the failure of Pius XII to condemn publicly the very great sins perpetrated in the 1940s under Hitler, a Catholic by birth and baptism although he repudiated Christianity. The brave denunciation of breaches of the concordat, and of signs of Nazi paganism, which Pius XI launched in 1936 was not followed up. Hitler's withdrawal from plans for mass euthanasia in the 1930s after protests by Catholic bishops suggests that had the rise of Nazism been condemned as immoral the maturity of evil in the 1940s might have been restrained, for the Führer was always surprisingly sensitive to German public opinion. Instead, on the ground the Roman Catholic Church became largely (not completely) identified with the triumphs of Mussolini's Fascists in Italy and Franco's Falangists in Spain; bishops gave no support to those few Germans who refused to serve in Hitler's army; and until the Americans' entry into the war, Pius XII seems to have accepted very sadly the inevitability of a Nazi victory, although he privately condemned Nazi excesses and did what seemed to him possible to help Jews and other victims. The argument often used in his defence, that a more public condemnation would have been futile and would have brought suffering to many Catholics living under the Nazis, is of course not to be dismissed. But the caution of Pius XI is in striking contrast with the papal deposition of Elizabeth of England some 370 years previously. It is also in contrast with the inflexible resistance to Communism which the papacy led until the 1960s. Pius XI declared formally in 1937: 'Communism is intrinsically wrong and no one who would save Christian civilization may collaborate with it in any undertaking whatsoever'.

However, in the more strictly religious sphere papal power has grown in the modern age, and brief reminders may be offered about some of the reasons why many millions of Christians have been convinced that it has not always deserved 'the obedience of faith' or 'the religious assent of the mind'. These Christians have included the ancient Orthodox churches of the east, angered when Rome recruited dissident groups from their membership to form 'uniate' churches accepting papal jurisdiction. One such group attracted most of the Orthodox in Poland and the Ukraine in the 1590s. Another, the Melkites, emerged in the Middle East during the 1720s.

It is now widely known, and regretted, that the papacy did not welcome the truth that the sun, not our planet, is the centre of the solar system – a discovery vital to the rise of modern experimental science. (In 1600 Giordano Bruno, a pioneer in that rise, was burned by the Roman Inquisition.) In 1616, under Gregory V, the treatise of Copernicus (a priest) which had begun to demonstrate this truth about the solar system was placed on the 'index' of prohibited books established in 1559 and not ended before 1966. At the same time Galileo, a devout Catholic layman, was formally warned not to teach such a contradiction of the Bible. In 1633 under Urban VIII Galileo, then aged 70, was threatened by the Inquisition with torture when he had published a dialogue between an opponent and a supporter of Copernicus, making it clear (although not explicit) that he agreed with the latter. He was compelled to recant and to promise silence. His condemnation was not formally reversed until 360 years had passed. And the participation of many Roman Catholics in good scientific work has not entirely erased these blots on the record.

The papacy also lamented the birth of religious liberty in the modern world. In 1555 Paul IV condemned the Peace of Augsburg which ended the religious wars of the Reformation by allowing both Catholics and Protestants to exist in Germany, and in 1648 Innocent X denounced the granting of rights to Protestant minorities in the Peace of Westphalia, which ended thirty years of 'religious' war. In 1572 Gregory XIII publicly celebrated the most notorious incident in the French wars 'of religion' – the massacre of Protestants on St Bartholomew's Eve. One of the eighty 'principal errors of our time' attacked by Pius IX in his 'syllabus' of 1864 was the suggestion that 'other forms of worship' should be allowed by a state. In his view the Roman Catholic Church taught 'the only true religion' and had the right to use force during its mission. Summing up a tradition which essentially continued until the 1960s, the 1864 syllabus concluded triumphantly that it was an error to think that 'the Roman pontiff can, and ought to, reconcile himself to, and come to terms with, progress, liberalism, and modern civilization'. Four years later he pronounced more favourably on slavery, held by him to be contrary neither to Scripture nor to nature. Twice in the 1890s Leo XIII (who modified Pius IX's stance) formally warned all Christians against thinking that the separation of Church and State in the USA, with religious liberty for all, was the best model.

Other papal teachings on important matters have failed to command assent in the long run and have been revised. For example, in 1705 Clement XI prohibited the Christian adaptation of Chinese rites for the veneration of ancestors, thus causing the closure by the Chinese empire of a Jesuit mission which had been remarkably promising. This condemnation, although matched by the suppression of a similar experiment in India, was reversed in 1939. In 1794 Pius VI declared that even the use of a living European language in liturgical prayers would be 'false and foolhardy'.

In 1830 Pius VIII expressed 'horror' at 'grave crimes' in a reference to marriages between Catholics and Protestants, and he reaffirmed 'this firm dogma of our religion, that out of the true Catholic faith no one can be saved'. In 1863 Pius IX described the denial of this dogma as 'of course extremely (*maxime*) contrary to Catholic faith'. He also taught (to quote words used in 1854) that 'those who live in ignorance of the true religion, if such ignorance be invincible, are not subject to any guilt in this matter in the eyes of the Lord' – but that concession received less emphasis. In 1896 Leo XIII assured those who 'depart from the one and only enduring Church' that they were 'heading for destruction', and in 1928 Pius XI reaffirmed the traditional teaching that 'the unity of Christians can come about only by furthering the return to the one true Church of Christ of those who are separated from it'. Not even in order to spread this stern message were Roman Catholics to take part in ecumenical discussions or joint prayers. As late as 1954 Pius XII taught that any participation in ecumenical activities required the Vatican's special permission. This teaching was reversed when in 1965 Vatican II exhorted all the Catholic faithful to 'take an active and intelligent part in the work of ecumenism'.

As late as 1956 Pius showed what 'the return to the one true Church' would mean by demanding that Latin should always be used at Mass, except when the papacy gave a special permission as in 'uniate' churches allowed to use languages of the east. 'One would be straying from the straight path', he added, 'were one to wish to see the altar restored to its primitive table-form.' These positions, too, were cancelled during the 1960s.

Although often conciliatory, Benedict XIV demonstrated his adherence to a tradition inherited from the Middle Ages. In 1754 he condemned 'usury', defining it as 'that guarantee by which it is pretended that from what has been loaned more should be returned than the original loan'. Thereby he condemned all shareholders and bankers, although in the nineteenth century the papacy was to refine its criticism of capitalism and was to develop its own bank. This did not escape major scandals by its involvement in the often corrupt world of high finance in Italy, but is now controlled by an international group of respected senior bankers.

During the eighteenth century papal teachings showed very little awareness of the force of the protests of the philosophers of the 'Enlightenment' against the falsehoods and the intolerance enshrined in the Church. As in the period of the Reformation, critics were turned into enemies. In 1879 Leo XIII insisted that Catholics should regard as authoritative the thirteenth-century theology of Thomas Aquinas, at least as the basis for their own theology. He pronounced in 1893 that all the books in the Bible 'in their entirety were written under the dictation of the Holy Spirit'. He cautiously encouraged an intellectual elite but in 1907 his sterner successor, Pius X, reaffirmed that divine inspiration made everything in Scripture 'free from every error'. He denied any opposition may 'exist between the facts narrated in Sacred Scripture and the Church's dogmas which rest on them'. In 1910 a long oath (not officially replaced until 1967) was imposed on all clergy and others who claimed to be teachers of the Catholic faith, denouncing the 'Modernist' opinions which this pope or his equally conservative advisers had drawn out of an unfair interpretation of unnamed books. These opinions were said to constitute a systematic collection of all the heresies. To it was opposed a system of beliefs said never to change 'from one meaning to another' and to be error-free, and alleged deviations from this system of 'absolute and immutable truth' were hunted down in what has been correctly described as a reign of terror. A council of vigilance was established in every diocese, with a secret society to assist it by reporting suspects to the Vatican – among them two future popes, Benedict XV and John XXIII. Eminent scholars were censored, as was any priest who wished to write a letter to a newspaper. And in 1994 the situation was that Pius X was the last pope canonized as a saint.

This regime was somewhat relaxed when Benedict XV became pope in 1914 and (as I have gladly noted) Pius XII encouraged some freedom in the study of literary styles in the Bible. However, in *Humani Generis* (1950) Pius showed a renewed willingness to pit the papacy against modern thought and knowledge by sweeping condemnations, which led to the further discouragement of leading scholars. Existentialist thought was then denounced as a 'philosophy of error' because it left 'the unchanging essences of things out of sight'. The 'historical method' was rebuked 'if it confines its observations to the actual happenings of human life'. The idea that the human body evolved from other living matter was allowed, but only as a speculation – and only if it did not affect the belief that all humanity is descended from one individual, Adam. Pope Pius added: 'When the Roman pontiffs go out of their way to pronounce on some subject which has hitherto been controverted, it must be clear to everybody that, in the mind and intentions of the pontiffs concerned, this subject can no longer be regarded as a matter for free debate among theologians'.

Other beliefs taught with emphasis by the papacy, but often nowadays held by Roman Catholics and other Christians to have been errors, are mentioned elsewhere in this book. But this brief summary of the past may be enough if our main concern is to see whether the record of history justifies this catechism's claims about the papacy in the present. We may leave the history of the papacy with a verdict which Pius XI delivered about politics in *Quadragesimo Anno* (1936), although he did not apply it to his own power: 'It is an injustice, and also a grave evil and a disturbance of right order, to assign to a greater and higher association what lesser and subordinate associations can do'. As this catechism affirms, 'the way God acts in governing the world, which bears witness to such great regard for human freedom, should inspire the wisdom of those who govern human communities' (1884). We must turn our attention to the questions: are bishops' councils infallible, and if even they can err how does God maintain truth in his Church?

Infallible councils?

The bishops' councils that struggled to end the scandal dominating the early years of the fifteenth century had to proclaim their superiority to the rival popes in order to depose them. The Council of Constance accordingly declared in 1415 that a council 'has its power directly from Christ' and that the pope was 'bound to obey it even in matters relating to faith'. The pope who emerged out of this confusion, Martin V, had joined the unanimous vote of the council to this effect although he later repudiated the concession. In 1682 an assembly of the French clergy adopted this subordination of a pope to a council although Innocent XI instantly repudiated such 'Gallicanism'. In 1781 one of the last of the Holy Roman emperors, Joseph II, again tried to limit the power of the papacy by an edict in favour of himself and diocesan bishops. This 'Febronianism', so named after a theological book of 1763, was condemned in Rome, but it remained for a time strong in Germany.

However, these three peaks of a strong attempt to restrict papal power all crumbled into the dust. Among the reasons for these failures, two factors were decisive. The first was the link between 'conciliarism' and nationalism or imperialism. The rulers of the nations had great influence over their own bishops. This could discredit the bishops' theology, which might seem to be political expediency when it reduced the pope's power. But it also created the possibility that a pope could do a deal with an emperor or king, one ruler with another, so that in exchange for papal support in the politics of the day the governments' support for the bishops' claims was withdrawn. The other decisive factor was the pope's continuing activity in the religious sphere when the council had dispersed. Year by year, a pope could acquire a prestige and popularity which an occasional and untidy council lacked. This came to a climax in the influence of Pius IX in 1870. A pope also had money. The contrast with most of the bishops came to a climax when most of those at the Council of Trent (never a large number) depended on him financially. And a pope had power, whatever lesser bishops might say. He could simply cancel the decision of the Council of Constance that he must convene other councils regularly, at least once every ten years.

By the 1860s the tide in the affairs of the Church was running away from conciliarism. The great dramas of the French Revolution and the Napoleonic empire had demonstrated twin dangers: Christianity itself might be suppressed by the advocates of reason and democracy, yet governments might accumulate too much power while crushing revolutionaries. The dependence of Christianity on Catholicism, and of Catholicism on the pope, was now proclaimed by 'ultramontanes' who looked for authority 'beyond the mountains', most eloquently in France. When a French emperor abandoned the defence of the papal states it seemed more necessary than ever to stress and develop the papacy's spiritual dominion. This was done in the First Vatican Council, by the 'constitution' entitled *Pastor Aeternus* which has already been quoted. There had been opposition arguing that the definition of infallibility would be 'inopportune', specially from German and American bishops.

Criticism also came from the leading theologian, Newman, and the leading church historian, Döllinger, who were not present in the council. However, many such bishops abstained from voting and the minority which did vote against *Pastor Aeternus* submitted. Most Roman Catholics accepted the definition as stating what they had anyway assumed to be a part of their faith, and the numbers who joined the rejection by 'Old Catholics' (started in 1724) remained small.

When in 1959 John XXIII announced his decision to summon another council there was general surprise, for it had been thought that no council would be needed after Vatican I; and he himself had no clear plans for this strange event. But when the bishops met, it became evident that the 1960s were different from the 1860s. Opposition to lists of leaders and drafts of documents prepared by conservative officials in the Vatican showed a spirit of some independence. To some observers it seemed possible that this council might reverse the decision of 1870 that no council could reform a papal decision claimed to be infallible. At the least, there might be a formula of compromise such as the suggestion of the fifteenth century that the pope could not err when 'using the counsel and seeking the help of the universal Church'. In the event, the general (although not unanimous) verdict on the Second Vatican Council was that it brought new life and light. Thirty years later the absence of any equivalent in the Eastern Orthodox Churches can be seen to result in the absence of renewal and reorganization. But Vatican II reaffirmed the narrower definition of papal infallibility by Vatican I, and the continuing absence of any check on papal authority in practical affairs became obvious when the council also agreed to withdraw from its discussions the vital questions of birth control and married priests: the decisions were to be made by the pope alone (with disastrous consequences). Charles Davis, a prominent Roman Catholic theologian in England before he left the priesthood, wrote bluntly: 'At the Second Vatican Council there was a glossing over by everyone of the major changes in papal authority necessary for any serious acceptance of collegiality. This was a great mistake' (*The Temptations of Religion*, 1973, p. 75).

When a leading European theologian, Hans Küng, eventually decided to rebel against papal authority, he did not repeat the argument that a pope needed the agreement of a council of bishops in order to be assured of infallibility. In his book *Infallible?* (1970) he rejected the whole concept of infallibility which had been accepted by both Vatican Councils. Part of his argument was historical. The Roman Catholic Church regards fourteen councils held since 787 as ecumenical (representing the whole Christian world) although this classification was developed only in the sixteenth century, partly in order to authorize the Council of Trent. However, since a papal pronouncement in 1460, it has regarded as heretical the claim that a council may hear appeals from the authority of the pope. Eastern Orthodox, Protestant and Anglican Christians deny that these Roman Catholic councils were truly 'ecumenical', and it seems significant that the Eastern Orthodox, while claiming that they could hold such councils since they are the only true Church, have felt themselves able to do without guidance by any councils that could claim to have the authority of those held in 787 or earlier. Protestants specially deplore the burning of the Czech reformer Jan Hus by the Council of Constance in 1415 after being assured of his safety if he came to put his case to the bishops. Against the insistence of Hus that only holy people can truly belong to the Church, the council wisely decreed that the Church includes sinners. Unfortunately it proved it.

There are also problems about the councils held in and before 787. Seven of these (sometimes eight) have been revered by the Eastern Orthodox and the RC Church, and at least four (sometimes six) by Protestants and Anglicans, but it is not accurate to regard them as triumphant successes. They were rejected by large bodies of 'heretics', including the Arians who converted much of Europe to Christianity, the Monophysites who took it up the Nile to Ethiopia and the Nestorians who took it to Persia, China and India. These divisions between Christians, accompanied by much bitterness and violence, weakened their response to the Muslim invasions as the Arabs rapidly conquered Jerusalem, Antioch, Alexandria, North Africa and Spain between 637 and 711. Moreover at least five other councils which were convened as 'ecumenical' have not been treated as such even by Catholics and Orthodox. The first ecumenical council, Nicaea I in 325, was widely respected as uniquely authoritative, yet its creed did not prevent fierce doctrinal disputes breaking out. In 381 another council (Constantinople I) was convened in order to settle these disputes and a creed was produced in order to embody its decisions. This creed closely resembled the creed of Nicaea and wrongly became known as the 'Nicene creed'. When the next authoritative council met, at Chalcedon in 451, many of the bishops said that they had never heard of it but they endorsed it without dispute. Sixty years later the church in Constantinople began to use it in public worship, but when a bishops' council at Toledo in Spain ordered its use in 589 it was with the addition of 'and the Son' (*Filioque*) to the statement that the Holy Spirit 'proceeds from the Father'. In this expanded form the creed was ordered to be used in the emperor Charlemagne's dominions about 800, but about another two centuries passed before it was used in worship in Rome – with the addition of the extra words, although Leo III had strongly condemned the change in 810. The new catechism offers no apology for this unilateral addition to an ecumenical creed (247), but I have to add that the addition has also been preserved in many (not all) Anglican prayer books.

Hans Küng's later work has shown much sympathy with the modern criticisms of the over-ambitious theology of these 'ecumenical' councils, and the relevant questions will be outlined in the next chapter of this book. Meanwhile it may be suggested that one lesson taught by this complicated history is that a council is recognized as 'ecumenical' and authoritative in a process which may be neither rapid nor total. Ideally the whole Church's agreement is expressed by the Russian word *sobornost*, meaning 'free agreement in love', but in history the reality may be more complicated. Küng's main argument, however, did not depend on detailed historical considerations. An interpretation of the nature of Christianity led him to wish to substitute for 'infallibility' the technical term 'indefectibility' or the slightly more popular 'perpetuity in truth'. 'If the Church ceases to be in the truth', he wrote, 'it ceases to be the Church. But the truth of the Church is not dependent on any fixed, infallible propositions, but on her remaining in the truth throughout all propositions, including erroneous ones' (*Infallible?*, p. 150). After a much shorter book in which he argued that the Church was 'maintained in truth' although not infallible, in 1979 the Sacred Congregation for the Doctrine of the Faith acted with the approval of Pope John Paul II. It declared that Küng 'can no longer be considered a Catholic theologian nor function as such in a teaching role'. Thus he was sentenced to world-wide fame.

Authority in the Church

Recent dialogues between Roman Catholic and other theologians have attempted to move beyond this apparent impasse by exploring the idea of 'indefectibility' with more diplomatic finesse. The seed of the idea had been sown long before. For example, an Anglican scholar, T. G. Jalland, had concluded his major study of *The Church and the Papacy* (1944) by saying that 'belief in the infallibility of the Church seems to amount to this: it is the conviction that those interpretations to which the consensus of the Church has been given will correctly mediate the original *depositum*, and therefore cannot mislead' (p. 536). But such a definition had left many questions unanswered. What body of Christians is meant by 'the Church'? How extensive is the agreement required? Within what period must the 'consensus' be obvious? Once given, can it be withdrawn? Must the doctrines so endorsed be only 'interpretations' of the New Testament, or may they add new facts to those related in that 'deposit'? Above all, how can such a definition be acceptable to the RC Church, when Vatican I clearly decreed that infallible teachings of the pope do not require the consent of the Church?

In 1973 the Congregation for the Doctrine of the Faith issued from the Vatican a declaration intended to be reassuring (*Mysterium Ecclesiae*). 'God, who is absolutely infallible', bestowed upon the Church 'a certain shared infallibility' about faith and morals 'which is present when the whole People of God unhesitatingly holds a point of doctrine relating to these matters.' And in 1980 the official Lutheran–Roman Catholic dialogue in the USA ended in agreement that 'the ministry of the Bishop of Rome should be seen as a service under the authority of the Word of God. The doctrine of infallibility is an expression of confidence that the Spirit of God abides in his Church and guides it in the truth.'

In 1976 the first Anglican–RC International Commission of theologians reached a 'convergence' which was remarkable but scarcely less ambiguous than Jalland's conclusion. The Bible, it said, is 'a normative record of the authentic foundation of the faith'. Through it 'the authority of the Word of God is conveyed' and 'the Christian community is enabled by the Holy Spirit to live out the Gospel and so be led into all truth'. 'By reference to this common faith each person tests the truth of his own belief' and 'the Spirit of the risen Lord . . . safeguards their faithfulness to the revelation of Jesus Christ.' In this context, 'since the bishop has general oversight of the community, he can require the compliance necessary to maintain faith and charity in its daily life'. In this duty he is assisted by other ordained ministry, and the whole Christian community 'must respond to, and assess, the insights and teaching of the ordained ministers'. But when bishops meet in ecumenical councils, their decisions 'are binding in the whole Church' since 'they express the common faith and mind of the Church'. The ambiguities in these agreed words arose in part from the avoidance of any explicit suggestion that errors may be found in the Bible, or in the teaching of the ordained ministers, or in the faith of the 'Church' as this is expressed at any one time. Indeed, the commission agreed that 'when the Church meets in ecumenical council its decisions on fundamental matters of faith exclude what is erroneous'. These decisions, however, must be 'faithful to Scripture and consistent with Tradition'. They are not necessarily 'the only possible, or even the most exact' way of expressing the faith, so that 'the mode of expression may be superseded'. But 'restatement always builds upon, and does not contradict, the truth intended by the original definition'. It was not explained how faithfulness to Scripture and Tradition might be tested or how a truth 'intended' but not expressed originally might be discerned.

Difficulties increased when the commission considered the papacy in 1976, but the extent of the agreement is very remarkable:

The purpose of the episcopal function of the Bishop of Rome is to promote Christian fellowship in faithfulness to the teaching of the apostles. The theological interpretation of this primacy and the administrative structures through which it has been exercised have varied considerably through the centuries. Sometimes functions assumed by the see of Rome were not necessarily linked to this primacy: sometimes the conduct of the occupant of this see has been unworthy of his office: sometimes the image of this office has been obscured in interpretations placed upon it: and sometimes external pressures have made its proper exercise almost impossible. Yet the primacy, rightly understood, implies that the Bishop of Rome exercises his oversight in order to guard and promote the faithfulness of all the churches to Christ and one another.

In 1981 the commission responded to some criticisms of these careful words. It said more clearly that 'the New Testament contains no explicit record of a transmission of Peter's leadership'. It maintained that Vatican I 'need not be taken to imply that the universal primacy as a permanent institution was directly founded by Jesus during his life on earth'. It agreed that the pope 'has the right in special cases to intervene in the affairs of a diocese and to receive appeals from the decision of a diocesan bishop', but it explained that 'the jurisdiction of the Bishop of Rome is called ordinary and immediate (i.e., not mediated) because it is inherent in his office; it is called universal simply because it must enable him to serve the *koinōnia* (fellowship) as a whole and in each of its parts'. It added that Vatican II 'allows it to be said that a Church out of communion with the Roman see may lack nothing from the viewpoint of the Roman Catholic Church except that it does not belong to the visible manifestation of full Christian communion which is maintained in the RC Church'. It agreed also that the pope has the right to exercise 'responsibility for preserving the Church from fundamental error', although it noted that the term 'infallibility' is 'applicable unconditionally only to God'.

These 'clarifications' went a long way towards Anglican recognition of papal claims. However, they did not satisfy the Congregation for the Doctrine of the Faith, which in 1992 insisted that:

For the Catholic Church, the certain knowledge of any defined truth is not guaranteed by the reception of the faithful that such is in conformity with Scripture and Tradition, but by the authoritative definition itself on the part of the authentic teachers . . . The Catholic Church believes that the councils or the Pope, even acting alone, are able to teach, if necessary in a definitive way, within the range of all truth revealed by God . . . The Catholic Church sees in the primacy of the successors of Peter something positively intended by God and deriving from the will and institution of Jesus Christ. As is well known, the Catholic doctrine affirms that the historical-critical method is not sufficient for the interpretation of Scripture. Such interpretation cannot be separated from the living tradition of the Church which receives the message of Scripture.

This response made it completely clear that the Vatican now understands Christianity as a religion in which the pope, assisted sometimes by bishops' councils, defines truths authoritatively and precisely, so that the faithful are certain that they are true. The religion which has this character was, it is claimed, instituted by Jesus Christ. However, while noting that the Vatican discourages reliance on the 'historical-critical method' we may be forgiven for asking what the historical evidence tells us about the substance and style of Jesus Christ's own teaching.

Christian truth

The gospels of Mark, Luke and Matthew leave the impression that Jesus concentrated on the proclamation of the arrival of the Kingdom of God. He did not teach so much about the Church: his concentration was on transformed individuals and a transformed society, the transformation being brought about by the joyful acceptance of the overwhelming fact of God's miraculously outreaching love. He taught his disciples to pray for the complete power of God's government. He did not leave behind, either in writing or in speech, detailed instructions for the life and teaching of the community of his disciples. It was not even made clear whether this community was to be confined to Jews. What Jesus did was to tell stories and to utter pithy sayings which provoked thought about the coming of 'the kingdom', in promise and demand. These were remembered. Above all, Jesus left behind the story of his own life and the great utterance which was his death-and-resurrection. In many ways he was a man of his time and place, a Galilean Jew. He accepted many of the conventional practices and ideas of his teachers and contemporaries. He shared current beliefs about the authorship of the books in the Hebrew Scriptures, for example, or about demons causing diseases, as he shared current hopes that the end of that unhappy age was imminent. These beliefs are now generally regarded as erroneous. But his style of teaching as conveyed in these three 'synoptic' gospels meant that Jesus escaped making the far more damaging mistakes which are inevitable if anyone with a human mind dictates propositional dogmas and laws meant to be enforced by threats of excommunication or hell.

The admission that to be human is to be liable to error also seems to be thoroughly in keeping with John's gospel. There Jesus announces that he personally is 'the truth' and promised that the Father will give 'the Spirit of truth', 'to bear witness to me' and 'to guide you into all the truth' (14.6, 17; 15.26; 16.13). But in this gospel this 'truth' does not include all propositions about faith and morals, or about history, which can be connected with Scripture through Tradition. It covers what 'the Spirit hears' from the Father, what belongs to the Father and Jesus and 'what is to come' – in other words, what is eternally true, revealed by Jesus and vindicated at the End (16.13–15). This limited but all-important 'truth' reaches us through the Father's 'word' (17.17).

Did John interpret the Spirit's guidance as a promise of infallibility to the apostles, enabling them to repeat the teaching of Jesus exactly? The best answer to that question seems to be indicated by the fact that John never directly quoted any other passage contained in what the Church came to venerate as the New Testament, although it is generally agreed that he wrote after Paul, Mark, Luke and Matthew, and some passages in his own gospel suggest that he was aware of the traditions recorded by those authors of Scripture. Such was the limit of his reverence for the infallibility of the apostolic tradition. Or did John mean that through the ages the 'bishops' as successors to the 'apostles' could infallibly interpret that tradition by teaching doctrines or facts not recorded in Scripture? In support of the suggestion that he did, a text from the First Letter of John has been quoted: 'You have been anointed by the Holy One, and so you have knowledge' (2.20). But the readers of that letter were assured that this 'anointing' had already taught them 'all you need to know' so that 'you need no other teacher' (2.27). And in this fourth gospel the words 'apostles' and 'bishops' are not used.

John recorded his own tradition which at many points was incompatible with the other gospels, and most modern scholars are agreed that he did not hesitate to put his own words into the mouth of Jesus. So did the early generations of Christians accept that other teachers had the right to act as John had done, while claiming their teachings to be part of the 'apostolic tradition'? The answer is that four gospels, and only four, became accepted as recording the authentic teaching of the Lord and the apostles. Some ninety years after the completion of John's gospel, Irenaeus insisted that there could be only four and attacked the claim of the Gnostics that they could add to these gospels or to the rest of the apostles' teaching. This teaching was, he maintained, preserved by Scripture and by the churches which, through a succession of bishops or through 'men from everywhere', remained faithful to what the apostles had actually taught. He ridiculed the idea that there had been secrets handed down by the apostles but not known to Scripture or to those churches at that time, and he knew nothing of any idea that later Christians could infallibly 'explain' or 'develop' what the apostles did teach.

In what sense, then, is 'the Church of the living God the pillar and bulwark of the truth' (1 Tim 3.15)? I hope it will not seem too ridiculous if, having recorded criticisms of popes and councils, I expose myself to criticism by submitting concisely what I believe as one Anglican student of the New Testament and Christian history.

Infallibility is simply impossible for any human being or human group, for all of us can make mistakes. 'Inerrancy', meaning that a mistake has not been made, is a little less difficult and in this context I would adapt the phrase used by Aidan Nichols about the Bible (which I quoted on p. 22) to say: 'it is the entire Christian community as a self-correcting whole that enables us to identify the inerrant aspect of any one doctrine'. Amid the sins and errors – the destructive weeds, the useless fish, the guests not ready for the party or claiming places which are not theirs – the Christians who constitute the Church are given by God the Holy Spirit a grasp on the essential 'Gospel' or good news of God's reality and rule which the apostles did pass on from Jesus, as the foundation of the Christian faith. After all the complex history of the relationships between ecclesiastical and political authorities, the voice of the Lord can still be heard forbidding excessive claims on either side: 'Pay Caesar what belongs to Caesar, and God what belongs to God' (Mark 12.17). After all the spiritually splendid or tragic history of the papacy and other church leadership, the Church's one Lord can still be heard promising to make his follower Peter and other followers 'fishers of men' if following really does mean taking up one's own cross (Mark 1.17; 8.34). Despite all the misuse of the Bible, the Christian people has wielded a single sword, the sword 'which the Spirit gives you, the word of God' (Eph 6.17) 'piercing so deeply that it . . . discriminates among the thoughts and purposes of the heart' (Heb 4.12). The Gospel spread by the Christians, following with their golden crosses and blunt swords, remains the truth which sets people free (John 8.32) – free to accept from God all kinds of truth and progress, but above all free from the darkness of a world which does not know or obey God. This is 'the truth with which the Redeemer willed his Church to be endowed'. And through the Christians who are the One, Holy, Catholic and Apostolic Church in all the centuries and continents, many hundreds of millions of other people have found this truth and, through it, this life.

This kind of 'maintenance' in the essential truth despite human errors was part of the experience of Peter according to the New Testament. If it was not to be a Satanic temptation to avoid suffering, his confession of Jesus as 'the Messiah, the Son of the living God' at Caesarea Philippi needed to be corrected by the truth that Jesus was 'Messiah' in a sense not expected by him or (so far as we know) by anyone else apart from Jesus (Mark 8.27–33). A radically new understanding of that title was declared when it was asked: 'was not the Messiah bound to suffer in this way before entering upon his glory?' (Luke 24.26). In the Acts of the Apostles, we are told that Peter was the first Christian to baptize Gentiles, since after resisting the idea he came to understand that 'in every nation those who are God-fearing and do what is right are acceptable to him' (10.34, 35). Yet we have noted that Paul told the Galatians that years later Peter still did not fully understand the implications, for when he insisted in Antioch that 'Gentiles must live like Jews' his 'conduct did not square with the truth of the Gospel' (2.14). According to Acts, Peter described Jesus as 'a man singled out by God' who 'went about doing good . . . because God was with him' (2.22; 10.38). That primitive 'Servant Christology' would have been condemned as heretical by the ecumenical councils of the fourth and fifth centuries, but any error or inadequacy in it did not prevent Christians from arriving gradually at more fully truthful ways of obeying the instruction in the document called the First Letter of Peter: 'hold Christ in your hearts with reverence as Lord' (3.15). The New Testament presents Peter as one who shared the belief, common to the early Christians, that those were 'the last days' (Acts 2.17), when 'the end of all things is upon us' (1 Pet 4.7), but what mattered far more than any such error was the true belief about God: 'in his great mercy by the resurrection of Jesus Christ from the dead, he gave us new birth into a living hope' (1 Pet 1.3).

It seems that if, as this catechism claims, it was Peter's mission 'to guard this faith from every error' (552), he was not completely successful – and if the Bishops of Rome were meant to be infallible, or at least to deserve 'assent' always, history does not testify to their complete success either. But it does not follow that such human failures have killed the heart of Christian faith. That heart is the truth to which the Bible and the Church bear witness.

CHAPTER

4

The heart and clothes of faith

THIS CHAPTER is going to be shorter, but that is not because the subject is less important. The Bible matters because through it God is revealed. The Church matters because it is the instrument or 'body' of Christ. The God in whom Christians believe is infinitely more important than the Bible or the Church.

This chapter is going to be full of questions, but that is not because I disagree with what matters most in the Roman Catholic Church's teaching about God as Father, Son and Holy Spirit. The heart of Christian faith beats in all truly Christian hearts and it is not necessary to spell out all the agreements here. What needs to be washed from time to time, and occasionally may need replacement, is not faith's heart but faith's clothing.

Even after the Reformation most Christians were content to be simply orthodox believers in the traditional doctrines about basics. They raised very few, if any, questions of the sort that will be asked in this chapter. The ancient expressions, often set out in this catechism, were accepted as sacred. The Church of England, for example, ordered that the Apostles' or Nicene creed should be recited at almost every service and it often prided itself on its conservative orthodoxy, accusing the Roman Catholics of adding to 'that faith which God entrusted to his people once and for all' (Jude 3). That was the theme of Jewel's *Apologia* for the Church of England in 1562 and of Hooker's more elaborate volumes which began to be published in 1594. In the Anglican tradition since then there have never been lacking conservatives determined to hold that static faith, perhaps as a kind of Western Orthodoxy, perhaps as a system based on

'Scripture alone'. There is nothing exclusively Roman Catholic in the conservatism I shall question, and there is nothing distinctively Anglican in the questions I shall ask. What is, however, characteristic of the Church of England, and to a lesser extent of other parts of the Anglican Communion, is the freedom with which the questions have been asked in public during and since the eighteenth century. This freedom is not exclusively Anglican. It has been conspicuous in the history of the Lutherans, for example; there, famous theologians have said many things which would have horrified Luther. And in our time many Roman Catholics ask these questions – although often in a less public and perhaps less articulate manner, for the sense of loyalty to the Church's leadership is strong. So is the fear that if any question about 'the Faith' is asked too loudly, the whole house of Christianity will come tumbling down. It may therefore be the role of an Anglican (or of a Lutheran, etc.) to ask the questions without a Roman Catholic's inhibitions. Indeed, this role may be a duty owed to truth – and this duty may be an obligation even though raising these questions in ecumenical discussions makes agreement still more difficult, so that the diplomatic approach may prefer the many such discussions (the recent Catholic–Orthodox theological conversations, for example) which have ignored them.

The questions have to be confronted in connection with a task which this catechism acknowledges to be 'indispensable': the 'adaptation' of the teachings in this catechism which is 'required by the differences of culture, age, spiritual maturity and social and ecclesial condition' (24). 'Adaptation' is also required if the questions of our time asked outside the Church are to meet with a sufficiently serious response so that there may be evangelism, the commendation of the Gospel. But it is not a task which can always be discharged simply by producing summaries of the traditional doctrines, as indeed this catechism does – with the suggestion that they should be memorized (22). Shortening a dogma may be an aid to sympathy and understanding; in this chapter I am shortening my questions as an aid to the reader's patience. But even the abbreviated dogma may remain hard or impossible to understand or accept. Nor is it always enough to illustrate the dogma by a homely comparison or story. The illustration may then be appreciated while the dogma may still be thought incomprehensible or untrue. Sometimes it is necessary to communicate Christian truths by finding new words – words which translate old truths into the thoughts as well as the languages of cultures and generations remote from the ages which produced the Bible and the Church's orthodoxy. Sometimes in order to pass on the Gospel it is vital not to be too traditional.

This is obviously a dangerous process, for it may mean the abandonment of truths which the traditional words expressed. John XXIII conveyed warning as well as encouragement in the famous words with which he opened the Second Vatican Council: 'The substance of the ancient doctrine of the deposit of faith is one thing, the way in which it is presented is another'. Therefore it is healthy that when attempts are made at the restatement of basic Christian doctrines there will always be conservatives eager to spot mistakes and dangers, challenging the 'heretics', the 'innovators', the 'modernists', the 'liberals' or the 'radicals' to defend their claim to be evangelists rather than traitors. And it is understandable that no such attempts were made by Vatican II. But not to attempt the task is also to run risks, chiefly the risk of making the Gospel a fossil. Only in a superficial view is the revision of traditional expressions thought to be incompatible with the catholic and evangelical task of spreading the Gospel ('evangelism' or, in the preferred Roman Catholic term, 'evangelization'). And it is a short-term view to say that only exceptionally well educated people have difficulties with the truth or realism of what has been taught traditionally: obviously most people are not intellectuals, but it can be the duty of intellectuals to articulate disquiets felt by ordinary folk.

When the Christian Church is confronted by a persecuting enemy propagating a monolithic ideology, as has been the case under the Roman empire, under Nazism, under Communism, or sometimes under Islam, it is understandable that it usually adopts the strategy of affirming its own orthodoxy with as much intellectual rigidity and organizational resistance as may seem possible. It is a time for heroes. That has been Roman Catholic as well as Eastern Orthodox, or Protestant, experience; and in particular it has been the experience of the Pole who became Pope John Paul II. But when that enemy is defeated, the scene changes. Christians are no longer so prepared to be told how to think, behave or vote, or how to spend their Sundays; and people on the fringes of the churches, while grateful that the churches kept alive a spirit which was an alternative to the dominant ideology, are critical if church leaders now seem locked in the intellectual and social structures of the unhappy past. That, too, has been experienced in the second half of the twentieth century. After the initial euphoria of freedom which often applauded Christian humanism, obedience to church leaders and attendance at clergy-controlled churches have declined. The questions about traditional expressions of Christianity have surfaced. It is a time for answers.

When the Christian Church enters a non-Christian society which is heavily traditional and by modern standards uneducated, its task is twofold. It has to preach the Gospel in as simple a form as possible hoping that, despite the strangeness of its traditional expressions, its appeal will produce conversions; and it has to establish a network of healing and education in the hope that this will show that Christians seek the people's welfare. It is a time for missionaries. But when Christianity has been rooted in that new soil, the churches cannot safely be controlled any longer by foreign personnel or foreign ideas, for local Christians will sooner or later insist on developing their own expressions of the Gospel and on weaving their own clothes for the faith which responds to that news. At varying speeds, that process can be observed in the 1990s all over the Two-Thirds World. It is a time for 'natives'.

And it is a mistake to think that the restatement of the expressions which clothe Christian faith must always be too intellectual, too negative or too complicated to be acceptable to ordinary folk. Inevitably theologians develop a professional jargon and a habit of talking (mainly to each other) with an intellectual precision which tries to avoid questionable statements, but that is a style regarded as properly professional by conservatives as well as by others. It is also inevitable that the period of debate before clarity emerges may be long. To some extent, the New Testament is itself the record of a debate about the significance of Jesus Christ. The actual restatement which becomes truly public, however, may be effective on the conditions that it springs from, or relates to, everyday experience; that it is positive with a keen sense of human needs; and that it is as simple as possible. In these characteristics it will resemble the witness of the gospels to the teaching of Jesus Christ.

Faith and knowledge

First I ask whether it is right to rely on the First Vatican Council, as this catechism does, for the teaching that 'God, the first principle and last end of all things, can be known with certainty from the created order by the natural light of human reason' (36).

Such a confident statement is easier to accept in societies where the existence of God (or gods) is taken for granted by almost everyone, at least in the background of daily life. Jesus and the first Christians lived in such a society and this catechism quotes Paul: 'Ever since the creation of the world God's eternal power and divine nature, invisible though they are, have been understood and seen through the things he has made' (32). But, as the catechism grants, people can forget, misunderstand and even explicitly reject this 'intimate and vital bond with God' for causes which include 'a revolt against evil in the world' and 'currents of thought hostile to religion' as well as less honourable factors (29). The catechism is surely right to say that even in an atmosphere of doubt the existence of God can still be glimpsed by some 'in the natural light of human reason', by following and weighing the arguments. What results, however, scarcely amounts to 'certain knowledge': it is faith.

In particular, faith in God must seem different from 'certain knowledge' in a society where science, not religion, seems to most people to provide the most reliable way of knowing and proving. The catechism quotes, rather than justifies, Pius XII's lofty rebuke to sceptics or doubters in modern societies: 'The human mind is hampered in the attaining of such truths, not only by the impact of the senses and the imagination, but also by disordered appetites which are the consequences of original sin. So it happens that people in such matters easily persuade themselves that what they would not like to be true is false or at least doubtful' (37). The problem which the pope avoided is that people easily persuade themselves that what they do like is what is true.

Modern sceptics, whether atheists ('no God') or agnostics ('don't know'), are not all stupid fools or gross materialists. There are in our time many intelligent and highly moral people, self-denying, loving, utterly sincere in seeking the truth, who find it difficult to believe in 'God' if by those three letters is meant the Creator and Ruler who is father-like. To many Hindus, 'God' should not be characterized in that way, for 'God' may have many faces, father-like but also animal-like, creative and loving but also destructive; and this approach appeals to many outside India. To many people who adhere to traditional paganism (especially in Africa), the 'God' who created all things is, if believed in, remote (perhaps in the sky or up a mountain) and worship is directed to the god or gods of the tribe without necessarily denying the existence of other tribal gods.

To many others, more modern because more influenced by science, the universe seems too vast and too complex to be covered by a childish explanation. Human beings seem too animal-like to be able to know 'the first principle and last end of all things'. Despite all its order and beauty, this planet is full of things which do not seem to have come straight from a parent-like, divine love, and despite all its goodness life on this planet seems a sad affair, often in the events and always at the end. In the last analysis all existence can seem an absurd accident, the product of chance combinations of realities known to physics and chemistry – but an accident which produces its own iron laws of cause and effect, those necessities which take no account of any individual's merits but which on the whole favour the strong and crush the weak.

This view of the world can be taken by people who are more or less thoughtless, but atheism (the so-called 'death of God') is also accepted as the truth by many of the best educated and most reflective. Intellectuals have expounded it with a passionately serious care and artists in words or images have expressed it with honesty torn out of the heart. It is not a comfortable view and that is why its bleakness seems intolerable to many people who may usually conduct their lives on the basis that God does not exist for them, but who when challenged are reluctant to deny his reality altogether. Or if people cannot escape the conviction that they have been thrown by sheer chance into a world which is ultimately meaningless, they may try to attach religious significance to a reality which is not God such as Communism or nationalism or money-making. To such causes they may sacrifice a great deal, including themselves. Or they may try to escape the pain of life in a world which offers no God and no great cause by abusing sex, drink or drugs, by turning to the thrills of violence or by killing off the mind by television (for example). Or they may treasure fragments of religious experience in unbidden moments of ecstasy, in the power of music, in the delighted care of children or in the profound love which is true marriage. Or they may throw themselves into charities or festivals as substitutes for churches. Buddhists in particular concentrate on spiritual development, seeking No-thing-ness as the ultimate goal, without believing in the existence of 'God' as that word is understood by believing Christians, Jews, Muslims or other theists; and the idea of a religion without God has a wide appeal outside traditionally Buddhist countries. In recent years some theologians have tried to develop the idea of a 'Christian atheism'.

Such facts deserve to be considered alongside the reminders in this catechism that a 'frequent form' of atheism is 'the practical materialism which restricts its needs and aspirations to space and time' and that the spread of such materialism may be due in part to a lack of religious education or to the misbehaviour of religious believers (2124–2125). Under Communism or consumerism atheistic materialism has certainly been helped by the failures and sins of the religious and, in its turn, has certainly failed to take account of humanity's religious instincts. Yet modern atheism remains the most searching intellectual challenge in the history of religion. Believers do not serve the cause of true religion if they ignore or patronize this opponent.

This catechism is not content with saying that the natural 'knowledge' of God can be 'certain'. It also claims that for those who believe in God because they think that God has revealed himself, 'faith is more certain than all human knowledge, because it is founded on the very word of God who cannot lie' (157). The claim appears to forget that the belief that a word is 'of God' is itself an act of faith. One of Cardinal Newman's sayings is then quoted with approval: 'Ten thousand difficulties do not make one doubt'. But this piling of certainty upon certainty, refusing to allow any 'difficulty' to cause the slightest disturbance in what one 'knows', is fundamentalism. Some Christians have been, and still are, thorough fundamentalists – and their complacent dogmatism is a reason for thinking Christian faith stupid. But this attitude is not typical of Christian believers who are aware of the awkward questions of our time. Such believers (including many Roman Catholics) know that genuine faith cannot be forced on anyone, by arguments any more than by persecutions. Faith is well described as 'a personal act – the free response of the human person to the initiative of God who reveals himself' (166). It is a choice where another decision is possible, a leap where it is also possible to refuse to take a step over uncertain ground. At its strongest, the intellectual content of faith is 'a sense of converging and convincing arguments', as the catechism says (31) – but ten thousand arguments which can be contradicted do not make one absolute certainty. What is called 'moral certainty' is the belief that one is morally right to act despite remaining doubts. Always genuine faith includes doubt: otherwise it would be not faith but knowledge. It is not paralysed by doubt, for it is the exploration of a mystery, but always it is more or less tongue-tied as it reports what it is discovering about this mystery.

Sometimes this catechism echoes the modesty of advanced mystics and philosophical theologians, as well as of ordinary believers, who know that it is foolish to be cocksure. For example, it teaches that 'God transcends all creatures. We must therefore continually purify our language of everything in it that is limited, image-bound or imperfect, if we are not to confuse our image of God – "the inexpressible, the incomprehensible, the invisible, the ungraspable" – with our human representations' (42). That quotation comes from a great and orthodox theologian of the fourth century, John Chrysostom. The thirteenth-century Thomas Aquinas is often regarded as a theologian who exaggerated the capacities of the intellect in religious matters. Indeed, his famous definition of faith is quoted in this catechism: 'believing is an act of the intellect assenting to the divine truth by command of the will moved by God through grace' (155). But he is also quoted there as teaching this uncomfortable truth: 'concerning God, we cannot grasp what he is, but only what he is not, and how other beings stand in relation to him'. And although people and things in the world can be used when thinking about God, a council of medieval bishops is quoted as admitting that 'between Creator and creature no similitude can be expressed without implying an even greater dissimilitude' (43). But the catechism does not explain how all this welcome acknowledgement of the limits of religious thought and language is combined with claims which are far more disputable – as when it is asserted that 'knowledge' of God can be 'certain' after merely thinking about the world and that an even greater certainty comes after the revelation which the bishops expound and which the faithful should receive with an unquestioning assent. It is surely better to say with this catechism: 'We do not believe in formulas, but in those realities they express, which faith allows us to touch' (170).

It seems to be the case, whether we like it or not, that faith in God is not knowledge like our knowledge of things which can be known through the impact of the senses. In so far as faith in God resembles our knowledge, the comparison has to be with our 'getting to know' another person, a relationship which is deepened when love opens the two hearts. In other words, this faith is not like learning from a scientific experiment or some other research, but it is a bit like learning from a friendship or a happy marriage. It leads not to certain knowledge, but to stable trust. Certainly this is today the character of the faith of many Christians, who are well aware of many strong contemporary challenges to that faith. They can say with one of the most learned RC theologians of modern times, Karl Rahner, that 'the concept "God" is not a grasp of God by which a person masters a mystery, but it is letting oneself be grasped by the mystery which is present and yet ever distant' (*Foundations of Christian Faith*, in English, 1978, p. 54). But they can also say with Luther: 'That to which your heart clings and entrusts itself is really your God'. And they can add with a late voice in the New Testament, a voice which certainly does not advocate a faith that is vague: 'I know whom I have trusted' (2 Tim 1.12).

The power of God

For many people in our time who face the challenge of atheism, faith in God is not made any easier by some interpretations of the traditional words 'omnipotent' and 'almighty'. In this catechism we read that God is 'the Lord of the universe, whose order he established and which remains wholly subject to him and at his disposal. He is master of history, governing hearts and events in keeping with his will' (269), with 'absolute sovereignty' (303). The world is 'in a "state of journeying" towards its ultimate perfection. In God's plan this process of becoming carries with it the appearance of certain beings and the disappearance of others, the existence of the more perfect alongside the less perfect, constructive and destructive forces of nature' (310). But many now ask how these impressive words connect with reality.

To cling to God in trust is to believe that his power will prevail, that he will in the end be the Ruler over all – in Greek *pantokratōr*, a less misleading term than the Latin *omnipotens* which suggests 'all-powerful' like a dictator. For Christians, that is the faith in the Kingdom of God, a faith held in the light of the belief that God raised Jesus from death. But Christian trust does not forget that Jesus had to go through death after going through isolation and crucifixion. Christian faith is not untouched by doubts when it thinks of natural disasters which cause great human suffering, or of the evils experienced in every human life and death, to the point of agony for many. In this darkness, Christian commitment cries with the crucified: 'My God, my God, why have you forsaken me?' (Mark 15.34).

Therefore it seems probable to many Christians – probably to most who have entered at all deeply into the dark world of suffering – that God has limited his power in order to create a world with a large measure of independence. Nature has to take its course once its 'laws' or regularities have been established; the sun shines, or rain falls, on good and bad alike (Matt 5.45). Events also have to take their course although individuals suffer the consequences, including individuals who pray for deliverance; the collapsing tower falls on good and bad alike (Luke 13.4). Amazing 'miracles' may or may not occur, but that is what is normal in nature or in history and our understanding of God's sovereignty has to be adjusted to these ugly facts. The Christian believes that 'in everything he co-operates for good with those who love God and are called according to his purpose' (Rom 8.28), but the Christian is marked by the sign of the cross, an exhibition of 'the weakness of God' which was not seen before the first Easter to be 'the power of God' (1 Cor 1.24–25). That is the power in which Christians may now trust, although with 'horror and anguish' (Mark 14.33), 'loud cries and tears' (Heb 5.7) and 'sweat like drops of blood' (Luke 22.44). This catechism could have been strengthened by making it clearer that its faith in the power of God has passed through Gethsemane.

Three ways of being God

When teaching about the Holy Trinity, this new catechism rightly stresses that here is a 'mystery beyond human expression, infinitely beyond all that we can humanly understand' (251). That is a welcome change from the mood of the so-called 'Athanasian' creed, which roundly condemns as doomed 'to perish everlastingly' anyone who does not agree with its overconfident definition of the Trinity. This creed seems to have originated in Gaul (France) in the fifth century. It has never been regarded as authoritative in the churches of the east although it has been printed in some service books. It was used in worship in the churches of the west during the Middle Ages and even since the Reformation, but this use has declined near to the point of oblivion. And in contrast with the tone of that creed, many Christian preachers and teachers in our time ask: need the truth about God as Trinity be put in all the old words?

I am therefore one of those who ask whether the word 'persons' is the only right term to indicate the distinctions between God the Father, God the Son and God the Holy Spirit. We are told in this catechism that Father, Son and Spirit 'are not simply names designating the modalities of the divine being, for they are really distinct from one another' (254), and we may readily agree to reject any theory which claims that the Holy Trinity is 'simply' anything. But when using simple English words to think about this far from simple mystery, it may be less dangerous to distinguish between 'ways' than to distinguish between 'persons'. At least it may be asked whether this alternative is a legitimate way of expressing the diversity which exists in God's being as well as in his revelation.

It is usual to avoid the plural word 'people' to classify Father, Son and Spirit. This has been thought necessary in order to avoid the frequently made charge (central to many Jewish and Muslim criticisms of Christianity) that Christians worship three gods. With a passion equal to anyone else's, the Christian has to say 'He is the One!' In this catechism it is once again stated that 'Christians are baptized in the name of the Father and of the Son and of the Holy Spirit: not in their names, for there is only one God' (233). 'We do not confess three Gods, but one God in three persons' (253). The word 'person' is used, we are reminded, in a sense peculiar to 'the Church's own terminology' (251). Indeed it is. It comes from the Latin *persona*, used by Tertullian (not long after 200) to point to Father, Son and Spirit, who had one *substantia*. The Greek equivalent is *prosōpon*, which originally meant an actor's mask. In order to say that Father, Son and Spirit were not merely masks of the Godhead, Greek-speaking theologians took to using *hypostasis*. That word appears in the Letter to Hebrews, which says that faith gives *hypostasis* to our hopes (11.1), and it is usually there translated as 'substance'. (Basically it then meant 'support'.) Greek-speaking philosophers, however, later used *hypostasis* to answer the question 'which is it?' rather than 'what is it?' To answer the second question, they now used *ousia*, which may be translated as 'substance' or 'being'. Greek-speaking theologians did the same when struggling to express their own Christian ideas, but it seems reasonable to ask whether what was intended by the old terminology in the doctrine of the Trinity could now be communicated better by using a term such as 'ways of being God'. It may even be suggested that this alternative could be preferred in loyalty to the Jesus who daily recited the *shema* – 'Hear, O Israel: the Lord our God is the one Lord, and you must love the Lord your God with all your heart, with all your soul, with all your mind and with all your strength' (Mark 12.29).

Using a term such as 'three ways of being God' need not mean denying God's personality. As many theologians have taught, the Creator who has created us as personal beings cannot be less than personal. As countless ordinary people have discovered with delight, this God often communicates with us in ways which are at least personal, like a ruler talking with subjects, a friend with friends, a parent with children, a lover with the beloved; and we are invited to treat him as '*Abba*, Father'. That Aramaic word used by Jesus was quoted by Paul at least twice in his letters (Gal 4.6; Rom 8.15). For many, it has been the heart of the Gospel and of prayer. This is surely right, for love is the supreme characteristic of the God revealed by Jesus and the human loves with which we have to compare this supreme relationship are person-to-person affairs. But God must also be more than personal, or must be more personal than we are, for he cannot be subject to the limitations of human personality. God cannot be in eternal reality 'a person' as people are persons. It is legitimate and helpful to think in terms which reflect this obvious truth, and the Bible is full of non-personal images of the 'persons' of the Trinity. For example, the section of this catechism on 'Symbolism of the Holy Spirit' (691–705) usefully collects images used in the Bible about the 'Third Person' of the Holy Trinity: wind, water, fire, cloud, light, a seal, a finger, a dove. It could have added that to describe the Spirit as 'love' is again to use a term which does not suggest 'a person'. Ever since the Trinity was described (by Augustine and others) as the Father loving the Son and the Son loving the Father, the Spirit being the love between them, many Christians have been deeply moved – and practically motivated – by the thought that human loves and communities ought to reflect the eternal society of the Godhead. But in this tradition the Spirit has been thought of as a relationship rather than as a person, and that is a reminder that the lack of similarity between the 'triune' God and any human group has to be greater than the similarity.

In this catechism the term 'modalities' is rejected on the ground that the three persons of the Trinity are 'distinct in their relations of origin'. If we inquire what these 'relations of origin' were, we are told that the Lateran Council of 1215 taught that 'it is the Father who generates, the Son who is generated and the Holy Spirit who proceeds' (254), as if that settled the matter. But these are no more than words pointing to a mystery. The fatherhood of God cannot be more than a metaphor, since God has no child conceived by sexual intercourse. The word points to God's parent-like tenderness, but as the catechism observes this can also be expressed by the image of motherhood (239). The 'procession' of the Spirit must be another metaphor, for in eternity the Spirit does not literally move away from the Father (or from the Father and the Son). Nor can this 'procession' be literally by 'inspiration' (*spiratio*, Latin for 'breathing'), for the Father does not breathe. The catechism's claim that the Council of Florence 'explained' this mystery in 1436 (246) is exaggerated.

We are told that 'the real distinction of the persons among themselves does not divide God's unity, but resides only in their relations, which refer them to one another'. And the Council of Florence is quoted: 'Everything is one where there is no opposition of relationship' (255). That is a summary of the subtle theological discussion by the Cappadocian Fathers in the fourth century of the 'penetration' (in Greek *perichōrēsis*) between the 'persons'. However, here again human understanding is getting out of its depth because there is no human experience to provide a firm footing. What we can begin to experience and understand before death is the work of the 'triune' God as this work affects us; in terms used in the Eastern Orthodox tradition, not God's 'essence' but his 'energies'. Yet this catechism tells us that this energetic work is 'one and the same operation', the only noticeable distinction between the three divine persons when at work being that 'each performs the common work according to his unique personal property' (258). The Son and the Spirit are not excluded from the work of creation; the Father and the Spirit are not excluded from the work of salvation; the Father and the Son are not excluded from the work of inspiration. Here, then, are not three people at work if by 'people' we mean three centres of activity independent enough for it to be possible to tell them apart. It is hard to see how this work of the 'triune' God is not covered by some simpler words used by Athanasius in his letter to Serapion: 'The Father himself through the Word and in the Spirit has made and has given all things'. The New Testament and countless Christian prayers across the centuries often refer to God the Father alone as 'God', to be approached through Jesus Christ in the power of the Spirit. In this tradition this catechism says, for example: 'God has fully revealed "the plan of his good pleasure" by sending us his beloved Son, our Lord Jesus Christ, and his Spirit' (50). That seems enough for Christian prayer and life.

If we use a term such as 'ways' (or 'modalities') rather than 'persons' to point to the work of God the three-in-one as we experience it, we need not fall into the heresies which were condemned in the past. We need not be identified with the 'modalism' of Sabellius and others which was condemned by the Roman church early in the third century. So far as we can recover it, this teaching failed to distinguish between work which is indicated when we say 'Father', the work which is indicated when we say 'Son' and the work which is indicated when we say 'Spirit'. Nor need we be accused of the 'Arianism' condemned by the Council of Nicaea about a hundred years later. We do not regard the Son as some sort of half-god, different in being from the Father as well as from humanity, who was created before he created the universe. The one real God is met in Jesus and in the Spirit. Nor need we be 'Unitarians' in the style of the eighteenth and nineteenth centuries. We say that Jesus was a prophet but also more, bringing not merely a message but also the Spirit. With full conviction we can say with Paul that 'God was in Christ' (2 Cor 5.19) and we can see why Paul spoke of the Spirit as 'the Spirit of God' (and 'the Spirit of Christ') as well as 'the Spirit'. God has made himself known to us human beings in 'the grace of our Lord Jesus Christ, and the love of God, and the fellowship of the Holy Spirit' (2 Cor 13.14). What is revealed by implication (not completely) is, as Karl Rahner put it in his book already quoted, 'three modes of subsistence in the one God' (p. 304). 'Three modes of being' was the expression preferred by the greatest Protestant theologian of the twentieth century, Karl Barth, in his exposition of the Trinity at the beginning of his vast *Church Dogmatics*. Both theologians were anxious to interpret, not to destroy, what was meant by the ancient Church's terminology. And many humbler teachers and preachers, seeking to expound the great mystery of the Trinity to non-theologians in our time, have said that the One God is known in three ways – in creation, salvation and inspiration.

The embodiment of God

Jesus was a man. There is no conceivable way of becoming human except by becoming a girl or a boy, a person, and this catechism rightly reasserts 'the full reality of Christ's human soul, with its operations of intellect and will, as well as with the full reality of his human body' (470). He 'loved with a human heart' as this catechism adds, and so he embodied God's love for all. Unfortunately in its enthusiasm the catechism also adds something which cannot be true about a 'true human intellect' (472) when it says that 'Jesus knew and loved us each and all during his life, his agony and his passion' (478). But it also gives us a magnificent quotation from a bishops' council in 853: 'There is not, never has been and never will be, a single human being for whom Christ did not suffer' (605). Jesus could not know everyone, but in his great love he accepted suffering for the sake of everyone. And he assured his disciples that he would go on loving them, by communicating with them after his death not as a ghost but as a conqueror 'alive for evermore' (Rev 1.18).

Faith in that resurrection rightly implies that the man Jesus must remain a human person in eternal life. Christians have always hoped to remain people after their deaths; no less is believed about the Lord. We should like to know how the human person of Jesus is related to God the Father in eternity, but we cannot know this while we are in the conditions of this mortal life; we do not even know what 'we shall be ourselves' (1 John 3.2). We have to be content with the hope that 'we shall be like him' and with the picture that Jesus is 'at the right hand of the Father', sharing the glory of God. That is the picture given to us by the New Testament and by the experience reported of Christian saints from the martyred Stephen's dying cry to Jesus (Acts 7.55–60) onwards. It can be found to be enough until we are in a position to make a cry of delighted adoration after our own deaths.

One question asked by many in our time is about the 'miracles' surrounding Jesus or performed by him. All or many of them seem contrary to what is known of nature through science. It is asked: must a modern Christian 'believe' them all? It is also asked: do the miracles that deserve credence mean that Jesus was so abnormal as not to be truly human?

The right answer to the second question is clear: Jesus of Nazareth was human. But as the embodiment of God in a human life, was he able to suspend the normal processes of nature marvellously? Nowadays there is a division between Christians who do, and those who do not, accept some or all of the miracles as physical, historical facts. It is not a division which runs in a clear-cut way between the RC church and other churches. Like the Eastern Orthodox, Roman Catholics tend to be more conservative than Protestants and Anglicans, but many individuals in the more conservative group of churches are doubters or sceptics and many in the more liberal group of churches have been, and are, strongly conservative. All I can offer here is a very short summary of my own reactions to the new catechism.

I am surprised that the historical question is nowhere taken seriously. No effort is made to distinguish between the 'nature' miracles in the gospels (such as the cursing of the fig-tree), some or all of which may be legends, and the 'healing' miracles some or all of which are more easily understood by modern doctors as the triumph of mind over matter, of faith over the brain's surrender to disease – a triumph expressed in terms of the expulsion of demons, as was natural at the time and is still natural in surviving pre-modern societies.

As I have already noted, both the 'Virginal Conception' and the 'Virgin Birth' are affirmed in this catechism. That is, however, done without any serious considerations of what is admitted to be 'the silence of St Mark's gospel and the New Testament epistles' (498). It might have been granted also that there is no clear reference in John's gospel and that the only evidence supporting the Virginal Conception is the lovely and loved (but not easily harmonized) stories which are given to us by Luke and Matthew but which are plainly not accurate history. Their very beauty is a signal that these evangelists were not reporters to newspapers, let alone gynaecologists. The confidence of Christians inclined not to take the stories of the Virginal Conception and Birth literally is not strengthened when we are told that 'the Church sees here the fulfilment of God's promise given through the prophet Isaiah, "The virgin shall conceive and bear a son"' (497), for biblical scholars are agreed that these words about a young woman (in Hebrew *almah*), were not intended as a prediction about Jesus despite the mistranslation 'virgin' in the Greek version of Isaiah 7.14. Nor is any discussion offered by the catechism about how a boy could be conceived without sex; it is 'a divine work which surpasses all human understanding and potential'.

The catechism's teaching about the Resurrection of Jesus is also not related to the questions of our time. Almost all Christians will agree that the Resurrection was 'a real event', but the catechism fails to notice that nowadays it is often noted both by scholars and by ordinary readers that the accounts in the New Testament give no clear picture. Although the catechism treats all the NT's lists of witnesses as being equally accurate, it is impossible to reconcile them all except by arguments which will appear to many as dishonest. All the stories of the appearances are also accepted here, with the consequence that the clothed body of the risen Lord is believed to have been able to talk unrecognized, to enter a room through a closed door and to eat a meal, but the catechism rightly teaches that 'no one could say' how the Resurrection 'came about physically' since it was 'not a return to earthly life' and this mystery 'transcends and surpasses history' (646–647). The essential Christian faith that 'he rose from the dead' could have been commended more persuasively in our time had there been a greater acknowledgement of this element of mystery, and therefore of uncertainty, in the only accounts available to us. That would have helped questioners to believe in what Christian faith holds to be the real event of the Resurrection of Jesus Christ from the dead, an act of God as significant as the creation of the universe.

Another question asked by many in our time concerns the meaning of the catechism's language about Jesus as 'the Father's one perfect and unsurpassable Word' (65). Every person is unique, but no human person can be perfect or unsurpassable in every respect. In what way, then, was Jesus uniquely, perfectly and finally the Son or Word of the One who 'spoke in many and varied ways through the prophets' (Heb 1.1)?

This catechism deserves to be questioned when it claims that 'In him God has said everything; there will be no other word than this one' for 'he has no more to say' (65). To claim that is to be in danger of suggesting that all truths not recorded in the evidence about Jesus of Nazareth are exclusively human discoveries. God the Holy Spirit would then be excluded from the whole history of religion, philosophy, science and great literature outside the tiny contents of four (or three) gospels. Yet this catechism is of course concerned to safeguard faith in the divine inspiration of the Church's tradition after the completion of the New Testament: 'even if Revelation is complete, it has not been made completely explicit; it remains for Christian faith gradually to grasp its full significance over the course of the centuries' (66). That seems to be an acknowledgement that God did not in fact 'say everything' in Jesus. What, then, is the status of the many truths which have come from the divine source of all truth? In the catechism criticism is directed towards non-Christian religions which are ' "revelations" that pretend to surpass or correct the revelation of which Christ is the fulfilment' as well as towards 'private' revelations which may be claimed to 'improve or complete Christ's definitive Revelation' (67). And any believing Christian will reject 'revelations' intended to replace Jesus Christ. But it does not follow that God has been silent while truth has been spoken outside the gospels. On the contrary, as the catechism declares: 'all goodness and truth' are 'given by him who enlightens all men that they may at length have life' (843).

What is really unique, perfect and unsurpassable in Jesus is rightly called in this catechism the 'new and definitive covenant' (66) which he began by his words and actions. This 'covenant' is a new agreement between God and humanity. 'God was in Christ reconciling the world to himself' (2 Cor 5.19).

The new covenant was sealed by Christ's life-blood (1 Cor 11.25) and inevitably this death creating life was compared by Christian Jews with the sacrifice of bulls, and the uniting of altar and people by flinging blood over both, which had marked the older covenant in their traditions about Moses (Ex 24.3–8). As this catechism says, 'Christ's unique sacrifice completes and surpasses all others' (614). The new covenant brought freedom, and in days when slaves yearned for freedom inevitably this death as the climax of this life was celebrated as a ransom 'for many' (Mark 10.45), as this catechism says (608). The new covenant brought a life freed from the power of evil, and inevitably in an age when demons seemed everywhere it was believed that the 'Son of God appeared for the very purpose of undoing the devil's work' (1 John 3.8), as this catechism says (394). Pope Gregory the Great, who sent its first archbishop to Canterbury, used the theory of Augustine, Bishop of Hippo, that the devil was tricked into accepting Christ's death as payment for his rights over sinful humanity – and clinched the bargain without realizing that

Christ would rise again. Some five hundred years later another Archbishop of Canterbury, Anselm, drew on the custom in feudal society that an outraged overlord demanded 'satisfaction' for a vassal's disloyalty. He propounded the theory, repeated in this catechism and by many other authorities (including Anglican prayer books), that Jesus 'atoned for our iniquities and made satisfaction for our sins to the Father' (615). The Roman Catechism of 1566 taught that by this 'satisfaction' the Son 'entirely appeased the wrath and indignation of the Father', but we may note gratefully that this catechism does not repeat that.

In our time animal sacrifices are usually thought wrong, outright slavery is rare, belief in devils is often mocked as superstition, the feudal system is a curiosity of medieval history and the punishment of an innocent substitute for a guilty person is not thought to be justice. But it is possible to express in more contemporary ways the truths which were expressed in those biblical terms, for Christ is still seen to be the martyred witness to the forgiving love of God and the liberator who leads into new and eternal life. He 'came down from heaven' to Calvary, plunging into our world of sin, illness, sorrow and despair. And it is still seen that, so far from God needing to be reconciled to us, 'all this has been the work of God' (2 Cor 5.18). The new catechism provides welcome summaries of the older doctrines about Christ's at-one-ment of God and humanity, but would have added to its value had it more definitely encouraged new images in order that people who have never sacrificed an animal, or met a slave or a devil, or satisfied a feudal lord, can be persuaded to be at one with the God whose 'very being is love' (221). In many generations Christians have asked this question because (so to speak) Jesus steps out of the pages of the gospels, out of the conditions of life in the days of his flesh, out of the tomb where he was buried, into their hearts asking them: 'And you, who do you say I am?' (Mark 8.29).

It seems unsatisfactory that this catechism reprints (in 467), but does not stop to explain, the most comprehensive and authoritative answer to this question given so far in the Church's history, the definition by the Council of Chalcedon in 451.

As the catechism wisely acknowledges, 'the Church had to develop its own terminology', but 'by doing so, the Church did not submit the faith to human wisdom, but gave a new and unprecedented meaning to these terms' (251). Yet these are not terms used by philosophers, let alone by ordinary Christians or inquirers, on the eve of the twenty-first century and it is not enough to authorize certain English or other words as translations of the Greek. Nor is it enough to say that expert theologians committed to the definition of 451 have advanced subtle explanations of the 'hypostatic' union of Christ's two natures, divine and human. For many in our time, some questions are inescapable. How can a man be 'perfect in divinity'? How can the Son be 'perfect in humanity' if he is 'one person' and that 'person' is divine, not human? Is 'human nature' which does not belong to a person possible? How are we to distinguish between Christ's 'two natures' if they are 'without division or separation'? How are we to understand their union if they have 'one substance' yet are 'without confusion'? Do they mean that Jesus had two minds or two different kinds of power? And in an age of psychiatry how are we to understand the further decision, by a council in 681, that 'Christ possesses two wills and two principles of operation, one divine and one human', which 'co-operate' because his human will 'submits to his divine almighty will'?

The difficulties in answering all these questions are such that it seems to many Christians in our time that this is the situation: if we renounce the imaginative attractions of mythology (stories about happenings in a life which is not history) and the intellectual attractions of metaphysics (speculation about what may exist beyond what we can know in our physical world), we cannot understand the relationships between Father, Son and Holy Spirit in eternity. Nor can we understand the depths of the unique (not split!) personality of Jesus, Son of Man and Son of God. 'No one has ever seen God'; God's Son (or God the Son) has 'made him known'; yet the Son has never told us exactly how 'the Word became flesh'. We cannot know how the eternal entered history, how the changeless and the infinite became something. We cannot rely on the words in John's gospel where Jesus speaks of the glory which he had with the Father before the world began, for it is generally agreed by the scholars that those were not the words of the historical Jesus. We cannot even know exactly what John meant when he used the term *logos* in the magnificently poetic prologue to his gospel (not in the gospel itself), possibly quoting a hymn. The English translation 'Word' rightly suggests the connection with the 'Word of the Lord' in the Hebrew Scriptures. But the first readers of John's basically Jewish gospel, who needed to have Jewish terms and customs explained to them, may well have had in mind the use of *logos* in some of the philosophy of the time to point to Order, Reason and Meaning in the world. And if we treat John's gospel as the expression of John's spirituality rather than as the self-expression of the historical Jesus, we are unlike the theologians who engaged in the controversies leading up to Chalcedon. Indeed, we are unlike almost all Christians who were aware of the gospel before the last hundred years. Even theologians who are strong traditionalists have, however, come to see that the words used in 451 were neither the whole truth nor wholly untrue. Thus in 1967, in conversations between theologians from the Orthodox churches (which accepted Chalcedon) and the Oriental churches (which did not), it was agreed: 'Ever since the fifth century we have used different formulae to confess our common faith in the One Lord Jesus Christ, perfect God and perfect man'.

Mark's gospel says that Jesus asked: 'Why do you call me good? No one is good except God alone' (10.18). And John's gospel keeps to the standard practice of the New Testament (and of this catechism), which normally refers only to the Father as 'God'. Yet towards this gospel's end doubting Thomas says to the risen Jesus: 'My Lord and my God!' (20.28). No explanation is given about this use of a title which was claimed by some Roman emperors, but every committed Christian knows what essentially is meant. 'To know Christ', said Melanchthon, 'is to know his benefits; it is not to contemplate his nature or the manner of his incarnation.' But we have met God in Christ. We hear that Word. We love and obey that Son. For us, Jesus is *Emmanuel*, 'God with us' (Matt 1.23). We can repeat the frequently recited prayer of the Eastern Orthodox: 'Lord Jesus Christ, Son of God, have mercy on me, a sinner' – and the concise creed of the first Christians: 'Jesus is Lord!' (1 Cor 12.3), using the word *kyrios* which was used about God in the Greek translation of the Hebrew Scriptures but meaning also our submission to our Lord in our behaviour. And so most Christians taking part in the Eucharist are very willing to repeat the expressions which became orthodoxy in 381, linking themselves with the millions who have used that creed across the centuries and around the world, but often seeing this as the meaning of the ancient words: 'the one sole, true God poured himself out in love in Jesus Christ for our final and decisive salvation, calling us to return to him in love'. That was the conclusion formulated by two brothers who were Anglican biblical and patristic scholars, A. T. and R. P. C. Hanson (*The Identity of the Church*, 1987, p. 77). And it was the conclusion of major books about the New Testament evidence and modern thought such as Edward Schillebeeckx's *Jesus* and *Christ* (in English, 1978, 1980) and *Born Before All Time?* by K. J. Kuschel (in English, 1992).

That is not to say much if what we want is a drama of religious mythology or a scheme of theological metaphysics. It is not enough if we feel obliged to agree with the Sacred Congregation for the Doctrine of the Faith, which in *Mysterium Filii Dei* (1972) pronounced that the beliefs that 'God, in revealing himself, was present in the highest degree in the human person Jesus', and that 'Jesus can be called God because God is supremely present' in him, are 'beliefs far removed from true belief in Christ'. But it seems to be enough if what we want is to enter a new life through the biblical faith that 'Jesus is the Christ, the Son of God' (John 20.31). The catechism quotes the Roman Missal's Preface of Christmas:

in Jesus 'we see our God made visible and so are caught up in the love of the God we cannot see' (477).

For all nations

If it is agreed that this is the biblical faith which the ancient councils expressed in terms borrowed from the philosophy of their times – if we agree with Karl Rahner's book already quoted that the official doctrine of the Church 'develops the basic assertion: God in his *logos* becomes man' (p. 286) – a vital task remains. It is the task of expressing this essential assertion of faith in terms which seem more powerful to believing Christians who, as the catechism says, have 'differences of culture, age, spiritual maturity and social and ecclesial condition'. It is a pity that this catechism offers no definite encouragement to this task by approving – or mentioning – any of the experiments which have been made, and it is a greater pity that in the twentieth century some theologians making these experiments have been censured, silenced, forbidden to teach as Catholics or driven out of the priesthood by the Vatican. The already well-known names of Küng in Germany and Boff in Brazil will probably be quite prominent in church history among the blots in the record of the papacy, but examples of censorship in other European and American countries, Africa, India and elsewhere have also made Christian thinkers who are not Roman Catholics feel that supervision by the Vatican would not be a help in their own delicate experiments. In 1989, 163 German-speaking theologians made a joint protest about this negative attitude of the leadership of the Church they wished to serve.

All this is sad because as a result of experiments already made it seems possible to glimpse new ways of stating Christian truths. Ours is a time of many questions. It is also a time when Jesus is being encountered as the Questioner. He may seem dead in the eyes of many in traditionally Christian lands, but he is 'lifted up from the earth' and found to be alive and attractive. In this connection I refer, of course, to the Catholic or Orthodox church life which has outlived Communism in lands once officially godless and to the Evangelical, Pentecostal and Charismatic movements which have swept millions into their enthusiasms, but there are also other movements full of vitality and promise. For example, the movement to see Christianity from women's points of view has been articulated in the many experiments of feminist theology. It is sad that instead of mentioning these experiments in this catechism, the Vatican has insisted that the word 'men', not 'people' or 'all', should be used in the English translation.

In the industrial or post-industrial nations which are becoming increasingly science-based in their cultures as well as their economies, the spiritual and moral vacuum left by the decline or disappearance of definite religious belief also grows. No answer to this crisis will seem convincing if it depends on mythology or metaphysics. This modern or post-modern world of thought wants things it can see and touch, the rest being thought of as 'imagination' or 'emotion' or 'guesswork' or 'personal preference'. And so if it wants a religion, it wants one which stands within the limits of experience alone although it may reach out to a mystery beyond. Religious faith can never be testable and verifiable (or falsifiable) by the strict standards of science, for it points to a mystery transcending our world, and it needs what Schleiermacher called 'a sense and taste for the Infinite' producing 'a feeling of absolute dependence', but at least Christian faith can reply that it speaks of this mystery by relying on something within solid, human experience. 'We have heard it; we have seen it with our own eyes; we looked upon it, and felt it with our own hands; our theme is the Word which gives life' (1 John 1.1).

If the language about the Father begetting the Son in eternity has lost its power, it can be affirmed that 'what God was, the Word was'. Although it was natural for people sometimes to personify *logos* (as in the female figure of Wisdom in Proverbs and the Wisdom of Solomon), essentially what was meant by Christians was, it seems, this: God expressed his own meaning in the love that became a human being as Jesus Christ, as he also expressed himself in the beauty and the order that became the universe around us. Seen in this light, the universe is not entirely meaningless and indifferent to human life. On the contrary, despite all the elements of chance which were necessary if novelty would emerge in evolution, the process was in some sense 'programmed' to give birth to life and human life on this planet. And one individual in the species *homo sapiens* was (as it were) programmed to reveal the potential of human life as 'glory'. As John Macquarrie has written, Jesus was 'not a chance mutation thrown up in the course of evolution but the one in whom is concentrated that progressive penetration of the universe by the *logos* that has been going on from the beginning'. And 'if we think of Jesus in all the relationships that went to constitute him as a person, in his continuity with Israel on the one hand and with the new Christian community on the other, then it is within this complex human reality that God has come to expression in the new and fuller way that we call "incarnation"' (*Jesus Christ in Modern Thought*, 1990, pp. 22, 294).

That is good news for science-based societies and the vision has been spread by (for example) the writings of the Jesuit Teilhard de Chardin, who suffered much when silenced by official disfavour but achieved much before his death in New York on Easter Day in 1955, ten years before the translation into English of his *The Phenomenon of Man*. As further examples of such experiments, I may point to two books published in 1993 by clergy of the Church of England: *Credible Christianity* by Bishop Hugh Montefiore and *Theology for the Scientific Age* by Dr Arthur Peacocke.

In the poorer countries of the world, theological responses to such challenges may seem less central to the relevant restatement of the Gospel, because the important question is not whether God exists (his existence is either taken for granted by the many or dismissed as ridiculous by the few) but whether his government can come. Can there be justice on earth for women or men in confrontation with the daily realities of dehumanizing poverty? In this world without much science or much hope, it becomes very significant that when Paul quoted an early Christian hymn to the church in Philippi (2.1–11), his emphasis was not on the Christ who was 'in the form of God' but on the Christ who 'made himself nothing, assuming the form of a slave . . . even to the point of death', leaving an example. The theology which arises among the poor, and is usually inspired by the personal experience of theologians who share the thoughts of the poor, is controlled by the example of Jesus of Nazareth, poor among the poor, for whose sake Christians must make a 'preferential option for the poor'.

In that humble life liberation is offered to the world – first of all freedom from the spiritual chains of custom, lethargy and defeatism and the physical chains of drug-addiction or other pathetic escapism, but also freedom from structures of economic slavery which resemble the slavery of Israel in Egypt before Moses led the Exodus. The extensive development of liberation theology in Latin America has enjoyed the blessings, and even leadership, of some of the local bishops and can appeal to some of the pronouncements of regional bishops' conferences in 1968 and 1979 – although the Vatican has recently taken care to appoint more conservative bishops. It has stimulated Christian leaders in many parts of the world – although apparently less in the Vatican, where attention has been given to condemning the uses of Marxist categories in analysing the plight of the poor. The Congregation for the Doctrine of the Faith's *Instruction on Christian Freedom and Liberation* (1986) was reckoned by many to be unjustifiably patronizing. Some Latin American theologians do seem open to the charges of vagueness and naïveté in the advocacy of 'socialist' solutions, but it seems entirely possible to combine their religious and moral vision with greater realism about economics. The charge that they have ignored the human need of spiritual liberation would not survive any fairminded study of their work – for example, the books by Leonardo Boff, including *Jesus Christ, Liberator* (in English, 1980).

In Africa and Asia (with big exceptions) urgent problems of material poverty exist alongside rich religious traditions which may include sophisticated religious philosophy. In these countries Christian theology does not have many material resources, but it is challenged to translate what is essential in Christian faith into the terms bequeathed by the strongly religious past, whether tribal, Muslim, Hindu or Buddhist. Already African Christianity has expanded in spirit as well as numbers, with a triumphant joy amid its suffering, with a discipleship ready for martyrdom as it follows in the dusty road behind Jesus the Prophet, the Healer, the Chief, the God whose body was never white. I see no reason to withdraw the suggestion in my 1987 book on *The Futures of Christianity* that the most hopeful future lies in Africa. And already at least one major theologian has appeared in this Two-Thirds World, the Indian Catholic scholar Raimundo Panikkar, author of *The Unknown Christ of Hinduism* (1964) and *The Trinity and the Religious Experience of Man* (1975). He approaches the mystery of the Son with the aid of Jewish and Muslim teachings about God's self-revelation. But he also approaches the mystery of the Father with the help of Buddhist meditations about No-thing-ness – and the mystery of the Spirit with the help of Hindu celebrations of the link, and even the identity, of the deepest reality in the human spirit with the ultimate divine reality. At a more popular level, many 'Asian faces of Jesus' have been glimpsed, as in the collection of essays with that title edited by R. S. Sugirtharajah in 1993.

There are dangers in these pioneering theologies and despite some vaguely worded papal blessings the Vatican and Vatican-appointed authorities have often been quick to point out the dangers and to discourage the experimenters. This catechism is eloquent in its silences and in its insistence on a very Roman kind of Catholicism. It quotes Irenaeus: 'The churches established in Germany have no other faith or Tradition, nor do those of the Iberians, nor those of the Celts, nor those of the East, of Egypt, of Libya, nor those established at the centre of the world' (174). However, even in his day (about 180) Irenaeus was not being accurate about the diversity that existed, whether or not he knew about it; and it is significant (although unmentioned in the catechism) that he protested when a Bishop of Rome tried to condemn a tradition about fasting held in Asia Minor, writing that 'we should keep peace with one another' since 'difference in fasting confirms agreement in faith'. In later periods church history exhibits considerable differences between Celtic Christianity (for example) and Rome, or between Alexandria and Antioch in the east. To go back earlier, honest biblical studies show that to accept Scripture means to accept diversity. If that was the case then, it seems realistic to expect that in the centuries to come there will be no

uniformity between women and men equally 'in Christ', or between
Catholics in Europe (for example) and Catholics in tropical Africa or the
Pacific Islands, or between Catholic theologians at work in the USA (for
example) and in India or Japan. It also seems realistic to expect that the
dangers run as a genuinely feminist or local Christianity emerges will be
no greater than the dangers incurred by the Catholic Church in Europe
when Christian images were given the setting of a Renaissance palace, or
when reconciliation to the Father through the crucified Jesus was
compared with the feudal practice of 'satisfying' an offended lord, or
when Thomas Aquinas used (to the indignation of many fellow-
theologians) the pre-Christian philosophy of Aristotle. Dangers were run
in an earlier period when terms used in the metaphysics of Greek
philosophy were also used in dogmas which after acrimonious debates and
excommunications became compulsory through disciplines modelled on
the laws of the Roman and Byzantine empires.

To be sure, theology is necessary. But every theology, like every
picture and every song, is human work. Try as we may (and how fruitful
Christian attempts have been!), we cannot pin down the mystery of Jesus
of Nazareth, who did not strike his neighbours in his village as being
more than a carpenter but who was followed by his disciples into life and
death with the disturbed awe which is appropriate to the encounter with
the Creator.

5

A loving look
at sexuality

THE NEW CATECHISM has once again shown what a contrast there is between the current teaching of the Roman Catholic Church about social justice and its official teaching about sexual morality. The contrast was reaffirmed by the encyclical *Veritatis Splendor* (1993).

Nowadays when the Church's leadership considers society, it ponders the complexities of history as well as the ideals of Scripture. It condemns all violence, oppression and corruption, praising governments which serve the people; affirming lesser associations that deserve the State's respect and help because in them the people combine for justice and progress; pleading for justice and peace between nations, races and classes. Yet the Church's leadership has become largely pragmatic about particular questions in politics and economics. It has forbidden clergy to belong to governments or legislatures (in contrast with the Middle Ages) and, however reluctantly, it has come to terms with legislation (about divorce, for example) not to its liking. Bishops have learned not to become too involved in day-to-day politics (in the rise or fall of Christian Democrat parties, for example), and few parish priests try to dominate everything that goes on locally. In modern times the Vatican has not attempted to identify the Gospel and the Church with one side or the other in an international conflict. At its highest level the Church has neither approved nor denounced the possession of nuclear weapons since 1945, and even their use has not been the subject of a completely clear and firm doctrine. Thus the RC bishops of the USA moved towards the position that any first use would be immoral, while for the sake of deterrence the West German bishops were unwilling to handicap NATO's potential response to aggression. Most of the American bishops supported the Vietnam war, while Europeans including Paul VI deplored it. John Paul II condemned the Gulf war but did not impose his views on others. And the weapon of excommunication has not been used against those who have disagreed with the social teaching of popes and bishops. For example, the RC bishops in the USA took no steps against the many lay people who in practice ignored their carefully compiled Pastoral Letter on *Economic Justice for All* because it seemed to be preaching socialism.

This approach to social problems is non-dogmatic in comparison with much of the past and that has its dangers, for the papacy incurs criticism (at least) for not condemning Nazism in time – or nuclear weapons. But its wisdom has to be argued about case by case. It has not been without influence and it offers some hope for the future when, on a planet already tormented by international and civil wars and by acute poverty, and already polluted, the population is expected to double in the next hundred years if AIDS and other epidemics can be controlled. In cities, towns and even countryside already made sordid and dangerous by crime, drugs, unemployment, boredom and the breakdown of family life, the sense of despair is also likely to increase. In this human crisis Christianity could contribute a vision (not a detailed plan) which would help to create hope and determination. It could communicate the vision of a society in which justice and health for all are sustained within peace by material resources which are both increased without damaging the environment and shared without damaging personal incentives to enterprise and work. It could make 'a civilization of love' more than a fine phrase. And the recent social teaching of the Roman Catholic Church makes it reasonable to look in that direction for the moral leadership of the world. In particular, a pope has an unrivalled opportunity to articulate the aroused conscience of humanity with all the benevolent power of religion. He would – like all prophets – encounter prejudices and suspicions, but no other religious leader, no national leader and no official of an international organization inherits such awesome prestige. When teaching morals, no other authority can so easily command the attention of the media and the admiration of the public including non-Catholics and non-Christians. Perhaps the future was glimpsed when at Assisi in 1986 John Paul II presided over a gathering of leaders of different Christian bodies and of different world religions, to face the planet's problems.

When dealing with sexual morality, however, the leadership (*magisterium*) teaches that people who do not accept one or other of a number of its doctrines should not be admitted to Holy Communion, and this signal is registered even when the pastoral practice of parish priests, or the practice of communicants who offer themselves at the altar, is less strict (as it often

is). These doctrines are based mainly on an interpretation of 'natural' law –
an interpretation which is very widely rejected by those whose human
nature is involved in their sexual activity, whether outside devout
membership of the Roman Catholic Church or within it. Or they may be
based on an interpretation of the Bible – an interpretation which is very
widely regarded as oversimple by those who study the Bible with care.
And many Roman Catholics have seen the results of these doctrines in
human lives as often tragic.

Clergy who cannot accept these doctrines may be deprived of their
teaching posts, not made bishops, reprimanded or disciplined, or
eventually persuaded by their own consciences that it is wrong to exercise
the priesthood under such a regime, while many other Roman Catholics
who would make good priests may be deterred from ordination by the
doctrines about sexuality culminating in the demand that they themselves
must never marry. RC laity who dissent may cease to consult the clergy or
may cease to mention sex when doing so. Or they may withdraw from all
regular worship in Church, although quite often with a haunting sense of
sorrow or with anger at their exclusion.

Women, who have so often been classified by (male) 'spiritual' or
'ethical' teachers as the Eve-like seducers of men, have been made to feel
inferior or guilty. They have been condemned because as sexual creatures
they enjoy making themselves attractive and even making love in suitable
circumstances, with the modesty and the faithfulness to one partner which
are also parts of the normal woman's nature. By its imagery and by its
arrangements for the selection of its leadership and for the celebration of
its saints as much as by its words, the Church may seem to have approved
thoroughly of only a few women – the Mother of God who was also a
perpetual virgin, virgins who were nuns or martyrs, other heroines who
have sacrificed themselves in caring for the poor. Family life has indeed
been praised, but the sexuality in which it originates may seem to be
denigrated as dirty or evil. Adolescents who relieve their strong urges by
masturbation may begin this psychologically dangerous association of sex
with shame. Wives who (it is hoped) have matured healthily and are now
devoted to God, marriage and family (often plus a job) may feel forced by
the ban on artificial contraception to have more children than they can care
for adequately, or more than is good for their health or their marriage. Or
they may feel forced to abandon all hope of children because it is said to be
wrong for their husbands to use any artificial aid to insemination.
Husbands who feel sexually rejected may turn to mistresses or prostitutes.
People who are trying to make a lasting success of a second marriage after
the searing tragedy of a divorce, and who may be innocent of cruelty or
adultery, will be officially excommunicated. 'Practising' homosexuals

whose condition is not their choice will also be rejected at least to that extent. And Roman Catholics in all these categories may not be able to get rid of the implanted fear that, because of an unconfessed sexual sin which is 'mortal', they will end up in hell.

A mountain of misery may be built up by these rulings, or at least hypocrisy and evasion may develop as a spiritual cancer when clergy form sexual relationships (as is common in some regions) or when devout laity 'shop around' for a priest prepared to sympathize with their predicaments more than the bishops do (as is common in many towns). Among Roman Catholics who depend less on the clergy, some loyalty will remain but for practical purposes it will be very limited. For example, in the best sociological study of *Roman Catholic Beliefs in England* (1991), Michael Hornsby-Smith found that 'Catholics generally accept the Pope as an authoritative guide but reserve the right to make up their own minds in most areas of their lives' (p. 134). According to a Gallup Poll in 1993, 84 per cent of American Catholics reject papal teaching about contraception (and 76 per cent think that priests ought to be allowed to marry). The declining birth rates in Italy and Spain, allied with the dramatic spread of pornography, are suggestive about the practices in such traditionally Catholic countries.

Outside the Roman Catholic Church, many people find it hard to separate doctrines about sexuality which they may be permitted to call foolish and destructive from the sound and creatively important elements in the Church's teaching. It is asked: 'if the pope and the bishops appointed by him understand so little about sex, a subject on which almost everyone else has to become something of an expert, how reliable are they when they teach about religious topics which to most people remain very mysterious? And how far are they to be trusted as wise when they discuss social problems which are often caused by the results of sexuality?'

In the fifth Christian century Augustine, who passionately disapproved of him, quoted some words taught by a fellow-theologian and fellow-bishop (and bishop's son), Julian of Eclanum. In the opinion of many, it would have served sanity and morality if the new catechism had endorsed them. 'God made bodies, distinguished between the sexes, made genitalia, bestowed affection by which the bodies would be joined, gave power to the semen, and operates in the secret nature of the semen – and God made nothing evil.' What seems to many necessary now is that the leadership of the Church should add to the wisdom of its recent teachings about society by teaching about sexuality with more regard to the given realities.

Changes about war

It is often objected that a suggestion such as that made in my last sentence is nothing more than sentimentality camouflaging the disgraceful idea that the *magisterium* should lower the Church's standards preserved as the way to holiness through many centuries. To this objection, it can be replied that in human experience war has been almost as important as sex and even greater as a cause of misery; yet like other churches, the Roman Catholic Church has changed – indeed, reversed – its doctrines about the ethics of warfare in response to pragmatic considerations. Such changes are not untypical of the history of the social teaching of the churches. For many centuries bishops blessed emperors and kings, and theologians (including Anglicans) supported their right to rule as 'divine' or God-given (in Roman Catholicism, subject to claims about the rights of popes and bishops). The papal states in Italy were run in a style totally incompatible with the praise of democracy which became dominant in twentieth-century teaching and the church which provided this model was heavily involved in thoroughly hierarchical societies such as feudalism or the class system which emerged after the Middle Ages, often preaching about the necessity of 'order'. Slavery was still being justified in the middle of the nineteenth century. Like lesser preachers, popes condemned the 'usury' practised by capitalists but also 'idleness' and disobedience among the employed, and did not seriously consider the relations of capital and labour before the 1890s, or the economic causes of the poverty of most of the world's population before the 1960s. Today the situation is very different and I hope that I have already shown how much I admire what is now taught. But the changes in teaching about the ethics of warfare have been specially dramatic. Before the present position there was militarism – and before that, pacifism.

The new catechism (2302–2317) teaches that 'all citizens and all governments are obliged to work for the avoidance of war'. But it also quotes the Second Vatican Council: 'As long as the danger of war persists and there is no international authority with the necessary competence and power, governments cannot be denied the right of lawful self-defence, once all peace efforts have failed'. It adds: 'Public authorities in this case have the right and duty to impose on citizens the obligations necessary for national defence. Those who are sworn to serve their country in the armed forces are servants of the security and freedom of nations. If they carry out their duty honourably, they truly contribute to the common good of the nation and the maintenance of peace' (2310).

No mention is made of any moral obligation to refuse to kill, but some other important limits are placed on a Christian's obligation to perform military service. For the first time in official RC teaching, Vatican II (as quoted here) recommended provision 'for those who, for reasons of conscience, refuse to bear arms': they are 'obliged to serve the human community in some other way'. It neither affirmed nor denied the moral legitimacy of the possession of nuclear weapons in order to deter aggression, but it condemned 'without hesitation' actions in war aimed at the destruction of whole cities and widespread areas. Those serving in the forces are now warned not to take part in genocide, the inhumane treatment of non-combatants, prisoners or the wounded. They are told to disobey other orders 'deliberately contrary to the law of nations'. 'Those responsible for the common good' are warned that 'legitimate defence by military force' cannot be morally justified unless there is no other means of putting an end to serious aggression and unless 'serious prospects of success' are present without involving 'more serious evils and disorders than the evil to be eliminated'.

With these clearer restrictions, the teaching of Augustine and Thomas Aquinas about the 'just' war is reaffirmed. But the caution in this reluctant approval of some military actions contrasts with papal enthusiasm for many past wars waged, it was proclaimed, on behalf of the Faith or the Church. No medieval crusade would have passed the tests set by the catechism of 1992. Equally, the catechism's concessions to war contrast with the teaching and practice of Christians during the first three Christian centuries.

No teaching permitting a Christian to take part in warfare has survived from that period. Before about 170 no Christian is known to have served as a soldier and most of those who did so after that date were probably non-combatants doing what was virtually police work (except on the empire's turbulent eastern frontier). Every major theologian of these centuries is known to have urged other Christians to follow the way of love rather than violence. Non-resistance was, they repeated, the way of the crucified Lord who challenged his followers to turn the other cheek, to go the second mile and to love any enemies (Matt 5.39–44). No attention was paid to the problems of a Christian emperor, or a Christian citizen in a Christian empire, who might need to be prepared to kill an aggressor, because before the 'conversion' of Constantine such a phenomenon seemed a very remote possibility if conceivable at all.

This virtually pacifist position was rapidly abandoned when Constantine was converted by the belief that the cross of Christ would make him the conqueror in a civil war, and when his successors made the Church the heart of an empire where the army was the strong right arm. The clergy and the monks were still expected to refuse to enter the army and a soldier-saint such as Martin of Tours was admired for opting out of a battle with the simple words 'I am a soldier of Christ; I cannot fight'. But by the fifth century Christian participation in military service and in warfare was so extensive, and so reliable, that the emperor Theodosius II could order that none but Christians should be enlisted. In later centuries, few Christians felt obliged to protest against the frequent wars, and in 1914 a militant patriotism killed talk about peace and friendship before it nearly killed Europe. Since then it has been generally regretted that Christians have in the past not been more selective in their support of wars, and the brave witness of the pacifist minority has been tolerated and even admired. But there is still no general agreement of the Christian conscience with the idea that pacifism is the only morally legitimate position.

Probably most Christians now share my own belief that the limited concessions made by this catechism to the need of the nations to deter or resist aggression are the best that can be said in a situation which results from sin. And this non-pacifist position has been held, although with much heartache and soul-searching, in a time when an uneasy peace was preserved between some nations through a 'balance of terror' in the possession of weapons which morally as well as emotionally must be horrifying. In order to win the prize of peace Christian realism has been willing to go to that dreadful extreme, the nuclear deterrent. Yes, there have been changes in Roman Catholic attitudes to war.

What is natural?

We have to ask why the *magisterium* of the Roman Catholic Church has so far refused to change those parts of its teaching about sexuality (and its consequences) that are rejected by many as unrealistic.

Sexuality has made countless people foolish and unhappy. Everyone who has reflected on this fact – which means, almost every adolescent or adult – will agree that 'chastity', meaning self-control, is needed when handling emotions which get out of control all too easily. As this catechism rightly teaches, it is both possible and necessary both for the unmarried and for the married (2349). Yet often sexuality is joyful and good. The words of this catechism are healthily positive although the English translation could have been improved by mentioning 'her': 'Sexuality affects all aspects of the human person in the unity of his body and soul. It especially concerns our affectivity, our capacity to love and to procreate, and, in a more general way, the aptitude for forming bonds of communion with others. Everyone, man and woman, should acknowledge and accept his sexual identity' (2332–2333). And sexuality is endowed with such powerful instincts and such ecstatic pleasures because it is intended by 'nature', or as believers will say by nature's God, to be the most used source of human happiness, self-sacrifice and creativity. It is the earth out of which the flowers of love grow. It opens the school in which most people learn most about God's own creative and healing love. The first chapter of Genesis teaches that as the climax of his material creation which was itself 'good', God made human beings in his 'own image and likeness'. There has been much discussion about the meaning of this 'image of God'. Two meanings stand out in Scripture and in human experience. One is that the love which is the nature of God is reflected in human nature at its most basic, for human nature is relational: 'male and female he created them'. The other is that human creativity is like the Creator's (although also unlike). Their own nature makes men and women want to 'be fruitful and increase, fill the earth and subdue it'. In countless ways humanity longs and toils to be creative; that includes making children and that is part of what God himself thinks 'very good'. Some theologians inclined to be hostile to sexuality have sometimes speculated that if Adam and Eve had not sinned they would have been fruitful without sex, but Scripture contains no hint of this impossibility. On the contrary, Genesis allows us to glimpse some fairly early stages of the glad acceptance of married sexuality which has consistently been a feature of the Jewish tradition. This feature is reported to have been endorsed by Jesus: 'At the creation, "God made them male and female". "That is why a man leaves his father and mother, and is united to his wife, and the two become one flesh"' (Mark 10.6, 7).

Why, then, is the *magisterium* thought by so many to have gone so wrong in its teaching about sexual morality? It is not because celibate priests know nothing at all about sex. They are themselves human – and as priests they hear many confidences about problems in the sexual activities and temptations of lay Catholics. And the explanation is not that official Roman Catholic theology is superficial. It has a long history, it is based on a coherent philosophy, and it has been defended by men who deserve respect for their intellects as well as for their pastoral experience and their high office. John Paul II, for example, has while pope only developed the teaching which he gave in his book on *Love and Responsibility* (1960), and no one who has studied it will call that book superficial. His encyclical *Veritatis Splendor* (1993) has not been criticized for being cheaply popular.

Conservative Roman Catholics are not the only people who admire the very firm teaching repeated in this catechism. It seems to be a dam against a flood of vice. It has been said that the only alternative to the proclamation of moral laws which are absolute, universal and unchanging is 'situation ethics', meaning by that ambiguous term the naïve belief that morality depends entirely on each individual deciding within a particular situation what ought to be done without reference to anyone else. Almost everyone would agree that such extreme selfishness is simply immoral – and is specially dangerous when sexual passions have been aroused. But the only alternative to crude immorality is not 'natural law' as defined by the Holy Office of the Vatican when in 1956 it condemned 'situation ethics' in favour of 'the objective right order determined by the law of nature and known with certainty from that law'.

Responsible modern advocates of 'situation ethics' have pleaded only that 'love your neighbour as yourself' should be decisive in the application of moral principles to particular situations, since 'the whole law can be summed up in a single commandment' (Gal 5.14). Obviously the question then arises: what is 'love'? This catechism quotes the unsentimental wisdom of Thomas Aquinas: 'To love is to will the good for another' (1766). Immanuel Kant is not cited in the catechism, but his famous summaries of 'the moral law' provide further guidance: 'Act only on that maxim through which you can at the same time will that it should become a universal law' (we may add: for people in that situation) and in all cases 'act in such a way that you always treat humanity, whether in your own person or in the person of any other, never simply as a means but always at the same time as an end'. And within the RC Church, the long tradition of casuistry, whether in textbooks of moral theology or in the advice given by priests to penitents, has related moral laws to personal situations, lovingly.

In part the mistakes of the *magisterium*, as illustrated by this catechism, seem to be due to the fact that men who have never had a fully sexual relationship – or who have never had one fully approved by their consciences – claim to be unquestionable authorities on sex. We have noted that the pope and the bishops even claim that under certain conditions their teachings on morals may be as infallible as their teachings on faith, although fortunately this general claim has not yet been applied definitively to any particular teaching. 'The Church', we are told (2419), 'has received from the Gospel the full revelation of the truth about man' – and by 'the Church' is plainly meant its leadership, just as the word 'man' includes women who are all excluded from that leadership. That claim is made in connection with teaching about society, but obviously it also covers teaching about sexuality. Thus the opinions of the *magisterium* may be held to be 'the splendour of the truth' even when they conflict with what many millions of Roman Catholics who have personal experience of sexual activity affirm to be true and believe to be moral.

However, a rude reaction of that kind ought not to be the only response of those of us who criticize the *magisterium* for its failure to understand the sexual activities which it observes from a distance (and even when hearing a confession, a celibate priest is at a distance). We ought to be more sympathetic, acknowledging fully some factors which do much to excuse any insensitivity towards the sexually active.

The calling of a Christian to be celibate (permanently unmarried and without any other genital expression of sexuality) is a calling to be Christlike in a specially costly manner, since Jesus sacrificed marriage to his own mission involving a cross. It is called 'virginity for the sake of the kingdom of heaven' in this catechism (1618–1620) and it has been rightly honoured by almost all Christians as the authentic vocation of a minority. Celibacy is a commitment which 'not everyone can accept, but only those for whom God has appointed it' (Matt 19.11). Within this vocation many virtues can be practised and many rewards can be received. Jesus called his apostles to leave everything in order to be with him in his brief and urgent mission to proclaim the dawn of the Kingdom of God, and the promise in Mark's 'gospel for martyrs' (10.29, 30) has always had an intense meaning for those who have sacrificed marriage to later missions: 'Truly I tell you: there is no one who has given up home, brothers or sisters, mother, father or children, or land, for my sake and for the gospel, who will not receive in this age a hundred times as much – houses, brothers and sisters, mothers and children, and land – and persecutions besides; and in the age to come eternal life'. Among the other rewards (for men and women alike) have been liberation from domestic responsibilities and anxieties with the accompanying freedom to be devoted to spiritual, pastoral, missionary or intellectual work. It is no innovation and no wonder that in this catechism the celibate leadership of the RC Church is eloquent about the high calling of 'virginity for the sake of the kingdom'.

But people who remain celibate because of their religious commitment do not cease to be human and therefore to be affected by their sexuality 'in all parts of their persons'. If they are not to betray their ideals and to break their vows by giving genital expression to their sexual urges, for many life must be a constant battle of the will against the flesh and the imagination – or at least, must be until with advancing years the flesh and the imagination no longer tempt so insistently to physical activity. To 'fall in love' would be for them to fall into sin. It is not surprising that in their statements about sex popes and theologians have tended to stress the superiority of the reasoning will over the luring emotions. They have found here the heart of the contrast between 'the spirit' and 'the flesh' – although the Bible understands 'flesh' in a much wider sense, as the whole of human nature when not inspired by the Spirit of God.

In this catechism (1763–1767) 'passions' are defined as 'feelings or emotions of the sensitive appetite which incline us to act or not to act, for the sake of something felt or imagined to be good or evil'. It is well said that 'they are morally qualified to the extent to which they effectively engage reason and will . . . Strong feelings are not decisive for the morality or holiness of persons.' Yet for many who are not merely sensual, irrational and weak-willed, who are not blind to the difference between right and wrong, and who know that true love is not the same thing as sentimentality or exploitation, this sharp distinction between the reasoning will and the emotions will seem unrealistic and this treatment of the passions will seem too dismissive. And we may be allowed to ask why.

The catechism was written or edited by unmarried men who are called not only to chastity but also to celibacy. Their personal situation seems to have influenced their insistence that 'the alternative is clear: either man governs his passions and finds peace, or he lets himself be dominated by them and become unhappy'. They teach that 'the chaste person maintains the integrity of the powers of life and love placed in him' and that chastity raises truly human sexuality above 'belonging to the bodily and biological world'. In an apparent reference to the myth that Adam was originally both male and female, Augustine is quoted: 'It is through chastity that we are gathered together and led back into the unity from which we were fragmented into multiplicity' (2337–2340). In response, all Christians would agree that it is obviously dehumanizing and therefore immoral for a man or a woman to be promiscuous or to want only the body of a sexual partner. But to people who know a true love and a happy marriage from the inside, the emphasis in this catechism, and in much traditional teaching behind it, will seem somewhat misplaced. In what the catechism splendidly calls 'the complete and lifelong mutual gift of a man and a woman', peace and happiness may be found partly by self-control but largely by self-giving and by delighted and sustained self-surrender. Restraint is essential, but what unites a man and a woman is not restraint.

One of the most moving records of the struggle to attain peace through celibacy is to be found in Augustine's *Confessions*. In the fourth century, he was overwhelmed by his sexiness from the age of sixteen. He lived for thirteen years in a faithful, but not a married, relationship with a woman who, presumably amid much use of contraception, bore one child, a son who died. He remained restlessly dissatisfied with himself and did not find his true identity until he had rejected both a new mistress and the imminent possibility of a high-class marriage. He went on to found a religious community and to be a busy and famous bishop and theologian, but was dismayed to experience both in his own body and in his pastoral work the continuing pressures and fires of sexuality. He defended dignified marriages which produced children with as little passion as possible, as he defended friendships with as little sexual content as possible. He did not pour contempt and hatred on women, as did his contemporary Jerome. But he wrote with anger about the disgust felt by a man of high ideals who has an erection against his will, with indignation about the power of sex to distract from the spiritual life, and with compassion about the suffering inflicted on parents by the pains and dangers of childbearing and the defects or deaths of children. To read the autobiography of Augustine, who has had more influence than any other teacher on the official Catholic teaching about sexuality, is to understand why under his tuition the evils in the human condition have often been regarded as punishments for the 'original' sin of Adam, resulting immediately in shame about nakedness, reactivated by the lust involved in every act of sexual intercourse and transmitted through that act from generation to generation. Nor is it hard to understand why that dark vision has often seemed the truth about the human condition. There has been widespread disgust at the sexual habits of societies ancient or modern.

Paul began his letter to the Romans with a spirited denunciation of the 'vile desires' and 'consequent degradation' of men and women who have worshipped 'created things' instead of the Creator. That attack on idolatry might have led into an attack on a man's worship of a woman and *vice versa*, but actually Paul condemned homosexuals who 'burn with lust' for one another because that was not 'natural'. A Christian congregation must be an oasis of clean living in this desert of wickedness, and Paul wrote in chapters 5–7 of his first letter to the Christians amid Corinth: 'You must have nothing to do with those who are sexually immoral'. He ignored (if he knew about) the inclusive habits of Jesus who was known as the 'friend of prostitutes'. He urged self-respect on Christians tempted to make use of the trade of prostitution (which flourished in that great port), for their bodies were limbs of the body of Christ and temples of the Holy Spirit. He would like every Christian to be celibate like himself, but he knew that 'it is better to be married than to burn with desire' and that it was 'the Lord's ruling' that the married should not divorce. So he taught that 'in the face of so much immorality, let each man have his own wife and each woman her own husband', giving each other 'what is due' and not claiming their bodies as their own. Some of his followers were more positive about marriage, as is shown by the letters to Timothy and Titus. Within a hundred years of his death, however, the negative side of Paul's teaching surfaced again. It was being taught widely in the Church that the divine Spirit had the more easy access to bodies which had not been filled by the heats of sexual desire. So ordination was thought to involve the renunciation of sex, and married Christians who aspired to the higher stages of holiness did well to live 'as brother and sister'. When millions of people conformed to Christianity in the fourth century without abandoning most of the ways of the world, many thousands of ardent Christians fled to the deserts of Egypt, to seek God in a celibate holiness, heroically denying sex as well as other human hungers.

The background to such denunciations (and somewhat grudging permissions) was a society in which sex was in the air. No doubt many people were models of self-control while unmarried and of faithful marriage. Certainly praises of gentlemanly, maidenly or wifely conduct have survived. But other evidence agrees with the impression conveyed by Paul's letters that from erotic tales about the gods to songs in the streets, that ancient world was sexy. Young men were expected to enjoy bisexual experiences and older men were not criticized for drawing them into homosexual relationships. Most marriages were arranged by families and involved a financial transaction. After such marriages at an early age, wives were expected to remain faithful but the hope was often not fulfilled; and such an ambitious hope was seldom held about husbands. Slaves were often abused sexually and male and female prostitution was publicly recognized. Clumsy contraceptives were used but abortions were frequent and many infants, particularly daughters, were left in the open air to die. Divorce was easily available to restless men and under Roman law a woman could divorce her husband. Jewish law gave her no such right but had never repealed permission for polygamy. Some rabbis taught that a man might divorce his wife if he disliked her cooking or discovered someone more beautiful. Prostitutes are plentiful in the background of the gospels (most of them divorced wives) and in the story of the woman taken in adultery there is no proposal that the man should be stoned. The strength and purity of Jewish family life, rightly admired in the ancient world as in later centuries, had these limits in the period which Jesus of Nazareth addressed.

Liberalism amounting to immorality is, of course, not typical of all non-Christian societies. Tribal life in Africa, for example, or village life in India is full of restraints on sexual behaviour which are enforced by public opinion and if need be by violence. Communist China has been repressively puritanical. And even in the Roman empire, there was much teaching that a wise man must practise *severitas* (the control of all human weakness) and a woman must be a pure virgin or wife. But the evidence suggests that the society into which Christianity entered was in practice often quite like the 'permissive' societies observed in the twentieth century by the teachers of the Roman Catholic Church, in many countries but not least in Rome itself. Paul was not isolated in expressing disgust. It is not strange that spiritual teachers in Rome in our own time should also be indignant.

These teachers have inherited a long and praiseworthy struggle to prevent Christianity being identified with either of two extremes, both advocated by various 'Gnostics' in the early Christian centuries and not without later exponents. Either Christianity is said to be totally against nature and the flesh, an escape from this world which if not actively wicked is illusory, so that sex is simply banned – or Christianity is said to be so successfully spiritual that sex is simply accepted, without moralizing. But the teachers of the RC Church, resisting those follies in religion, and counselling the millions whose flesh is frail, have perceived that it would not be enough to rely on a call to Christian conversion and holiness – the call to which they have themselves responded – if they wish to diminish the sexual laxity of the bulk of the population. It is not safe to rely on most people becoming saints. A more reliable alternative seems to be teaching about what is 'natural'. This catechism says that 'the natural law, present in the heart of each man and established by reason, is universal in its precepts and its authority extends to all men' (1956). Although unfortunately experience suggests that those words are overconfident, we may agree that people are willing to listen when advised to be 'natural'.

But the question must arise: what is natural? 'Nature' can mean the survival of the fittest and can therefore encourage brutality, exploitation and slavery. Nature is so often morally ambiguous that Jeremy Bentham called the whole idea of natural law 'nonsense on stilts'. To many people, nothing seems more natural than sexual enjoyment, and many or all of the practices condemned by Christian teachers in sexually lax societies have been defended as 'doing what comes naturally'. As this catechism notes, 'the precepts of the natural law are not perceived by everyone clearly and immediately. In the present situation sinful man needs grace and revelation so moral and religious truths may be known "by everyone with facility, with firm certainty and with no admixture of error"' – a quotation from Pius XII (1960). 'Nature' must therefore be defined selectively. In this context it has to be understood as human nature, which however must also be defined selectively. As we select features for our admiration, we find ourselves making moral judgements. What is admirable is, we think, what is 'truly' human and therefore 'truly' natural.

What, then, is the function of sexuality in human nature?

Unfortunately the understanding of sexuality as the energy which makes people relate and create was reached only slowly in the history of Catholic (and other Christian) teaching. The emotional side was not sufficiently stressed in comparison with the physical acts needed to produce children. Love as an 'end' or purpose of marriage was not clearly emphasized by the *magisterium* until the 1960s brought the Second Vatican

Council. Before that, married love had of course been mentioned and praised, partly because it is commended in the Bible, as in 'husbands, love your wives, as Christ loved the Church' (Eph 5.25). As an onlooker, Paul observed that the aim of husband and wife is to please each other (1 Cor 7.33–34). But more stress had been put on other 'ends' of marriage emphasized by Paul and Augustine. In the canon law of the RC Church marriage was for long regarded as a 'contract' in which partners gave each other the exclusive right to the body for acts 'apt for procreation'. The bond was rendered indissoluble by the first act of sexual intercourse, and subsequent acts were often referred to by unenthusiastic theologians as 'the marriage debt'. This restricted view was, however, not an exclusively RC emphasis. In the Church of England the 1662 Book of Common Prayer taught that marriage was needed if children were to be conceived and 'brought up in the fear and nurture of the Lord' but that married sex was 'a remedy against sin and to avoid fornication' – a chillingly negative view of the marriage bed.

It is difficult to resist the impression that the great emphasis on reproduction as the main, or only, purpose of sexual passion has owed too much to observations in the farmyard. Many animals have numerous offspring, most of which die prematurely, and they are stimulated to go about the necessary business by the mating season. But men and women can be aroused sexually at almost any time, at most times when they make love they will not make babies, and from puberty onwards they are the sexiest creatures alive. Why? Many of their children die prematurely, but many others survive through a long period of dependence on parents and the welfare of humanity depends on this period as much as on any other factor. While many animals co-operate to feed their young, it seems specially natural for human parents to stay together with tasks which are as much emotional as physical, and the evolutionary advantage gained by the successful performance of these tasks is stimulated by the need for two to co-operate in the intense enjoyment of sex. Such understanding of what is distinctively human lies in the background to the modern emphasis on the priority of love in marriage. We admire love because love is human nature's most significant need and work.

I have repeated obvious and stale answers to the question 'What is natural in human sexuality?' I have done so because the question about nature matters to Christians as well as to everyone else. The Bible cannot be the Christian's only guide. It throws light on what is truly natural, yet it does not provide a detailed code of sexual behaviour which is authoritative permanently and universally, excusing us from all further thought. What the Bible provides, we discover, is a vision of holy love.

This has to be related to our knowledge and experience of the energies which the Creator has given us through nature. That sounds complicated – but so is real life. And the Bible is like life itself, in that it challenges us to make many decisions which are our responsibility. Almost all Christians will agree with the teaching of *Veritatis Splendor* that the function of the conscience is 'to apply the universal knowledge of the good in a specific situation' and that 'only the freedom which submits to the Truth leads the human person to the good'. But in many situations Christians who are guided by the biblical vision find that the Bible leaves them to the guidance of their own informed consciences as they have to work out what is good because truly natural.

The biblical vision

Conditions in biblical times were reflected in biblical laws and they continued almost unchanged for many centuries in the history of Christianity. There were great differences not only from pagan promiscuity but also from what are usually reckoned to be morally respectable standards in modern times. Most people who survived infancy died before their fortieth birthday, allowing between ten and twenty years for a marriage. The need for many children to provide hands to do the work was urgent. It was assumed that most young people would accept a marriage arranged by their families, for a woman when recently past puberty, for a man a little later. The spouses would be expected to have many children, to work in the home or at least within walking distance of it, and to live in a small and stable community. It was also assumed that women would be humbly obedient, first to their fathers and then to their husbands. Very few women were able to earn their living independently, except as prostitutes catering for other women's husbands. And it was assumed that all homosexuals were sinful perverts who could have enjoyed 'natural relations' and a normal family life. Under these conditions the Hebrew Scriptures included many laws regulating the relations between the sexes although there was no law against the fruitful polygamy practised by the revered patriarchs and long after those times by a few of the rich. In the Hebrew Bible, King Solomon was condemned not because he had 'seven hundred wives and three hundred concubines' but because their paganism 'turned his heart' from the true religion (1 Kings 11.3).

Jesus, so far from endorsing or revising the mass of biblical legislation in any detail, is said to have swept it aside for the sake of his own new vision on at least two occasions. Instead of citing with respect the law that permitted a man to give a note of divorce to a wife who 'does not win his

favour because he finds something shameful in her' (Deut 24.1), he taught
that all divorce went against the Creator's plan for humanity (according to
Mark 10.2–9). But, instead of approving as legal the stoning to death of
anyone caught in the act of adultery (Lev 20.10; Deut 22.20–22), he is
said in John's gospel (8.1–11) to have stopped an execution because the
accusers were also guilty of sexual sins. And he is not presented by the
other gospels as a cold and precise legislator who expected laws (old or
new) to be obeyed literally: on the contrary, his most characteristic words
were piercing because startling. In Matthew's gospel (5.28, 29) the
Sermon on the Mount teaches: 'If a man looks at a woman with a lustful
eye, he has already committed adultery with her in his heart. If your right
eye causes your downfall, tear it out and fling it away!' In Luke's gospel
(14.26), we read: 'If anyone comes to me and does not hate his father and
mother, wife and children, brothers and sisters, even his own life, he
cannot be a disciple of mine'. Yet it is remarkable how little time in the
gospels is spent on the condemnation of sexual sinners. And everyone who
has known this Lord has known how amazing, and how promising, it is
that he, the Holy One who summoned sinners to repentance, was called
the friend of prostitutes.

Jesus, it seems clear, proclaimed not a detailed code of regulations for
marriage and family life, or for any other field of life in the present world,
but the total coming of the Kingdom of God – and at first the summons to
share in this proclamation was so urgent that a man called to this mission
must not wait at home for his father to die: 'Follow me, and leave the dead
to bury their dead' (Matt 8.21, 22). Paul included at least a strong
element of this visionary excitement in his own teaching, for he shared the
early Christian belief that 'the time we live in will not last long. While it
lasts, married men should live as if they had no wives' and the unmarried
should remain in his own unencumbered state (1 Cor 7.26, 29). After his
death much of the Church settled down more conventionally, for example
expecting a presbyter-bishop or deacon to be 'the husband of one wife' (1
Tim 3.2, 12). The 'household codes' included in this late stage of the
writing of the New Testament echoed non-Christian teachers of respect-
ability, with the male head of the household controlling women, children
and slaves firmly but without harshness. And other Christians have made
other responses, more heroic or less. The challenge is always how to obey
the all-demanding vision of holy love in the Kingdom of God alongside
the fact that men and women are naturally filled with the creative,
although troublesome, energies of sexuality. That is a challenge to our
time, when questions are asked with a bold honesty not matched in any
earlier age.

Questionable ethics

The Second Vatican Council showed that the RC Church had moved away from some old patriarchal or sex-shy teachings which had been rejected by many consciences, and accordingly the new catechism says some fine and true things about the man–woman relationship and about marriage. 'Each of the two sexes is an image of the power and tenderness of God, with equal dignity though in a different way' (2335). The substantial teaching about marriage begins with the insight that 'the matrimonial covenant, by which a man and a woman establish between themselves a partnership of the whole of life, is by its nature ordered to the good of the spouses and the procreation and education of offspring' (1601). Scripture, we are reminded, affirms that man and woman were created for one another: 'it is not good that the man should be alone' (1605). Since the Fall 'marriage helps to overcome self-absorption, egoism, pursuit of one's own pleasure, and to open oneself to the other, to mutual aid and to self-giving' (1609). Equally edifying is the teaching about the delights and duties of the Christian family (2197–2233). But to many conscientious Christians, the catechism does not seem to have moved far enough away from some other traditional teachings about sexuality. In the discussion about marriage and the family, idealism is proper. But sexuality is still a force outside marriage's ring of gold and the happy family circle. So it is necessary to think honestly about some subjects which are not so polite.

Masturbation is comparatively unimportant and is not clearly mentioned in the Bible, yet it is the first of these supplementary questions to be treated in this catechism (in the section on the Ten Commandments) and the treatment sets the tone for much of what follows. The act is defined as 'the deliberate stimulation of the genital organs in order to derive sexual pleasure'. 'Both the *magisterium* of the Church, in the course of a constant tradition, and the moral sense of the faithful', we are told, 'have been in no doubt and have firmly maintained that masturbation is an intrinsically and gravely disordered action', because 'sexual pleasure in this case is sought outside of the sexual relationship which is demanded by the moral order' (2352). Yet repeated surveys have shown that masturbation is practised by most young men; as is often reported, by almost all. It is also common among older men who are not otherwise sexually active, and among women of all ages. The extent of the practice by faithful Roman Catholics open to advice seems to be acknowledged when the catechism proceeds to say that pastoral counselling must take account of 'the individual's affective immaturity, force of acquired habit, conditions of anxiety and other psychological and social factors'.

It may be suggested that those giving advice might take into account the fact that for many millions masturbation is a relief from sexual tensions which must otherwise distract, disturb and depress. These tensions arise because the human body is in part a machine which suggests and facilitates sexual intercourse, partly by adding intense pleasure to that act and even to the real or imagined prospect of it. It is hard to see how the relief of these tensions is an activity which is completely 'outside of the sexual relationship'. Indeed, many therapists recommend it as a preparation for that relationship. Although many young children masturbate when experimenting with their bodies, it is well known that this relief is sought particularly by young people who are at their peak of sexual potency but below the age at which society encourages them to marry; by adults who are also sexually potent but have not found a partner (perhaps because they are celibates); and by married people who for one reason or another cannot have intercourse or who wish to express their mutual love without risking conception. The act causes no physical harm, despite numerous ignorant warnings by so-called authorities in the past, and it seems to do no psychological harm unless it becomes a humiliating obsession or a cause of failure to form a sexual relationship with emotional content. What does very often cause harm is the connection between sex, shamefaced secrecy and confused, unrepented feelings of guilt – a link which has been encouraged by solemnly and unhesitantly calling every such act 'intrinsically and gravely disordered' as in this catechism. In the American catechism *The Teaching of Christ*, revised in 1984, it was said that 'the Church has clearly and persistently taught that the performance of such an act is a mortal sin' and 'has also explicitly defined the teaching that those who die in actual mortal sin enter their unending punishment immediately after death' – unless, it is later added, their deeds were done 'without sufficient understanding of their malice' (pp. 316, 515, 522). This catechism would have been wise to move right away from the identification of the Church's authority with such harsh attitudes.

Fornication is defined as 'carnal union between an unmarried man and an unmarried woman' and it is said to be 'gravely contrary to the dignity of human persons and of human sexuality, which is naturally ordered to the good of spouses and to the generation and education of children' (2353). This moral condemnation has much wider and stronger support than the verdict on masturbation, because in such a relationship women and men can easily inflict or suffer unhappiness, psychological damage or venereal disease. No thoughtful person, and of course no Christian, would applaud promiscuity or other 'easy sex'. Countless people (including myself, if that matters) have managed to adhere to the standard that sexual activity should be confined to marriage. But it may be questioned whether all acts of 'carnal union' outside marriage deserve equal condemnation as being 'gravely contrary' to the dignity and spiritual growth of the persons involved.

The catechism denounces all relationships where the man and woman 'refuse to give juridical and public form to a liaison involving sexual intimacy'. In all such cases, it asks scornfully, 'what can "union" mean when the partners make no commitment to one another, each exhibiting a lack of trust in the other, in himself or in the future?' It declares: 'all such situations are contrary to the moral law. The sexual act must take place exclusively within marriage. Outside marriage, it always constitutes a grave sin and excludes one from sacramental communion' (2390). But strangely, no moral distinction is made here in this catechism between commercial sex with a prostitute, or drunken sex with a stranger, and the tender but physical expression of a relationship between already intimate and trusting lovers who honour each other.

In particular it may be questioned whether sexual intercourse is always wrong between people whose 'living together' may amount to a socially recognized 'partnership' or 'common law marriage' or who may strongly hope or intend to be married formally, in many cases by a formal and public engagement to marry. In many societies traditional or modern (Britain and the USA being two contemporary examples), sex before marriage but within love is very common and is not thought wrong either by the bulk of public opinion or by most of the many Christians who rightly or wrongly enjoy it. It has recently been encouraged by the two beliefs that couples can now prevent the births of unwanted children and ought to prevent hasty and sexually inexperienced marriages which can lead to disaster and divorce. In sad fact, babies may be born who will not be able to rely on parents united by a stable commitment, and marriages contracted after 'living together' may fail because even now the partners have no real commitment to lifelong fidelity, but it is not ridiculous to try and hope to avoid these consequences. In traditional rural or working-class societies church weddings have often taken place after a pregnancy or birth, and currently most of the clergy seem willing to preside over the marriages of couples giving the same address. In many societies in our own time strongly Christian families accept 'living together' by some of their own members. It seems therefore that the Christian conscience may be moving away from the catechism's simplicity in excommunicating all people guilty of 'fornication', without any attempt to discriminate. In England the leading Roman Catholic writer on sex and marriage, Dr Jack Dominian, has observed that 'very few, Christian or not, reach the wedding as virgins. What I am suggesting is that the anticipation of sexual intercourse before marriage is . . . an expression of an insight that sexual intercourse is a signature of commitment and love which may occur before the actual ceremony of the wedding' (*Tablet*, 5 March 1994).

Contraception is said in this catechism to be 'both a positive refusal to be open to life and a falsification of the inner truth of conjugal love, which demands personal, integral self-giving'. Accordingly, the catechism describes as 'intrinsically evil' 'every action which, whether in anticipation of the conjugal act, or in its accomplishment, or in the development of its natural consequences, proposes, whether as an end or as a means, to render procreation impossible' (2370). The teachings of Popes Pius XI (*Casti Connubii* in 1930), Pius XII and Paul VI are cited in support of these propositions which are, however, in practice rejected by most Roman Catholics who are married in societies where contraception is readily available. It may be questioned whether this refusal to accept the teaching of the *magisterium* is morally wrong. The use of contraceptives by conscientious married couples was thought allowable by the Lambeth Conference of Anglican bishops in 1930 (reversing their condemnation in 1920). It seems clear that the majority of the bishops in Vatican II had come to the same conclusion. This change was recommended by 58 (out of 62) on the commission of experts set up by Paul VI in the 1960s to advise him when it seemed possible that the official teaching might be changed. The commission worked for three years and many of its members changed their minds in the process.

Two main arguments have been advanced by experts on ethics (and by others) on countless occasions during and since the 1960s in support of the millions of married Roman Catholics who practise contraception.

The first is that sexual intercourse renews, supports and increases married love, which the catechism affirms as an 'end' of marriage before it also affirms the conception of children. This strengthening of the marriage bond becomes specially important when the birth of children is feared because it would further damage the wife's health of body or mind, or because it would further increase strains on the marriage caused by poverty or overcrowding. And it is also of special importance in a time such as our own when unhappy spouses have access to divorce in most countries, for intercourse is the natural way for a married couple to end a row or to relieve stress. Quoting Paul VI's encyclical *Humanae Vitae* (1968), it is taught in this catechism that 'periodic continence, methods of birth control based on self-observation and the use of infertile periods conform to the objective standards of morality'. Indeed, it is added that 'such methods respect the spouses' bodies, encourage tenderness between them and contribute to authentic freedom' (2370). Yet Pius XII, in the 1950s, was the first pope to allow explicitly methods other than 'periodic continence'. It may be questioned whether the time has not come to allow methods which resemble these in not being intended to be open to 'the transmission of life' but which are more reliable. As has been found by many RC couples who have remained obedient to the *magisterium* in this matter, effective 'self-observation' counting the days of fertility requires a degree of methodical thoroughness which to many women is either very uncongenial or psychologically impossible – and 'infertile periods' are not always infertile. It is asked: when a blessing has been pronounced on some sex without conception, why not bless the condom, the pill or some developing or future technology of contraception which is less off-putting than the condom and which has fewer side effects than the pill? It is also asked: if legitimate advantage may be taken of a woman's presumed infertility during the rest of her monthly cycle, why not use contraceptives if intercourse seems desirable for some good reason during the remaining days? In answer to those questions it is often said that only 'natural' methods are permissible. But thermometers and charts are still needed for the 'natural' methods – and nowhere else in human life is it claimed that 'nature' must never be stopped from bringing about situations which human beings do not desire. In medical practice, 'natural' illnesses are very frequently frustrated; day by day we frustrate the tendencies of 'nature' to make us cold, hungry or dead; and this is thought to be highly moral. Christians think that these acts against 'nature' are willed by God.

The second reason often given for supporting married Roman Catholics who practise contraception is that the world's population is growing at a pace which causes misery through poverty and overcrowding, and disease or death through malnutrition. Injustice and inefficiency in the development and distribution of Earth's resources add to the problem, but the catechism does not argue, as some other Roman Catholics have argued to their shame, that there is no great danger that the resources may run out. It briefly acknowledges this feature of the world's current crisis when it teaches that 'the state has a responsibility for its citizens' well-being and so may legitimately intervene to direct population growth by supplying objective and respectful information' (2372). But at the same time governments are warned not only against 'authoritarian coercive measures' (which seems to imply a reference to Communist China) but also against the encouragement of 'immoral means of regulating population' (which seems to advocate discouraging the supply or sale of contraceptives) and against substituting itself 'for the initiative of spouses, who have the primary responsibility for the procreation and education of their children' (which presumably suggests strict limits for sex education in state-run schools). It may be questioned whether this response to a crisis which may result in very widespread distress, conflicts and famines is morally adequate, specially when it is remembered that two of the regions most threatened by population growth are Latin America and Africa south of the Sahara, where the RC Church has great influence. The slowing down of the growth of Mexico's population when contraceptives were made available widely and legally taught a lesson.

The control of births by abortion is much more clearly repugnant to the Christian conscience. But is the catechism right to demand that 'the law must provide appropriate penal sanctions for every deliberate violation of the child's rights' – meaning in this context, for every procured abortion (2273)? Although the New Testament is curiously silent on the subject, the catechism will be widely understood and applauded, often with passion, and often by people who are not Roman Catholics, when it says: 'Since the first century the Church has taught the moral evil of procured abortion. This teaching has not changed and remains unchangeable' (2271). Yet even here some questions have often been asked.

Is it right to base this application of 'the inalienable right to life of every innocent human individual' on the teaching that 'the embryo, like any other human being, must be treated as a person from conception' (2273–2275)? In 1974 the Sacred Congregation for the Doctrine of the Faith declared that it did not wish to pronounce on the question 'at what time the spiritual soul is infused' and theologians and other deep thinkers about ethics have refused to classify a newly conceived embryo as 'a person' or (as Pius IX did in 1869) 'a soul'. Augustine and Thomas Aquinas also refused; the latter thought that the foetus was 'animated' at forty days for a boy and ninety for a girl. In 1566 the Roman Catechism taught more cautiously that 'according to the order of nature, the rational soul is united to the body only after a certain lapse of time'. Innumerable natural miscarriages have been grieved over, to be sure, but not in quite the same way as the death of a child. The number of such miscarriages may be 40 per cent of all pregnancies. It is of course agreed that a foetus is a potential person and becomes capable of independent life at about 28 weeks, but there is no complete agreement about the moment before birth when what was potentially becomes fully human. So questions are asked. Is it always right to deny an abortion to a woman who may have become pregnant under age, or through rape or incest or under the influence of drink or drugs, or who may be judged by doctors to be in grave danger of losing her physical or mental health, or who may be judged to be incapable of caring for a baby known to be seriously abnormal? Is the date within the pregnancy irrelevant to moral considerations? Is the comparative physical safety with which such operations can now be performed also irrelevant? Or in some circumstances, may an abortion be the lesser of two evils, like the sacrifice of innocent lives as a side-effect of war?

These are not merely questions for a debate. It is estimated that about sixty million abortions take place in the world every year. About half are done outside the law of the land and about a million women die as a result.

It may also be asked whether the unchangeable and very widely accepted teaching that procured abortion is always morally evil will always be accompanied by refusals to leave some moral problems to the consciences of the individuals concerned and to the medical profession, in a choice between two evils. Already it has been agreed that when a womb is cancerous it may be removed even if it contains a foetus, and there has been a change in the teaching that when a terrible choice has to be made between the life of a mother and the life of a foetus the mother's life should be sacrificed. These developments sanction 'indirect' killing, but it may be questioned whether the termination of a pregnancy might escape the penalty of excommunication in a few other very hard cases, particularly in those early weeks when it is not clear whether or not the foetus in which the brain has not yet developed is an animated or ensouled person.

In some marriages couples experience a very different cause of unhappiness, because it proves impossible to conceive children by the normal method. As the catechism says in its teaching (2374–2379), they 'suffer greatly'. It therefore encourages 'research aimed at reducing human sterility'. But at the same time it describes as 'gravely immoral' techniques that intrude a third person between father and mother. This condemnation will seem right to most Christians and to most other people. But the catechism will not command such wide agreement when it goes on to describe as 'morally unacceptable' all artificial methods for implanting the husband's seed in the wife. It is said that these methods entrust 'the life and identity of the embryo into the power of doctors and biologists'; yet no such objection is raised to the assistance of births by Caesarean operations. It is also said that 'procreation is deprived of its proper perfection when it is not willed as the fruit of the conjugal act'; yet the question is not faced: what is the most loving action to take when after many attempts the couple are unable to fulfil their strong will to conceive a child without help? In other imperfect situations Christians are encouraged to be creatively compassionate.

In some sexual relationships there is no such possibility because both of the partners are exclusively and permanently homosexual (in Greek *homos* means 'the same'). The catechism teaches that Sacred Scripture always presents homosexual acts as 'acts of grave depravity' and that the Church's tradition 'has always taught that such acts are "intrinsically disordered". They are contrary to the natural law, for they close the sexual act to the gift of life and do not proceed from an authentic effective and sexual complementarity. In no case can they be approved' (2357).

The Christians who have agreed with this stern teaching have included many homosexuals who in obedience to it have sacrificed much of their own happiness and sense of fulfilment. Many, whether heterosexual or homosexual, have found it impossible to see how homosexual acts can be right morally because they seem wrong biologically. They seem to be what they were called in the Hebrew Bible (Lev 18.22), 'an abomination', even if it is not added that both homosexuals 'must be put to death' (Lev 20.13). Yet modern research into this phenomenon can be interpreted as changing some of the facts on which these moral judgements have been based.

As the catechism notes, homosexuality 'has taken very diverse forms through the ages and in different cultures'. In our time, the number of men and women who have deep-seated homosexual tendencies is not negligible. They do not choose their homosexual condition; for most of them it is a trial. They must be accepted with respect, compassion and sensitivity (2357–2358). Consequently, questions may be asked – and not only by Christian homosexuals.

Although the catechism says that the 'psychological genesis' of this condition 'remains largely unexplained', it is increasingly agreed by those who have studied the research that homosexual tendencies are present, although not dominant, in most people. When these tendencies are dominant one of the causes (to which childhood experiences may be added) is a variation in the genes dating from conception, inherited from the mother and resulting in a variation in the physical structure of the brain. It has also been found that a dominantly homosexual orientation can seldom be altered by treatment, however much this may be desired. In these ways homosexuality seems 'natural'. If that is the case, the Congregation for the Doctrine of the Faith was cruelly wrong to declare in *Personae Humanae* (1975) that since no homosexuals are 'incurable . . . the hope should be instilled in them of one day overcoming their difficulties and their alienation from society'. That teaching resembles a suggestion that the way to deal with the problem of racism is for black people to develop white skins. And in the light of our knowledge of this unalterable condition, it may be asked whether it is clearly right to say that for all homosexuals without exception 'chastity' must mean 'celibacy'. Is it not possible that some homosexuals have a vocation to renounce all sexual activity – and some do not? Physical expressions of sexuality by homosexual lovers faithful to each other are obviously less creative than heterosexual intercourse producing children. But are they always 'acts of grave depravity' in which a 'genuine affective complementarity' is simply impossible?

Recent research into church history has produced evidence that homosexuals enjoyed considerable acceptance among Christians before the twelfth century, and in the twentieth century Christian tolerance has greatly increased. The biblical passages to which this catechism refers have been shown in many studies to be not entirely relevant to modern reflection on medical knowledge. One is a story (Gen 19.1–11) about angels disguised as men and given hospitality by Lot in Sodom. They are surrounded by a crowd of men demanding to 'have intercourse'. Lot rebukes them for wickedness – it may be because they refuse the proper alternative offered (intercourse with his 'two daughters, virgins both of them') or because 'these men have come under the shelter of my roof'. Then the wicked crowd is struck by blindness. The story does not seem decisive for modern ethics. Similarly indecisive, if not completely irrelevant, are the story of the love of David and Jonathan, 'surpassing the love of women' (2 Sam 1.26), and the emphasis in John's gospel that Jesus 'loved' one of his disciples, a man. Other passages from the New Testament deserve more serious consideration in the ethical assessment of homosexual acts. But when writing to the Romans (1.24–27) Paul evidently thinks that the men and women whom he denounces have become homosexuals after 'giving up natural relations' with the other sex. In other words, they are perverts, not homosexuals by nature. This understanding or misunderstanding of homosexuals governs the other two hostile references (1 Cor 6.9 and 1 Tim 1.10, now translated 'perverts'). Jesus is not reported as having taught on the subject, except in the calm and far from hostile observation that 'some are incapable of marriage because they were born so' (Matt 19.12).

Remarriage after divorce is treated in this catechism in the same severe style as the treatment of abortion, artificial insemination and homosexual acts. Other churches have found all these subjects difficult to handle, but officially the RC Church does not. As the catechism says:

In fidelity to the words of Jesus Christ – 'Whoever divorces his wife and marries another commits adultery against her; and if she divorces her husband and marries another, she commits adultery' – the Church maintains that the new union cannot be recognized as valid, if the first union was. If the divorced are remarried civilly they find themselves in a situation that objectively contravenes God's law. Consequently, they cannot receive Eucharistic communion as long as this situation persists . . . Reconciliation through the sacrament of Penance can be granted only to those who repent for having violated the sign of the covenant and fidelity to Christ, and who are committed to living in complete continence. (1650)

Accordingly popes and bishops have used all their influence against any provision for divorce under the law of the land. However, it is added that divorced and remarried Christians 'may often keep the faith and desire to bring up their children in a Christian manner'. They should 'not consider themselves cut off from the Church, in whose life they can and must participate as baptized persons' (1651).

Here again many Christians, including many who are not Roman Catholics, will agree with the catechism's firm teaching. But almost everywhere the *magisterium* has failed to deter legislation; for example, in 1974 almost 60 per cent of Italians voting in a referendum wanted some provision for divorce. It has become a major issue for Christians, particularly since on recent trends in countries such as Britain and the USA one recent marriage in every three will end in divorce. This epidemic is often said to result from a low view of marriage, but in fact modern marriage, specially when undertaken by Christians, demands a high view of the potential in the human beings who are joined. It is based on a voluntary contract between equal partners who are attracted to each other by their sexuality and their common interests; they are 'in love'. If and when the strength of their sexual union diminishes, it has to be based also on friendship, co-operation and gratitude, making an emotional together-ness in an age when not many conventions about the status and role of either sex are thought by everyone to be obviously right. If and when children are born, it has to take a new form which acknowledges their rightful demands and growing independence. It has to be related to other adults who may feel free to form a close friendship with either of the spouses and even to make sexual advances. It is unlikely to be needed for the purpose of joint work in the fields or elsewhere, and both partners will probably think that they could survive a separation financially, even if with difficulty. They will also probably think that a divorce decreed under the laws of the State would be basically acceptable. And modern marriage is expected to last for far longer than was normal in the time when people usually died younger; over half a century may be lived through before a death. In that time one partner, once like the other full of love and hope, may grow away so far that the aim of a new partnership, or of independence, seems worth the cost of a sacrificed home.

Each year many tens of thousands of 'annulments' are granted to Roman Catholics, declaring that the marriage 'never existed', usually on the grounds that at the time of the wedding there was inadequate 'free consent' by the partners, or that they were impeded by some 'natural or ecclesiastical law' (1625–1629). The procedure is, however, slow and it means that a tribunal must ask intimate questions about sexual attitudes and practices, perhaps referring to the distant past. It may offend the conscience by the statement, which may seem hypocritical, that a union marked for a time by authentic love and hope, by firm intentions and perhaps also by the birth and rearing of children, was never a true marriage. And it inevitably involves judgements by religious courts which, however conscientious, are not infallible. (Thus the papacy may well be praised for refusing to grant an annulment to Henry VIII – but had it been right to grant one to Louis XII of France a few years previously?)

As the catechism notes, in response to these problems 'today in many countries numerous Catholics have had recourse to civil divorces and have contracted civil unions'. As it does not say, but as happens, many Roman Catholics in this position receive eucharistic communion either with the parish priest's assent or without finding it necessary to consult him.

The catechism also does not say how the new marriage can be expected to flourish as a new start in life (almost a resurrection) when it is under the censures and handicaps imposed by the official rulings. Nor does the catechism deal clearly with the moral situation of those who have entered into marriage with an understanding different from the RC Church's. The presence of a priest at the wedding was made compulsory for Catholics only in 1215 (but a deacon or a designated layman may adequately represent the Church according to the 1983 code). Marriage was first defined as one of the seven sacraments in the same thirteenth century. The Church has dissolved many marriages in which one of the partners was not baptized, yet the teaching of Jesus about God's plan for humanity was addressed to the unbaptized. Nor does the catechism discuss the moral problem connected with a vow to do something jointly when that becomes impossible because one of the partners has broken that vow and not renewed it. In Christian marriage the partners very solemnly exchange vows to live together in love until death whatever comes, and many Christians have felt obliged by that vow before God to stay indissolubly married, despite any problem or any claim to be divorced. Yet it may be asked whether this thoroughly praiseworthy heroism is the only legitimate interpretation of vows taken together to live in love together – for it takes two to do that.

The problem of how to care for Christians whose marriages have broken down irretrievably – which is usually one of life's most deeply distressing experiences, more sordid than death – has concerned pastors of the Church from the earliest days. The quotation of 'the words of Jesus Christ' in this catechism (Mark 10.11–12) shows traces of an editorial hand, since under Jewish law it was impossible for a wife to divorce her husband; Jesus would not have needed to condemn this. But it is clear that Jesus did teach that divorce by a husband was against God's plan for humanity. That was, as Paul wrote to Corinth, 'the Lord's ruling'. The question may still be asked whether it was intended as legislation prohibiting any remarriage at all. Was it a new law, binding people who had remained imperfect and so had received this concession in the Law of Moses 'because of your stubbornness' (Mark 10.5)? It seems more probable that in a society where divorce was easy for men it proclaimed the ideal and the challenge of permanently faithful and loving marriage. If so, its rigorous character would resemble adjacent sayings that an adult must become 'like a child', that a man with great wealth must 'sell everything you have and give to the poor', that a disciple must be baptized with the baptism of martyrdom, and that a leader must be 'the slave of all'.

In Luke's gospel (16.17, 18) the saying that a man who divorces his wife according to the Law of Moses and marries another commits adultery follows immediately after an emphatic endorsement of that Law in every detail, but in the Sermon on the Mount this confusion is reduced. The first part of the saying in Mark's gospel is repeated here, but what is condemned is the divorce of a wife for any cause 'other than unchastity' (Matt 5.32). ('Unchastity' here translates *porneia*. The Greek word has been held to refer to marriage within the forbidden degrees of blood relationship, but it seems improbable that Matthew would have used a word usually meaning 'sexual immorality' in general to refer only to an action so specific and quite rare.) This limited permission to divorce an adulteress is striking since no exception is made to the other moral challenges gathered in the Sermon. Remarriage after such a divorce is not allowed there explicitly, but in Jewish society those able to remarry were generally expected to do so, and later in Matthew's gospel when remarriage is condemned generally an exception is made if the divorce has been after 'unchastity' (19.9). This 'Matthean privilege' is believed by the Orthodox churches, as in many others, to sanction some second marriages. It is limited by Matthew to men whose wives are adulterous, but it has often seemed reasonable to Christians to extend it to women's rights and to cases of cruelty or desertion as constituting a 'matrimonial offence' making divorce morally permissible. Paul said that he had no relevant 'instructions from the Lord' but taught that a Christian deserted by an unbelieving (which could include Jewish) spouse was not bound by that marriage since 'God's call is a call to live in peace' (1 Cor 7.12–15, 25, 27). The simplest interpretation of that passage is that Paul thought such a Christian free to marry again within the Church. Like the Sermon on the Mount, Paul seems to be making a concession amid a tragic problem. The catechism draws attention to the saying given to us by Mark, interpreting it as Jesus' 'unequivocal insistence on the indissolubility of the marriage bond' (1615). But it does not mention the passages which show exceptions being made for pastoral reasons within the New

Testament. This selective use of the Bible is strange and it may be asked whether it deserves our assent.

I am not suggesting that the Roman Catholic Church ought to agree officially with my own answers to all these often debated questions. My own answers do not always echo exactly the teaching given by the bishops of my own Church of England in their report on *Issues in Human Sexuality* (1991). I am not an authority on 'moral theology' and I have no doubt been influenced by personal, as well as pastoral, experience. My point is that what this catechism teaches is not necessarily what Roman Catholics or other Christians now believe to be right about sexual morality. To us, this teaching does not seem to possess the real splendour of truth. Nor is it as full of love as Christians ought to be.

CHAPTER

6

Realism about unity

THE SECOND VATICAN COUNCIL aroused many hopes for Christian reunion and these persisted from the 1960s into the 1980s. The decree on ecumenism began with a roll of drums: 'Almost everyone, though in different ways, longs that there may be one visible Church of God, a Church truly universal and sent forth to the whole world that the world may be converted to the Gospel and so be saved, to the glory of God' – although on the last day before the final vote on the decree, Paul VI insisted that the 'almost' should be added at the beginning. It was hoped that courageous changes in the Roman Catholic Church would match changes in Eastern Orthodoxy and in the churches flowing from the Protestant Reformation; that prayer would feed friendship and collabo- ration; that a return together to Scripture and Tradition would show that past disagreements had resulted mainly from misunderstandings, from an over-emphasis on one part of the truth, or from influences more political or social than religious; that theological dialogues and official meetings would move quite swiftly through charity to courtesy and through courtesy to 'convergence' leading to a 'substantial' agreement on all 'essential' matters; that the present 'partial' communion would develop quite easily into 'full' communion; that loyalty to the 'apostolic faith', and to sacred institutions and doctrines inherited from the past, could be combined quite smoothly with a welcome to 'diversity' and with a freshness in restating what Scripture and Tradition 'affirmed' and 'proclaimed' in their 'witness', using 'expressions' more suitable to changed conditions; that a new spring in the Church's long history would be followed quite soon by a summer when the Great Church would be open to the sunshine of the Spirit, to the variety of the whole world and to the energies needed for the tasks of the future; that, in short, renewal would produce reunion.

In the 1990s the cause of 'unity' has taken root in that Christians belonging to separate churches are much more aware of each other and often more sensitive to each other, and in many places there is a feeling that more 'unity' would be a good thing. Many laity and local clergy ignore denominational differences in many situations. But at the official level the ecumenical movement has apparently ceased to move. Few reunions between denominations have been achieved or are being negotiated. We have seen that although the new catechism quotes extensively from Vatican II, on the whole it invites its readers to breathe a more wintry atmosphere. This change of mood in the leadership of the Roman Catholic Church is contemporary – rather than happily harmonious – with a new, but even more conservative, self-confidence in Eastern Orthodoxy after its victory over Communism. The authoritarian tone of the catechism also agrees – in psychology rather than in actual doctrines – with the strong resurgence of denominationalism and fundamentalism in the Protestant world. Many enthusiasts have claimed the right to evangelize in lands traditionally belonging to other churches and those churches have responded vigorously; thus Roman Catholic bishops are said to be intruders into Eastern Orthodox territory in Ukraine or Romania, and Protestant missionaries are counter-attacked after their successful campaigns in Latin America, formerly seen as part of the Christendom of Spanish or Portuguese Catholicism. Anglicans are among those who have claimed the right to proceed with the ordination of women despite solemn warnings from Roman Catholic and Eastern Orthodox authorities.

The lack of agreement has not only become obvious in the relationships between churches. The labels are among the matters which are debatable, but within almost every denomination is to be seen a tension between what may be called conservatism or traditionalism (often secure in control of the institutions and their official declarations) and progressive, liberal or radical attitudes, often expressed less publicly or less systematically. Sometimes the tension results in an explosion of bitterness. Thus in the *Tablet* (22 May 1993) it was reported that Hans Küng had attacked the catechism as an example of 'inquisition from above' intended to discipline and rule priests, teachers, theologians and ordinary faithful. The catechism, he declared, had ignored thirty years of theological work in the spirit of Vatican II and had no more than to 'cement old convictions' and demand 'blind submission'. It would have no value for religious instruction – or for ecumenical dialogue. In a later meeting Küng lamented that 'much more attention is being paid to Roman doctrine and canon law than to the Gospel and figure of Jesus', while Leonardo Boff said it was significant that the new catechism did not once mention democracy, in spite of the fact that 'Christ passed his authority on to the whole community. It was only later that the bishops assumed all power, creating the dualism, which still exists, of an official hierarchy which speaks and of a people which obeys' (*Tablet*, 12 June 1993). But it may be more helpful to consider the positions of the conservatives with more sympathy.

The Gospel and the traditions

Cardinal Joseph Ratzinger, the theologian who in 1981 was called from the archbishopric of Munich to be Prefect of the Congregation for the Doctrine of the Faith, chaired the commission responsible for this catechism. In his 1987 collection of essays on *Church, Ecumenism and Politics* he did not deal directly with any of the cases where he has presided over the disciplining of bishops and theologians alleged to be unsound Catholics (including Küng and Boff), but he did show his own motivation. As would be expected from an ex-professor of intellectual stature and integrity, he wrote that 'the Church does not coincide with the truth. It is not the constructor of truth but is constructed by it and is the place where it is perceived. Truth therefore remains essentially independent of the Church . . . Theology *and* the Church's teaching authority are realities that are ordered to each other.' But he quickly added that 'it is the Church's function to delineate the boundary where theology dissolves its own environment, the Church' (p. 160). By 'the Church's function' in this context he meant, under the pope, the censoring work of the 'congregation' over which he presided, and by 'theology' he meant a discipline which, when its 'boundary' has been set by the authorities of the Church, never argues about the faith proper to the Church; it only explores and explains it. This 'boundary' does not infringe a Christian thinker's freedom, he argued, because 'the fundamental right of the Christian is the right to the whole faith' – as defined by the Church. 'The fundamental obligation that flows from this is the obligation of everyone, but especially the Church's ministers, to the totality of the unadultered faith' (p. 202). This faith is superior to scholarly criticism, for 'the unity of the findings of scholarship is of its essence open to revision at any time; faith is something durable' (p. 106). And 'it is only by sharing in faith with the Church that I have a part in that certainty on which I can base my life' (p. 113). Referring to the rebellion against ecclesiastical authority in the seventeenth and eighteenth centuries, Ratzinger noted the Enlightenment's motto *sapere aude*, 'dare to use your reason'. But for him, 'the enlightenment consists in the fact that I am no longer alone with a distant God, but that, living in and sharing in the life of the body of Christ, I myself touch the ground of all reality because this ground has become the ground of my own life' (p. 127).

Although I have quoted only a few fragments of it, the cardinal's book amounts to a conservative vision of Christianity. If my space allowed, I could quote psychologically similar expositions of an Eastern Orthodox faith or of a conservatively Evangelical faith. The traditions of Lutheran or Reformed dogmatics have also had firm teachers in our time. Even some Anglicans have taught with authority in a style not remote from the boast of William Beveridge, who died in 1708: 'the doctrine of our Church was so reformed that it agrees exactly with God's holy word, as understood and interpreted by the whole Catholic Church'. But for my present purpose I offer another quotation from a high Roman Catholic source.

In *Mortalium Animos* (1928) Pius XI attacked as 'quite illegitimate' the distinction 'between articles of faith which are called fundamental, some being accepted by all and the others being left to the free assent of the individual'. His own position was that

> the supernatural virtue of faith has as its formal object the authority of the God who reveals, an authority which does not allow of any distinction of this kind. That is why all the true disciples of Christ believe, for example, in the mystery of the august Trinity with the same faith as in the Immaculate Conception, in the mystery of the Incarnation of our Lord as in the infallible *magisterium* of the Roman pontiff, of course as defined by the Vatican Council.

Pius XI stressed that 'although they have been solemnly decreed at different times, even very recently, these truths are no less certain or worthy of faith' – for 'is it not God who has revealed them all?' But the truth as I see it may perhaps be put in this way. The person who thinks that a doctrine has been revealed by God in the form taught by the religious authority which he or she accepts (be it Bible, Church, experience or whatever) will have 'faith' and will not immediately discriminate between 'fundamental' and 'non-fundamental' faith. The response of faith is not optional for that person, because God is believed to have spoken; and to that person, faith may be very close to certainty. Yet believers do think that some truths are more important than others, and most Christians are more prepared to tolerate doubts about some doctrines than about others. Not all 'true disciples' do actually believe that the immaculate conception of Mary is as significant as the divine Trinity, or papal infallibility as the Incarnation, and theologians have often allowed for a difference between the Gospel (of the Bible or the Church, or of both) and 'traditions' or 'customs'. The Gospel, they have said, does not change as the good news about God, but traditions or customs may, and sometimes should, change because they express the faithful reception of that Gospel in particular circumstances.

More difficult is the issue about the inclusion of detailed beliefs about church order in the foundations of Christian faith. Many Christians believe that God has revealed that a particular shape of the Church's ordained ministry – the one they know best – is superior or essential. But the evidence which I have summarized in this book seems to show that if God has revealed this, the 'revelation' is not clear either in the Bible or in the tradition common to all Christians. Vatican II, as quoted in this catechism, acknowledged that 'holding a rightful place in the communion of the Church there are also particular Churches that retain their traditions' (814). The council had in mind mainly the 'uniate' churches which under six patriarchs retain eastern traditions but accept the pope's jurisdiction. In the decree on these Eastern Catholic Churches it was said: 'It is the mind of the Catholic Church that each individual church or rite retain its traditions whole and entire, while adjusting its way of life to the various needs of time and place'. And a key figure in Roman Catholic ecumenism, Cardinal Jan Willebrands, developed this recognition of legitimate diversity. He put forward the idea that different churches represent different 'types' – and not only in the east, and not only in liturgical or ethical traditions. In an address in 1972 he said: 'We find the reality of a *typos* in the existence of a long and coherent tradition, inspiring love and loyalty in men and women, forming and maintaining an organic and harmonious totality of complementary elements, each of which supports and reinforces the other'. He mentioned as elements in a *typos* a characteristic theological method and perspective, a canonical discipline, a liturgical expression and a tradition of spirituality and devotion. And he declared that 'the life of the Church has need of a great variety of *typoi* which show the plenitude of the Catholic and apostolic characters of the one holy Church'.

In the 1970s other contributors to the ecumenical discussion, particularly Lutherans, further developed the condemnation of uniformity by suggesting that any future unity between churches should itself consist of 'reconciled diversity'. That phrase was criticized because it seemed to imply an acceptance of too much continuing separation between denominations, but it need not be so interpreted. Indeed, Pope Paul VI, who was no Protestant, seems to have accepted 'reconciled diversity' to some extent. For example, in 1970 he said:

There will be no seeking to lessen the legitimate prestige and the worthy patrimony of piety and usage proper to the Anglican Church when the Roman Catholic Church – this humble 'servant of the servants of God' – is able to embrace her ever beloved sister in the one authentic communion of the family of Christ, a communion of origin and of faith, a communion of priesthood and rule, a communion of the saints in the freedom of love and of the Spirit of Jesus. Perhaps we shall have to go on waiting and watching in prayer in order to deserve that blessed day.

For how long need we wait?

The Eucharist of the baptized

In many dialogues between Roman Catholic and other theologians during and since the 1960s, it has been taken for granted that substantial agreement on at least the 'essential' beliefs of Christianity must come before full communion between Christians now separated into different churches. This emphasis on doctrine seems sounder than the once fashionable slogan that 'doctrine divides, service unites' and it has been a healthy corrective to the strong temptation to understand the ecumenical movement as no more than courtesy and collaboration in serving society. Differences over doctrine have often proved their power to sabotage working together, but the emphasis on theology need not be so divisive. In recent years careful dialogues have produced important agreements.

For example, Christians have not stayed stuck in the disputes of the Reformation era about whether Christians are 'justified' by God because of their 'faith' or because of their 'works'. It has been widely agreed that Christians can be reached by God's loving initiative if they trust in that gracefully forgiving (rather than deserved) mercy and if they express that faith 'in love' (Gal 5.6) as well as in emotions or words. The progress from 'conversion' to 'the sanctification of the whole person' is set out in this catechism (1987–1995). Accordingly the second Anglican–RC International Commission (ARCIC) announced in its 1987 report on *Salvation and the Church* that it was 'agreed on the essential aspects of the doctrine of salvation and on the Church's role within it'. Fierce arguments between theologians in the past (producing many unrighteous attitudes) were ended when it was agreed that God's grace 'imparts what it imputes. By pronouncing us righteous, God also makes us righteous.' Two moments in the history of the first ARCIC were also full of hopeful significance for the future. At an early stage the assembled theologians discussed the possibility of a wide-ranging exploration of basic beliefs, but it was quickly agreed that since the churches had such a large measure of agreement about the basics it was more urgent to see whether a similar agreement could be reached about the Eucharist, the priesthood minister- ing in it and the authority under which the priesthood serves. The second moment came when the members of the commission realized that they had reached agreement about the meaning of the Eucharist. In its critical response in 1992 the Congregation for the Doctrine of the Faith pointed out that the agreement was not complete and that 'there are still other areas that are essential to Catholic doctrine on which complete agreement, or even at times convergence, has eluded the commission'. In this connection the dogma of papal infallibility was mentioned, together with the Marian dogmas which that infallibility defined. But it was not said that the list of disagreements about essential doctrines is endless, or that further dialogues would be pointless.

If we look for encouragement in the quest for sufficient agreement on essential matters, we can take note of the fact that Baptism is being recognized increasingly as a bond between all Christians – yet a diversity of customs about Baptism is also acknowledged. In this catechism the Second Vatican Council is quoted as saying that 'men who believe in Christ and who have been properly baptized are put in some, though imperfect, communion with the Catholic Church . . . justified by faith in Baptism, they are incorporated into Christ; they therefore have a right to be called Christians, and with good reason are accepted as brothers by the children of the Catholic Church' (1271). The extensive teaching about Baptism (1213–1284) makes it clear that it is in the name of the Holy Trinity. It symbolizes a dying and rising with Christ as 'entrance into the life of faith'. 'By Baptism all sins, both original and personal, are forgiven as well as all penalties for sin.' The baptized are the Church. They are a 'royal priesthood' and 'participants in the divine nature' because 'members of Christ' and 'temples of the Holy Spirit'. It is not only RC clergy who are entitled to administer the sacrament which so decisively incorporates into the Christian Church. 'In case of necessity any person whether baptized or not, with the required intention to do what the Church does when she baptizes, can baptize, applying the Trinitarian baptismal formula.' Baptism so administered cannot be repeated (in contrast with the former practice of administering a 'conditional' baptism to Christians converted from another church). And it is generously recognized that in the Church of the baptized beyond the visible bounds of the Roman Catholic Church 'many elements of sanctification and truth' include 'God's written word; the life of grace; faith, hope and love, together with other interior gifts of the Holy Spirit' (819).

All this reflects the growing convergence among Christians, as is also illustrated by the 1982 'Lima' report from the World Council of Churches on *Baptism, Eucharist, Ministry*. But both in what it says about Baptism and in its section on Confirmation (1285–1321), the catechism confirms that a very considerable variety of customs between churches is accepted in the process of Christian initiation.

This process, we are told, 'has varied greatly through the centuries, according to circumstances'. It is admitted that there is no clear evidence for the baptism of infants before the second century. Vatican II allowed the Christian use of local initiation ceremonies in 'mission territories' and restored the catechumenate for adults, divided into several 'stages' as a training period. In the eastern churches, Catholic as well as Orthodox, the priest administers 'chrismation' with oil consecrated by the bishop and applied to various parts of the body, and then immediately gives Holy Communion, however young the new Christians may be. In contrast, 'the Latin Church reserves access to Holy Communion to those who have attained the age of reason'. The sacrament of Confirmation is administered at the 'age of discretion' by the bishop 'through the anointing with chrism on the forehead, which is done by the laying on of the hand and through the words: "Be sealed with the gift of the Holy Spirit."' But the bishop 'may, for grave reasons, concede to priests the faculty of administering Confirmation'.

Presumably other customs, with other theological interpretations, would be allowed in other churches which are not eastern, but the catechism does not discuss in any detail what would have to be agreed in that direction before 'full communion' could be achieved. What it does say is that despite the diversity in customs the communion based on union in faith and baptism with the Eastern Orthodox Churches is 'so profound' that (quoting Paul VI) 'it lacks little to attain the fullness that would permit a common celebration of the Lord's Eucharist' (838). All that is lacking in the Orthodox, it seems, is the acceptance of the papal claims. The present canon law of the RC Church therefore allows its members to receive communion from an Orthodox priest 'whenever necessity requires or genuine spiritual advantage suggests, and provided that the danger of error is avoided, when it is physically or morally impossible to approach a Catholic minister'. RC priests may 'administer the sacraments of Penance, Eucharist and anointing of the sick' to Orthodox who 'ask on their own and are properly disposed' (1844). And even other Christians who 'manifest Catholic faith in these sacraments' may be given them 'if the danger of death is present or other grave necessity' and 'they cannot approach a minister of their own community'. These provisions contrast the absolute prohibition, repeated in the 1917 code, of 'sacramental ministrations to heretics or schismatics, even those erring in good faith'. It is, however, not the approved Orthodox practice either to take or to give communion in such circumstances. And on the Roman Catholic side, official approval of eucharistic hospitality to Protestants (including Anglicans) remains severely limited, although local practice can be more welcoming.

This breakdown of the fellowship of the baptized at the crucial point of participation in what Paul VI called 'the Lord's Eucharist' is both puzzling and scandalous to many Christians, including many Roman Catholics. For it seems that the variety of customs and interpretations allowed in Christian initiation is forbidden elsewhere. All the baptized are a royal priesthood and participants in the divine nature – yet they cannot receive the Eucharist together.

In its *Observations* on the report *Salvation and the Church* the Congregation for the Doctrine of the Faith complained that 'a rather vague conception of the Church seems to lie at the base of all the difficulties'. It was alleged that the theologians had not adequately emphasized that the Church is 'the universal sacrament of salvation', 'already endowed with real holiness' and 'necessary for salvation'. Although it was said that 'the Church is first of all a mystery', in the background to this response from the Vatican was little sense of mystery about the identity of 'the Church'. When the Congregation asked for 'more rigorous doctrinal formulations' instead of 'symbolic language' which may leave open 'the possibility of twofold interpretation', it seemed to be asking for the rigorous endorsement of the interpretation familiar in its own tradition.

In its response in 1992 to the work of the first ARCIC, the Congregation welcomed some agreements endorsed by the Lambeth Conference of Anglican bishops in 1988 as being 'in substantial agreement with the Anglican faith'. One was that 'the Eucharist is a sacrifice in the sacramental sense provided that it is made clear that it is not a repetition of the historical sacrifice'. The Vatican also welcomed the agreement that, 'before the eucharistic prayer to the question "what is it?" the believer answers: "it is bread". After the eucharistic prayer he answers: "it is truly the body of Christ." ' It welcomed, too, the agreement that 'the ordained ministry is not an extension of the common Christian priesthood but belongs to another realm of the gifts of the Spirit', since the baptized and the ordained constitute 'two distinct realities which relate each in its own way to the high priesthood of Christ'. And it welcomed the consensus that after ordination which is 'a sacramental act' the ordained minister (and he alone) 'presides' at the Eucharist, and has 'played an essential part in the life of the Church' since New Testament times, being 'part of God's design for his people'. But when inspected in the Vatican these agreements were not enough. 'The faith of the Catholic Church' would have been 'even more clearly reflected' had there been some 'explicit' affirmations. One affirmation required was that in the Eucharist 'the Church makes present the sacrifice of Calvary', the 'real presence of Christ' being 'accomplished by the ministry of the priest saying the words of the Lord'. Moreover, 'because of its propitiatory character as the sacrifice of Christ, the Mass may be offered for the living and the dead, including a particular dead person'.

This response did not explain fully or convincingly why the agreement reached by the first ARCIC about 'the real presence of Christ' was insufficient. Despite ARCIC's curious reference to the priesthood as belonging to a distinct 'realm' of the gifts of the Spirit, the whole stress in modern eucharistic theology and devotion is on the community's celebration of the Eucharist, the priest being the president of the whole sacrament, not a magician reciting a formula. And to those (almost everyone today) who do not use the medieval philosophical categories of 'substance' and 'accidents' or 'species' to describe realities, it is not clear what is meant by insisting on the old wording, as this response does (with my italics). We are instructed that 'Christ in the Eucharist makes himself present sacramentally *and substantially* when under the species of bread and wine these earthly realities are changed into the reality of his body and blood, soul and divinity'. It seems both possible and right for a believer to say 'it is truly the body of Christ' without adding that 'it is no longer bread'. If the change during the eucharistic prayer is claimed to have taken place 'substantially', the question remains what that word means in our time. Does it mean what the catechism of 1566 said it meant – that the sacrament contains 'all the constituents of a true body such as bones and sinews'? If not, can its meaning be expressed intelligibly?

Nor did the response explain why such an emphasis on Christ's self-sacrifice as 'propitiatory' is necessary to the apparent exclusion of other biblical passages which present the cross not as appeasement of God's wrath but as the exhibition of his love. The expressions preferred by the Vatican are dangerous if they suggest that God needs to be 'propitiated' or appeased by the offering of the Mass day by day, in flat contradiction of (for example) the Letter to Hebrews in the New Testament. And we know that in popular Catholicism the Mass has often been thought to be a sacrifice which adds to the sacrifice of Calvary, an act performed by a priest whose essential function is 'to offer sacrifice for the living and the dead' (the terms used in the Sarum rite for ordination in medieval England). The practice of 'saying Mass' for 'a particular intention' became established in the ninth century as part of the wider development of the Eucharist into a ritual performed by the priest, not the people; in the same period, the laity ceased to receive communion frequently, the priest's 'private Mass' without a congregation was sanctioned and when said in public the priest's eucharistic prayer was usually said silently or in a very low voice. As Edward Schillebeeckx put it bluntly in *The Church with a Human Face* (p. 163), 'in this world the priest was regarded as a magical person: he performed the mystery of changing bread and wine into the body and blood of Jesus Christ'.

It would, of course, be unfair to blame the experts in the Vatican for all the misunderstandings that may arise in popular religion. This catechism teaches that in the Eucharist, 'the celebration recalls God's wonders in a memorial (*anamnesis*) . . . The Spirit then inspires thanks and praise (*doxology*) by awakening the Church's memory . . . Christ's paschal mystery itself is celebrated, not repeated. It is the celebrations that are repeated, and in each celebration there is an outpouring of the Holy Spirit that makes the one mystery present' (1103–1104). But it may be questioned whether even now the official position in the Vatican has moved far enough away from the medievalism of Leo XIII in *Mirae Caritatis* (1902). The Eucharist, he taught,

should be regarded as in a manner a continuation and extension of the Incarnation, for in it the supreme sacrifice offered on Calvary is in a wondrous manner renewed . . . And this miracle, itself the very greatest of its kind, is accompanied by innumerable other miracles; for here all the laws of nature are suspended; the whole substance of the bread and wine are changed into the body and blood; the species of bread and wine are sustained by the divine power without the support of any underlying substance; the body of Christ is present in many places at the same time.

In his *Credo of the People of God* (1968), Paul VI taught that 'in this sacrament there is no other way in which Christ can be present except through the conversion of the entire substance of bread into his Body and wine into his Blood, leaving unchanged only those properties of bread and wine which are open to our senses . . . In the order of reality which exists independently of the human mind, the bread and wine cease to exist after the consecration.' And in *Dominicae Curae* (1980) John Paul II taught that the priest performs 'a true sacrificial act that brings creation back to God' while the faithful offer 'their own spiritual sacrifices' – although the New Testament unites the whole Christian people in recalling the perfect sacrifice made by the one true High Priest and in offering 'your very selves to him: a living sacrifice, dedicated and fit for his acceptance, the worship offered by mind and heart' (Rom 12.1).

In its section on the Eucharist (1322–1419) this catechism includes statements identical with, or very close to, the disputable statements just quoted. But other teachings are more intelligible and acceptable to those who are nervous about 'the sacrifice of the Mass' as 'propitiatory', who do not use the medieval doctrine of 'transubstantiation' and who believe that priest and people together celebrate the Eucharist.

The Vatican insists that there is no alternative way to its own of expressing 'the real presence of Christ'. But there is a way and in recent years it has been explored by many theologians who deserve to be called Catholic. By using the term 'transignification' these theologians teach that after the eucharistic prayer and the work of the Holy Spirit the bread and the wine signify to the Church and to individual believers more than meets the eye or the tongue. They signify the life of Christ, born, crucified and risen as the embodiment of divine love. It is not necessary to insist that they cease to be bread and wine in a manner which suspends all the laws of nature and is beyond the reach of human senses and minds, any more than it is necessary to pretend that a note in paper coinage, once printed on, miraculously consists of gold or silver.

This theology protects Christians against any suggestion (which I do not accuse the Vatican of making) that when at his last supper Jesus said 'this my body' ('is' or 'will be' not being in the original Aramaic) he suggested that his body had suddenly expanded so that his disciples could become cannibals. He was a Jew. His first followers were all Jews who were to need much persuasion if they were to break the Jewish food laws, even then abstaining 'from blood' (according to Acts 15.29), but according to Luke (22.18) at his farewell meal he repeated his use of wine as a symbol of joy in the coming Kingdom of God, the Kingdom for which he was ready to shed his blood. At this meal which was a Passover supper (or according to John an event very like one) he did not suddenly command them to drink his blood literally. And it is good to see that in contrast with some interpretations of 'concomitance' to mean that the *bread* is in substance blood and the *wine* is in substance flesh, this catechism teaches that 'since Christ is sacramentally present under each of the elements, communion under the element of bread alone makes it possible for us to receive the grace of the sacrament in full' (1390). Faith in this 'grace' does not necessarily depend on the belief that a 'substance' changes.

Nor, it seems, is it necessary to think that God the Father needs to be reminded about the self-sacrifice of God the Son, or needs to see that sacrifice 'renewed' in the Mass, before he feels at liberty to change his wrath into love for the living or the dead. A careful student of the Bible seems entitled to conclude that God the Father is Christlike, is 'love' and 'light' not hatred and darkness; that this character in which we may trust never changes; that what seems to some sinners to be his 'wrath' is in ultimate reality his loving plan for their perfection; that in the Eucharist as the supreme act of Christian prayer we are invited to approach the Father through the Son in the power of the Holy Spirit, reminding ourselves of the divine love for all including all the dead; that, in the words of the First Letter of Peter, the whole People of God 'must form a holy priesthood acceptable to God through Jesus Christ' (2.5).

Here as elsewhere in this book, it has not been my intention to give the impression that I am certain about the adequacy or necessity of the words which I prefer. My only purpose has been to deny that the words which according to the Vatican are 'what the Catholic Church believes' are compulsory for all Christians. It is not necessary to insist on them if the baptized are to share the Lord's Eucharist.

Priests: assistant, celibate, male?

The catechism quotes Vatican II as teaching that 'ecclesial communities derived from the Reformation and separated from the Catholic Church "have not preserved the proper reality of the Eucharistic Mystery in its fullness, especially because of the absence of the sacrament of Holy Orders." It is for this reason that Eucharistic intercommunion with these communities is not possible for the Catholic Church' (1400).

The Vatican's response to the first ARCIC illustrated the thinking behind this cold attitude. The commission had hoped that 'in what we have seen here both Anglicans and Roman Catholics will recognize their own faith'. But the Congregation for the Doctrine of Faith regretted that those theologians had not made it clear that 'it was Christ himself who instituted the sacrament of orders' and that 'priestly ordination implies a configuration to the priesthood of Christ'. It also asked for further 'clarification' of belief in apostolic succession, which 'the Catholic Church recognizes' both as 'an unbroken line in episcopal ordination from Christ through the apostles down the centuries to the bishops of today' and 'an uninterrupted continuity in Christian doctrine from Christ to those today who teach in union with the college of bishops and its head, the successor of Peter'.

Although it had delayed its final response for ten years after issuing preliminary Observations in 1982, the Congregation did not now pause to consider any objection to its interpretation of history. Some objections which seem to me convincing were outlined in Chapter 3. Others may be summarized by references to *Holy Order* by a Roman Catholic scholar whom I have already quoted, Aidan Nichols (1990):

The powers Christ had given to the Twelve . . . could not be generally transferred to the local ministry on the deaths of the original apostles. Why so? Because the 'corporate' type of presbyteral ministerial organisation had not yet developed a sufficiently clear personal organ which the full apostolic commission could be transferred – even though presbyteries were beginning to develop such an organ in some places. (p. 45)

Later, after 'the gradual dawning of the consciousness that the bishops had inherited the apostolic ministry' (p. 41), 'presbyters would belong to the apostolic succession only through their ordination by bishops who embodied that succession' (p. 46). But 'the earliest evidence for calling presbyters "priests" comes from memorials to deceased presbyters of the Asia Minor Churches around 360 . . . This was, of course, a natural consequence of the presbyter becoming the normal celebrant of the Eucharist' over which the bishop had previously been the normal president (p. 50). Already in the fourth century the bishop was often regarded as the Christian 'high priest', as is shown in letters from and to Bishop Cyprian, but this title for bishops was also a development from New Testament times. Despite the strong emphasis by Nichols that the apostles had a priestly character, he of course does not claim that any individual Christian is called a 'priest' in the Bible. The associations between that word and Jewish or pagan sacrifices in temples were too close.

Other objections may be made to the character of the present insistence on the authority of bishops. In this official teaching, priests and theologians are often put in their places as assistants or advisers. This decree of exaltation for the 'college' of bishops seems hard to reconcile with Paul's repeated insistence that all ministries in the Church are equally the gifts of the Spirit. It also seems to many an unrealistic reading of church history. Over the centuries, countless priests and other pastors have proclaimed and lived the Gospel in a manner which did not constantly refer to, and depend on, what was being taught or done by the bishops of the day. If in the Catholic tradition, these pastors have regarded themselves as authorized by a bishop and they have intended to teach and do what 'the Church' led by bishops teaches and does, but in practice they have exercised a considerable initiative, and even independence, in responding creatively to the needs of their neighbours or to the conclusions of their prayers and studies. In the Middle Ages it was widely stated that theologians shared with bishops the *magisterium* or teaching authority of the Church, and the Council of Trent treated bishops and priests as belonging to one 'order'. It can even be said that Trent was the council which made priests heroic in the Counter-Reformation style, while Vatican II was the council where bishops stressed their own authority. In our own time, it seems likely than an able young person may be deterred from undertaking a theologian's laborious training if the aim is to merely make suggestions to bishops and the danger is of being sacked for being honest. Equally, a lay person may be discouraged from preparation for the stressful work of a community's pastor if that work is regarded wholly as being delegated by the bishop, as it was not in the New Testament. A more balanced and attractive vision of priesthood is, however, set out in canon 835 of the 1983 code: 'the presbyters are in fact sharers of the priesthood of Christ himself so that they are consecrated as his ministers under the authority of the bishop to celebrate divine worship and sanctify the people'.

On earlier pages I attempted to sketch the historical background to the tradition that another function of the priest, derived from the bishop, is to 'forgive' or 'retain' sins. In this catechism (1420–1498) many things are said about 'the sacrament of Penance' which seem to be compatible both with the truth about the origins of the present RC discipline and with the spiritual needs of Christians. The central emphasis is that 'only God forgives sins', that 'the confessor is not the master of God's forgiveness but its servant', and that 'the Lord Jesus wanted his Church, in the power of the Holy Spirit, to continue his work of healing and salvation, even for its own members'. Yet this attractive exposition of God's forgiveness through the Church nowhere tackles the reasons why in recent years many fewer Roman Catholics have confessed their sins to a priest privately and regularly.

The catechism says that 'according to the Church's command, after having attained the age of discretion each of the faithful is bound by the obligation to confess serious sins at least once a year. Anyone who is aware of having committed a mortal sin must not receive Holy Communion, even if he experiences deep contrition, without having received sacramental absolution, unless he has a grave reason for receiving Communion and there is no possibility of going to confession' (1457). And the confession of everyday offences ('venial' sins) is strongly encouraged. 'A communal celebration of reconciliation with general confession and absolution' may therefore be used 'only in case of urgent need'. But the practical problems are that in many areas not enough priests are available to hear the regular confessions of all Roman Catholics – and when priests are available, they are not respected enough for most of the laity to think it their duty to confess their sins to them. And this lack of respect is not due only to the laity's widespread disagreement with the Vatican about sexual morality.

A large cause of the shortage of RC priests is the insistence, repeated by Paul VI in 1967 and in this catechism, that they are 'normally chosen from among believers who live as celibates' (1579). More than anything else, this insistence on celibacy suggests to the laity that the leadership of the RC Church is more interested in preserving the priesthood's distinction than in making the sacraments of the Eucharist and of Penance readily available to them, although canon 213 in the new canon law says that the laity have the right to receive the sacraments. The insistence on celibacy also seems to imply that sex is unclean, whereas to many of the laity (supremely, within married love) it is the most glorious thing in life.

John Paul II is reported to have said that 'Jesus proposed an ideal of celibacy for the new priesthood he inaugurated', a call which the apostles accepted (*Tablet*, 24 July 1993). Paul thought otherwise, asking: 'Have I not the right to take a Christian wife about with me, like the rest of the apostles and the Lord's brothers and Cephas?' (1 Cor 9.5). However, laws about ritual purity for priests in the Old Testament (although those priests were not celibate) were often quoted by church leaders down to Pius XII's *Sacrae Virginitatis* in 1954. When first bishops and then priests presided at the Eucharist, they were expected to be married (in accordance with 1 Tim 3.2) but to have abstained from intercourse on the previous night. When the Eucharist became daily in many churches in the fourth century, bishops including Bishops of Rome urged that married priests should be completely continent. This proved hard to enforce and when the priesthood became more remote from the laity, in the ninth century, pressure grew to confine it to the unmarried. This pressure was made law in the canons of the Second Lateran Council (1139), although many exceptions to the new rule continued in practice.

In the east, a bishops' council in 691–692 approved the clerical 'use' of marriage, but not when the clergy were 'handling holy things', which presumably meant when preparing for the Eucharist. Later in the east the custom grew that parish priests were expected to be already married but the superiority of bishops was illustrated by the rule that they must be celibates, and lingering doubts about the propriety of marriage were shown by adherence to the rule that priests must not marry after ordination, even if widowed. The difference in customs or rules between periods of church history, and between west and east, shows that it is possible for the Roman Catholic Church to make celibacy optional, for priests who have that vocation. A beginning was made when in 1967 Paul VI restored (mainly for use in the USA) the order of permanent deacons including men married before ordination. And some married men previously ordained in non-RC churches have been allowed ordination and work as RC priests, again mainly in the USA.

Obviously there are practical, as well as theoretical, arguments which can be used in favour of the celibacy of priests, and nowadays these appeal more to the laity. Being unmarried does release more of a man's time and energy 'for the sake of the Kingdom of God' (which is the emphasis in this catechism) and for the service of the community – and does enable the Church to pay him less than a family man would need. Being married to a priest does produce special difficulties for a woman, and having a priest for a father is not without its problems. But polls of public opinion in the RC Church in some regions show majorities for allowing marriage to priests: it seems 'natural'. In some other regions practically the same verdict is implied by the acceptance of priests' concubines. It seems that most (not all) of the RC laity accept that the world-wide Church will not get enough priests until marriage is allowed. So the end of compulsory (not all) celibacy seems to be needed for the sake of the Kingdom of God.

Another problem to be faced is the denial of ordination to one half of humanity solely because it is not male. The rule that 'only a baptized man can validly receive sacred ordination' is repeated in this catechism (1577) from the new canon law (1024). It is at present regretted by only a minority of the Roman Catholic laity, but it may be, and is, questioned. It applies even to deacons, although some women deacons survived in both east and west from New Testament times into the eleventh century. It suggests that for some, psychological difficulties are raised by the prospect of women near the altar, although the 1983 Code of Canon Law allows lay persons including women to preach, to lead prayers, to confer Baptism and even to distribute Holy Communion (230).

It seems strange that when the principle that 'men and women have been created by God in perfect equality as human persons' is well stated in this catechism (369), as recently as 1980 the Vatican forbade women to act as servers at the Eucharist. The denial of ordination to women has, however, been upheld by the Vatican on theological grounds, as in *Inter Insignores* (1977). The chief grounds then explained were: Christ did not include men among the apostles, women cannot adequately 'act in the person of Christ' when presiding at the Eucharist, and the imagery of the marriage between Christ and his Church is sacred. But responses to these objections have been offered in a long debate – a debate which led the most populated provinces in the Anglican Communion (for example) to decide that the theological objections to women priests are not decisive. In 1994 some 3,200 women minister in this way.

It would have been impossible in the ancient world, Jewish or Gentile, for a respectable woman, specially one not accompanied by her husband, to travel, speak in public and risk imprisonment and worse, as the apostles were evidently expected to do when they acted as missionaries. But in modern societies the position of women is vastly different, as is most of the work of the clergy. And the New Testament shows that even then women were active in the leadership of the settled congregations. Women are named in about a third of Paul's greetings to his fellow-workers in the last chapter of his letter to Rome. About the Church in our own time, this catechism teaches that 'in the ecclesial service of the ordained minister, it is Christ himself who is present to his Church as Head of his Body, Shepherd of his flock, high priest of the redemptive sacrifice, Teacher of Truth. This is what the Church means by saying that priests, by virtue of the sacrament of Holy Orders act "in the person of Christ the Head"' (1548). To many Christians including many Roman Catholics, it is indeed hard to see why a woman cannot preside over 'the Lord's Eucharist' if that is the manner of her representation of Christ, for women are already acknowledged to be strongly effective representatives of Christ in the life of prayer, in works of charity, in teaching or in the ministry of wives and mothers. Many women have already proved themselves in the leadership of religious communities and in the pastoral care of local congregations. Indeed, in many local situations in our time the effective leadership of the Christian community owes as much to women as to men, if not more. The relation has not ceased between Christ and those communities, expressed as 'marriage' (sometimes as the marriage of the Lamb of God) but also in other metaphors.

It therefore seems possible, even probable, that one day the Roman Catholic Church will ordain women as bishops, priests and deacons. At present its official teaching is that it is not 'authorized' to take this step, but over the last thousand years many councils have been held where only male Catholics accepting the papal claims have voted. These councils have authorized substantial and controversial developments in doctrine and discipline, including developments in the Eucharist and the priesthood, as this book has repeatedly demonstrated. And popes have made such changes on their own authority. The argument that the ordination of women is a uniquely 'grave' departure from tradition may be questioned.

The debate about women priests brought into sharp focus the question whether any one part of the Church has authority to make a change as important as this. It is a serious question, because there is an obvious danger of making a change which will further damage the unity of Christians. I am writing at a time when some of my fellow Anglicans are in a state which can without exaggeration be called mental anguish about the ordination of women. I do not share their objections to this particular change, because I have learned from history that Christian groups have in the end enriched others by following their own consciences in witness to truth, love and holiness. I believe, for example, that many of the protests by the sixteenth-century Protestants have been vindicated both by the spiritual quality of their Christian life and by the Roman Catholic Church's slow adoption of many changes then proposed. I cannot defend all aspects of the Reformation or of the subsequent life of the 'reformed' churches. I cannot defend the rhetoric of Luther, the sex life of Henry VIII, the harshness of Calvin, the bigotry including persecutions, the power of the State over church life, or the procedures by which these churches have made important changes country by country, or even city by city, without adequately consulting others. But at the time the improvements could not have been made without renouncing obedience to the papacy.

Need the fact that these changes have been made without its permission mean that the Roman Catholic Church now has to repeat that ministers ordained in these churches were not validly ordained?

In the eleventh century the Eastern Orthodox patriarchates finally affirmed their right to make their own decisions in ecclesiastical affairs (not changing the Orthodox faith) without reference to Rome. Between 1980 and 1988 dialogue between theologians representing the RC and Orthodox Churches produced three agreed statements on faith and sacraments but the last of these noted that 'the primacy of the Bishop of Rome constitutes a serious divergence between us' and in the 1990s it seems highly unlikely that agreement on this point will be reached by 2000, although John Paul II hoped in 1979 that 'the dawn of the third millennium will find us standing side by side, in full communion'. In the sixteenth century the churches of the Reformation, Lutheran, Reformed and Anglican, rejected papal jurisdiction while claiming to be Bible-based and to remain doctrinally orthodox – indeed, more biblical and orthodox than Rome. The present situation which results from those disputes is that the Roman Catholic Church does not ordain Eastern Orthodox priests who convert to it, but does insist on its own ordination for anyone previously ordained in one of the western 'ecclesial' communities (pointedly refused the title of 'churches' in this catechism). The question has often been asked whether this discipline is right.

Anglican ordinations

The Church of England, from which other Anglican churches have spread, may be taken as an example of an 'ecclesial community' under suspicion. It retained many Catholic traditions in the sixteenth century including the creeds, the sacraments of Baptism and the Eucharist, Penance and the threefold ministry of bishop, priest and deacon. Accordingly, Vatican II's decree on ecumenism declared that 'among communions in which some

Catholic traditions and structures continue to exist, the Anglican Communion occupies a special place'. But the theology of many leading Anglican churchmen under the Tudors, most notably Archbishops Cranmer and Whitgift, was decidedly Protestant and great influence over this church was exerted not only by the Tudor monarchy but also by a laity which became increasingly Protestant. Most Roman Catholics have therefore been convinced (at least since the 1560s) that the intention 'to do what the Church does' was lacking to a degree sufficient to invalidate Anglican ordinations, and in *Apostolicae Curae* (1896) Pope Leo XIII declared such ordinations to be 'absolutely null' (the Latin may also be translated 'ineffective') and 'utterly void'. Despite many protests by Anglicans and some pleas by Roman Catholics, that official verdict has never been reversed (I write in 1994).

Many questions have been touched on in this often heated discussion. Some have turned out to be marginal. For example, it was for long thought (and taught by the Council of Florence) that an essential part of the ordination of a priest in the Roman Catholic Church was the handing to him of the paten and chalice, the vessels to be used in the Mass, but in 1947 Pius XII pronounced against this theory and the practice has been dropped. Other questions have been more theological and more significant. For example, it has sometimes been reckoned fatal that the Anglican 'ordinals' of the 1550s were at least compatible with the eucharistic theology of Cranmer, which was somewhat confused but certainly different from the theology agreed by ARCIC in the 1970s. In 1555 Pope Paul V pronounced bishops thus ordained to be no true bishops. And other questions have been legal, for in the Roman Catholic Church's discipline bishops cannot ordain or exercise jurisdiction without the pope's consent, which was withheld from Anglicans after 1535. But it has still been possible for many Anglicans and some Roman Catholics to argue that enough of Catholicism was left in the 'reformed' Church of England to mean that ordinations were valid by Catholic standards. In the 1662 ordinal these solemn words were to be used by the bishop: 'Receive the Holy Ghost for the office and work of a priest in the Church of God, now committed unto thee by the imposition of our hands'. The bishop also conveyed the priest's power to 'forgive' and 'retain' sins and to dispense 'the word of God and his holy sacraments'. Moreover, care was taken that the bishops should themselves have been made priests and bishops in the forms legal in England at the relevant time. This included the consecration of bishops in the reign of Elizabeth I, when almost all the bishops who had led the Church during the restoration of Roman Catholicism under Mary refused to take part in the new ecclesiastical arrangements. Continuity was thought important, as was change. Since then, Old Catholic bishops recognized by Rome as valid (although schismatic) bishops have taken part in ordaining Anglicans as bishops or priests.

Doubts about these defensive arguments which have been put forward by Anglicans (and by some sympathizers) are at least understandable. After almost 450 years of attempts, it is difficult to see how either side can convince the other about the significance of events in the sixteenth century. But what matters much more, for the sake of the future, is that there should be an agreement about the present status of 'ecclesial communities' such as the Anglicans. It has therefore often been urged that because there is a 'new context' the Roman Catholic and Eastern Orthodox authorities should take a fresh look at what is said about the Eucharist and the ordained ministry in the current declarations of these churches which are under suspicion and above all in the prayer books now in use. Already important gestures have been made, as when Pope Paul VI gave Michael Ramsey, then Archbishop of Canterbury, an episcopal ring (which he wore until his death) and when John Paul II joined Archbishop Robert Runcie in prayers and blessings in Canterbury Cathedral. And it is a sign of hope that the published responses to the work of the Anglican–RC International Commission by the bishops of England and Wales, the USA, Canada and France were more positive than the response which eventually came out of the Vatican. It is said that many other responses were also positive in the main, but is was decided not to publish them.

In respect of the past, doubts on the Roman Catholic side could be laid to rest if a suggestion made by the Lambeth Conference in 1920 could be put into effect. The assembled Anglican bishops then said that

if the authorities of other Communions should so desire, we are persuaded that, terms of union having been otherwise satisfactorily adjusted, bishops and clergy of our Communion would willingly accept from these authorities a form of commission or recognition which would commend our ministry to their congregations, as having its place in the one family life.

During the subsequent seventy years little advantage has been taken of this possibility, one reason being that in reunion negotiations some Anglicans have protested against the 'ambiguity' of the proposed services of 'reconciliation'. (This protest was one of the factors which meant that there had not so far been a sufficient Anglican majority for reunion with Methodism in England.) But in the light of their history Anglicans are not really in a position to object to some 'ambiguity' and most are sure that it is wisest to leave many verdicts to God. In the right atmosphere the bold (but carefully phrased) offer of 1920 might be repeated. In Roman Catholic eyes the prayerful 'commission or recognition' of Anglican ministers could amount to 'conditional' ordination and Anglicans could feel that the humility of their willingness to accept such a commissioning was not a contradiction of their previous proclamation of the Gospel of Christ. And much would be gained by giving Roman Catholics full access to Anglican life through the mutual recognition of ministries as part of full communion between the sister churches. The 'conditional' ordination as RC priest in 1994 of Graham Leonard, formerly the Anglican Bishop of London, could be a pointer.

However, it is inconceivable that heirs of the Reformation, or the Eastern Orthodox, will ever accept all the claims now made for the college of bishops headed by the pope. The claims to freedom from error in certain circumstances, and to the more general right to assent and obedience by the faithful, have already been considered in this book. I turn now to some of the claims about jurisdiction over church life.

Hierarchy in the Church

It is of course proper that a church should have its own regulations reflecting its own doctrinal position. During the 1950s and 1960s the Church of England, which I am glad to serve, revised its canon law and was acknowledged to have the freedom to decide its worship and doctrine without the possibility of a veto by Parliament (although I am among those who want a complete end to the interference by politicians in the appointments and affairs of the Church). This church requires its clergy to assent to a declaration that it 'is part of the one, holy, catholic and apostolic church, worshipping the one true God, Father, Son and Holy Spirit. It professes the faith uniquely revealed in the Holy Scriptures and set forth in the catholic creeds, which faith the Church is called upon to proclaim afresh in each generation. Led by the Holy Spirit, it has borne witness to Christian truth in its historic formularies.' These are then listed, but 'Christian truth' is not identified completely with any of these written authorities.

The 1983 *Code of Canon Law* of the Latin Church was shorter than its predecessor of 1917 but far more elaborate than any Anglican canon law. It reflects a far longer and bigger tradition of law-making and law-administration, and a far more exact and extensive doctrinal position. Canon 833 obliges all who are to be made bishops or deacons, all priests entering in pastorates and all teachers of theology in universities or seminaries 'to make a profession of faith personally'. In addition to the 'Nicene' creed of 381, this oath is to be sworn:

I firmly embrace and accept all and everything which has been either defined by the Church's solemn deliberations or affirmed and declared by its ordinary *magisterium* concerning the doctrine of faith and morals, according as they are proposed by it, especially those things dealing with the mystery of the Holy Church of Christ, its sacraments and the sacrifice of the Mass, and the primacy of the Roman Pontiff.

To an Anglican it seems significant that the Bible is not mentioned in that oath and that Christian truth, instead of needing to be 'proclaimed afresh in each generation', appears to be identified with what has been taught by Roman Catholic bishops in union with the pope. It also seems significant that the 1983 code was promulgated (after extensive consultation but with a few last-minute changes) by the pope, not by any council or synod.

In comparison with previous codes in the RC Church, this code emphasizes the rights and duties of the whole Church, not merely of its monarch or of the rest of the hierarchy. Book II is called 'The People of God' instead of 'On Persons' as in the 1917 code. Leadership in the Church by bishops is repeatedly said to be a 'service' rather than a 'power'. At the Eucharist a priest 'presides' and the faithful are encouraged to take their own parts. The importance of the laity's contribution is set out in some of the many other changes from the spirit and the words of 1917. But in the spirit and words of 1983 there is little or no lessening of the actual power exercised by the Vatican over the world's bishops, by the diocesan bishop over the clergy of his diocese, or by the parish priest over his flock.

No legal limit whatsoever has been placed on the power of the pope over the Church. He issues or authorizes all books used in formal worship, since 'it is for the Apostolic See to order the sacred liturgy of the universal Church' (838); and this canon law contains many quite detailed regulations about worship. He has large powers in deciding the validity of ordinations or marriages anywhere in the world. Any kind of property in the Church is held under his supreme stewardship. 'The Supreme Pontiff freely appoints bishops or confirms those who have been legitimately elected' (377), the second group being a small number. All meetings of bishops, from ecumenical councils to national or provincial conferences, are subject to his decisions as to what is to be discussed or done. 'There is neither appeal nor recourse against a decision or decree of the Roman Pontiff' (333).

In his own diocese the bishop is virtually a monarch or at least the pope's viceroy. He controls all the worship within lines laid down from Rome. His control of teaching is illustrated by the provision that bishops have the duty and the right to demand that 'writings to be published by the Christian faithful which touch upon faith or morals be submitted to their judgement' (823) – although in this new code it is not said what will happen to writers or readers who fail to submit. The bishop appoints almost all the priests at work in his diocese and is expected to supervise all associations of lay Catholics. He is encouraged to consult a synod composed of diocesan officers and selected clergy and laity when new legislation is required for the diocese, but 'the diocesan bishop is the sole legislator' (466). A 'presbyteral' council (in which about half the priests are to be elected) and a 'pastoral' council of selected laity are also consultative, not legislative.

In relation to his parish the priest is also a kind of monarch or at least the bishop's viceroy. The parish council is authorized as an innovation in the 1983 code, and it gives its 'help in fostering pastoral activity' under 'norms determined by the diocesan bishop', but it makes no decisions. It possesses 'a consultative vote only' (536). The powers of the separate finance council in the parish, another innovation, are also decided by the diocesan bishop. For many of the laity (who may be not very interested in the higher levels of decision-making), this exclusion from responsibility in the parish is a sign that despite the new spirit spread by Vatican II the Church remains a hierarchy where the role of the laity is to obey. Even in the mundane matters about which the laity are likely to have more experience than the clergy – questions about fabric and finance, about the arrangement of voluntary work in the church, or about involvement in the neighbourhood – the laity are not allowed to share the right of the bishop or the priest to make the decisions. No doubt an amicable working arrangement based on mutual respect and affection is often achieved, but Christians who are not Roman Catholics seem to be entitled to say that here is no model of how the People of God ought to work locally. There is a gap between the position in canon law and the apostle Paul's question to the congregation in Corinth: 'It is God's people who are to judge the world . . . Are you not competent to deal with these trifling cases? Are you not aware that we are to judge angels, not to mention day to day affairs?' (1 Cor 6.2, 3). Partly for this reason, many Roman Catholics have voted with their feet, either by preferring other communities to the community of the parish or by making their visits to churches occasional and brief.

It remains to be seen whether this concentration of power in the hands of the pope over the lesser bishops, of the bishop over his diocese, and of the priest over his parish, will continue to be sufficiently acceptable or tolerable to Roman Catholics as a whole. Already it seems to many Roman Catholics wrong that the pope – which usually means in effect his assistants in the various departments of the Vatican – should have such powers over the adaptation of Catholic worship and teaching to local conditions. It seems wrong that he should defy the principle, always observed before the Middle Ages, that a diocesan bishop should be elected by representatives of the diocese (in many cases including laity, although their role was often imprecise). It seems wrong that when councils, synods or (more informal) 'conferences' of bishops meet they should not be empowered to decide their own membership, agenda and resolutions. It seems wrong that bishops alone should legislate about church affairs on the diocesan level, although it is usually agreed that they should be able to veto any proposals touching doctrine. It also seems wrong that parish councils should be merely consultative and in particular should be excluded from decisions about the use of finances contributed by the laity. In brief, the co-operation of pope and bishops, clergy and laity, seems to need strengthening. Many Roman Catholics are passionately convinced that it does – as are many other Christians.

In particular, many think that the role of the Bishop of Rome needs redefinition. Presumably developments are needed in the College of Cardinals and the Synod of Bishops, although it is not for an Anglican to enter into any detail. Suggestions made in public by distinguished Roman Catholics in recent years have included the election of popes by a body wider than the elderly College of Cardinals, and the end of election for a life which may continue long past a normal date for retirement. The biographies of popes often suggest that old age diminished both the vigour and the shrewdness of their leadership. It has also been suggested that the Synod of Bishops should be elected by all the bishops of the world for all its meetings, should meet regularly, should determine its own agenda, and should elect a cabinet. It should meet frequently in order to share with the pope control over all the departments of the Vatican, leaving much more responsibility to councils or conferences of bishops region by region. Further, it has been suggested that councils representing the world-wide Church, and including in some capacity eminent Christians who are not RC bishops, should meet more than once in a century, although considerations of expense would probably prevent a gathering of the (unprecedented) size of Vatican II. The absence of 'infallible' pronouncements by pope or council since 1950 should be continued indefinitely and the rights of the faithful to dissent from the ordinary *magisterium* in inessential matters should be established more firmly.

Perhaps the only contribution to the necessary debate proper for a member of the Church of England is to point to the role of a constitutional monarch, with almost no direct executive power, as a symbol and servant of unity and continuity in the nation and of friendship and consultation in a wider Commonwealth of Nations. There may be an analogy with the 'Petrine ministry' in our time, making the Bishop of Rome both the chief pastor of Christians glad to remain Roman Catholics and the president of a wider fellowship. Perhaps Bishop Christopher Butler had his English, as well as his Roman Catholic, background in mind when he regretted

> a monopoly of power in the Church which the popes have claimed and the Church, including other bishops, has been too willing to concede, and indeed to encourage: it is so much easier to leave the burden of decision upon the shoulders of a distant monarch than to take responsibility oneself . . . This misconceived idea that Rome is the fount not only of communion (which it is) but of everything in the Church finds expression in the notion that all canon law stems from the Pope, a notion which may need now to be vigorously contested . . . Should we not change our emphasis now, and propose the papacy as the centre of a reunited Christianity? Should we not admit that Peter too needed 'conversion', so that he might fulfil his task of – not reducing to uniformity, but – strengthening his brethren? (*The Church and Unity*, 1979, pp. 232–3)

Any such changes in the government of the Roman Catholic Church would certainly help other churches to welcome 'full communion' with that church under the Bishop of Rome as the president of their new fellowship. Such changes would probably leave many present features of Roman Catholic life little altered, so that other churches would not find a simple merger rapidly acceptable. But these changes would belong to the great renewal which was started by John XXIII and Vatican II. Despite many tensions between conservatives and progressives, despite a complete failure to obtain for themselves any effective share in the central government, the Synod of Bishops in Rome in 1985 did not halt many changes which other Christians are likely to welcome more warmly than the catechism as finalized. Developments blessed in that review of the consequences of Vatican II included ecumenism itself, more attention to the Scriptures and more active participation in the sacraments, the spiritual renewal of many groups including both parishes and non-parochial 'base communities', a more radical defence of human rights, a sense of the Church as a people on pilgrimage to the ends of the world and the end of time. Taken together, these officially approved developments may be said to have begun a new reformation.

The unity of the Spirit

'The vision that rises before us', said the Lambeth Conference of Anglican bishops in 1920,

> is that of a Church, genuinely Catholic, loyal to all truth, and gathering into its fellowship all 'who profess and call themselves Christians', within whose visible unity all the treasures of faith and order, bequeathed as a heritage by the past to the present, shall be possessed in common, and made serviceable to the whole Body of Christ. Within this unity Christian Communions now separate from one another would retain much that has long been distinctive in their methods of worship and service. It is through a rich diversity of life and devotion that the unity of the whole fellowship will be fulfilled.

'We believe', the bishops added,

> that the visible unity of the Church will be found to involve the wholehearted acceptance of the Holy Scriptures as the record of God's revelation of himself to Man, and as being the rule and ultimate standard of faith; the creed commonly called Nicene, as the sufficient statement of the Christian faith, and either it or the Apostles' Creed as the baptismal confession of belief; the divinely instituted sacraments of Baptism and the Holy Communion, as expressing for all the corporate life of the whole fellowship in and with Christ; a ministry acknowledged by every part of the Church as possessing not only the inward call of the Spirit, but also the commission of Christ and the authority of the whole body. May we not reasonably claim that the episcopate is the one means of providing such a ministry . . . ? We submit that considerations alike of history and of present experience justify the claim . . . But we greatly desire that the office of bishop should be everywhere exercised in a representative and constitutional manner, and more truly express all that ought to be involved for the life of the Christian family in the title of Father-in-God.

Here is a vision of two Communions 'united not absorbed' (to use the title of a contribution by Dom Lambert Beauduin to the unofficial and aborted Anglican–RC conversations in Malines in 1925). And it seems more realistic than the description of the goal by the Vatican or by any assembly so far of the World Council of Churches.

At New Delhi in 1961 the third assembly of the World Council declared its belief that the unity which is both God's will and his gift to his Church is being made visible as all in each place who are baptized into Jesus Christ and confess him as Lord and Saviour are brought by the Holy Spirit into one fully committed fellowship, holding the one apostolic faith, preaching the one gospel, breaking the one bread, joining in common prayer and having a corporate life reaching out in witness and service to all.

These Christians are 'at the same time united with the whole Christian fellowship in all places and ages in such wise that ministry and members are accepted by all, and that all can act and speak together as occasion requires for the tasks to which God calls his people'.

This definition has never been fully revised, yet it leaves many important questions unanswered. What diversity is allowable or welcome in loyalty to the 'one apostolic faith'? In what practical ways is prayer to be 'common' if much that is distinctive in traditions of worship is to be retained? What instruments are needed if they are to be so representative that it can be said plausibly that through them all the world's Christians – in number well over 1,500 million in the 1990s, even if the title 'Christian' is denied to those who are not so definite that they personally confess Christ as Lord and Saviour – can be 'one fully committed fellowship'? These questions were not answered in the Lambeth appeal of 1920, but a clue to the realistic answers was provided by that Anglican emphasis that diversity, no less than unity, is God's will and his gift to his Church.

At Uppsala in 1968 the fourth assembly of the World Council met when the excitement generated by the Second Vatican Council was still in the air. It called on the churches to 'work for a time when a genuinely universal council may once again speak for all Christians, and lead the way into the future'. But this development alarmed Eastern Orthodox representatives, presumably because of a basic worry that their traditions might be outvoted authoritatively in a council wider than the Pan-Orthodox Synod for which the preliminary preparations (not completed in the next quarter-century) were then being undertaken. Partly because of this reaction, in the next assembly of the World Council, at Nairobi in 1975, it was agreed that

the one Church is to be envisioned as a conciliar fellowship of local churches which are themselves truly united. In this conciliar fellowship each local church possesses, in communion with others, the fullness of Catholicity . . . To this end, each local church aims at maintaining sustained and sustaining relationships with her sister churches, expressed in conciliar gatherings whenever required for the fulfilment of their common calling.

This statement moved away from the more centralized visions of Rome and Uppsala in the 1960s into an emphasis on the 'local' church, which in Orthodox as in Catholic usage is considered to be the diocese or group of dioceses. It also moved away from the possibility of a council which could 'speak for all Christians' into an emphasis on fellowship in gatherings. But it, too, left unanswered the question: what does it mean for a 'local' church to be 'truly united'? Does it mean only one congregation in a village or only one organization in a town?

In its seventh assembly, at Canberra in 1991, the World Council agreed to a statement which went some way to an answer. It drew on the biblical idea of *koinōnia* (fellowship) which had emerged as the key idea in the theological dialogues between churches, and it declared:

The unity of the Church to which we are called is a *koinonia* given and expressed in the common confession of the apostolic faith; a common sacramental life entered by the one baptism and celebrated together in one eucharistic fellowship; a common life in which members and ministries are mutually recognized and reconciled; and a common mission witnessing to the gospel of God's grace to all people and serving the whole of creation. The goal of the search for full communion is realized when all the churches are able to recognize in one another the one, holy, catholic and apostolic church in its fullness.

Full communion would be expressed 'in the local and universal levels through conciliar forms of life and action'. Diversities, it was added, 'are integral to the nature of communion . . . yet there are limits to diversity'. This vision moved away from the 1961 or 1968 suggestion that 'all' would come together in one local congregation, to be represented in one universal council. Instead the emphasis was on 'churches' joining in councils and recognizing each other as churches in word and deed while also recognizing the value of some diversity. But this vision in 1991 still left unanswered the question whether in the unity there would be any place for anything resembling one of the present international denominations. Nor was the question answered clearly when in 1993 the World Conference on Faith and Order put 'communion' at the centre of the idea of unity.

It seems essential that in the unity which the ecumenical movement seeks the legitimate diversity which has been expressed in the separate churches should be recognized. Such 'communion' including 'reconciled diversity' would, however, constitute a major change from the insistence of many Lutherans, Reformed and Anglicans in the past that one church was the church of the nation or other region, entitled to penalize or even persecute others such as Roman Catholics. It would also be a departure from Eastern Orthodox theory, which has hitherto insisted that there should be one true bishop gathering the true Church in each place – although in practice, owing to past doctrinal disputes, more than one eastern bishop has claimed to be orthodox (as in Jerusalem, Antioch or Alexandria). Orthodox bishops in lands not traditionally Orthodox have had overlapping jurisdictions based on ethnic identities (Russian, Greek, etc.), as in New York or Sydney. And the acceptance of the degree of diversity envisaged in the Lambeth appeal of 1920 would be a sizeable development in the official teaching of the Roman Catholic Church, although some elements in that teaching appear to favour it.

This catechism includes passages which echo the courtesy of the Second Vatican Council towards fellow-Christians who are not Roman Catholics. 'One cannot charge with the sin of separation those who are born now into these communities and in them are brought up in the faith of Christ, and the Catholic Church accepts them with respect and affection as brothers' (818). Accordingly the catechism repeats the council's calls for participation in the ecumenical movement by an ongoing renewal including the conversion of the heart, by common prayer and mutual knowledge, by dialogue and ecumenical collaboration (821). But the council did not go so far along the ecumenical road as the Lambeth appeal had gone forty years before, when the Anglican bishops had made only modest claims for Anglicanism. They had wanted a church larger than their own – 'a church genuinely Catholic, loyal to all truth, gathering all Christians'. They had said that they were already bound to 'other ancient episcopal Communions in east and west by many ties of common faith and tradition'. They had also recognized that the ministries of churches without bishops 'have been manifestly blessed and owned by the Holy Spirit as effective means of grace'.

In contrast with such Anglican attitudes, this catechism quotes Vatican II: 'The sole Church of Christ is that which our Saviour, after his Resurrection, entrusted to Peter's pastoral care, commissioning him and the other apostles to extend and rule it . . . This Church, constituted and organized in this world as a society, *subsists in* the Catholic Church, which is governed by the successor of Peter and by the bishops in communion with him' (816). The words which I have italicized in the final draft of the English version of the catechism translate the Latin *subsistit in*. Another possible translation is 'most fully present in'; another, 'exists in'. These alternatives are of course loaded with alternative meanings and it is significant that the

Vatican has settled for the most cautious. The preceding debates showed that the majority of the bishops in the council intended a change from the previously firm exclusion of all who were not Roman Catholics from the Body of Christ. (The catechism of 1566 taught that 'heretics and schismatics are excluded from the Church . . . and belong to her only as deserters belong to the army from which they have deserted. It is, however, not to be denied that they are still subject to the jurisdiction of the Church and . . . may be punished.') Accordingly the Latin words have sometimes been interpreted as meaning that the Roman Catholic Church was regarded as one among many forms in which the Church exists. But the context in this decree on ecumenism shows that the catechism is correct in its unspectacular translation. It echoes the teaching of Vatican II that 'it is Christ's Catholic Church, which is the universal help toward salvation, that the fullness of the means of salvation can be obtained. It is to the apostolic college alone, of which Peter is the head, that we believe that our Lord entrusted all the blessings of the New Covenant, in order to establish, on earth, the one Body of Christ, into which all those should be fully incorporated who already belong in any way to the People of God' (816). The catechism also quotes Vatican II's warning: 'let us be very careful not to conceive of the universal Church as the simple sum or . . . the more or less anomalous federation of essentially different particular churches' (835). And it endorses the 1982 canon law's definition of 'schism' as 'refusal of submission to the Pope or communion with the members of the Church subject to him' (2089).

To many Christians, however, it seems more realistic to think that the unity of 'Christ's Catholic Church' was broken when substantial numbers in the east (now termed the 'Oriental Orthodox') could not accept the decisions of 'ecumenical' councils (specially since these were heavily influenced by the Byzantine emperors) – and unity was also broken, on a much bigger scale, when Eastern Orthodox, Protestants and Anglicans found the developed claims of the papacy unacceptable. The terminology used by Vatican II and this catechism is more generous than Pius XII's simple equation between the Roman Catholic Church and the Body of Christ, but it is still ambiguous about the inclusion of other Christians in what it calls 'the sole Church of Christ'. However, it is not my conclusion that the unity which Christians ought to seek because it is God's will and gift to his Church is a loose federation of local churches or international denominations without much contact with each other.

I am among those who in a 'rich diversity' within unity would expect many churches which can be called denominations (whether they like it or not) to retain a large measure of what was called in 1920 'distinctive methods of worship and service'. In that category would be not only many

Protestants or Pentecostalists, and not only the Eastern and 'Oriental' Orthodox, but also the Roman Catholic Church itself. However, these churches would not remain static. The new 'family life' of which the Anglican bishops spoke in 1920, and the 'sustained and sustaining' fellowship of which the World Council spoke in 1975, would help forward the agreements about doctrine and practice which have already been substantial and amazing since 1920. As their reasons for separation were seen as comparatively unimportant, some or many churches would be ready for mergers constituting what has been called 'organic' union. Anglicans, for example, might well renew their negotiations, locally or internationally, either with churches more Protestant or with the Roman Catholic Church. The choice between these two partners, if a choice had to be made, would depend on developments within the partners no less than within the Anglican tradition.

It seems essential to respect the consciences and emotions of those many Christians who have got used to the traditions of the separated churches and who feel threatened if it appears that it is proposed to dismantle those traditions insensitively. But it also seems essential that 'full communion' between the churches should be restored as quickly as consciences allow. By 'full communion' is meant being able to receive the Holy Communion together and being willing to develop a common life from that point of mutual acceptance. That, I believe, need not wait until the churches are able 'to recognize in one another the one holy, catholic and apostolic church *in its fullness*'. The words which I have put into italics in that quotation from the World Council of Churches in 1991 imply a stiff examination of sister churches and therefore a long wait before the renewal of communion. But all that churches really need to recognize in each other is Christ – who in Palestine enjoyed table fellowship with tax collectors and prostitutes.

In this book I have argued (I hope not too rudely) that the reasons given for the official Roman Catholic refusal of such communion are open to criticism. The authority of the college of bishops with the pope at its head is not sufficiently established as 'divine law' for all Christians (the phrase was used by Vatican I). The doctrines expounded in this catechism of the Catholic Church are not what has been believed 'always, everywhere by everyone'. This *Code of Canon Law* of the Latin Church is no model to all churches (as was partially affirmed when other canons for the Eastern Catholics were issued in 1990). The refusals or hesitations of other Christians when asked to accept the doctrines or practices on which the Vatican at present insists are not so obviously wrong and heretical that these Christians ought to be excluded from what Paul VI finely called 'the Lord's Eucharist'.

It has often been said that the pain of division at the Lord's table results in a passion to achieve first doctrinal agreement and then 'organic' union. That has certainly been the experience of some Christians who have been creatively committed to the ecumenical movement. But for many more, the impression has been conveyed that people excommunicated by the acknowledged authorities do not really belong to 'the sole Church of Christ' and therefore have little to contribute. The practice of 'intercommunion' probably led to Protestants not taking the scandal of the churches' disunity seriously enough when the desirable basis of unity was thought to be the common acceptance of a Protestant view of the Bible and when the ecumenical movement was almost entirely confined to Protestants. But the prominence of Roman Catholics and Eastern Orthodox in this movement during and since the 1960s seems to be a guarantee that the challenge to an ever-closer union with serious theology among its foundations will not be forgotten. The main danger now seems to be that people are deterred from backing the ecumenical movement by the fear that too close a union would end legitimate and valued diversity.

This catechism and this code of canon law have been reminders of the difficulties of the task confronting us, or future Christians, before there can be reconciliation and communion in truth and holiness. Yet the future of the Christian Church seems likely to be long: if Christianity lasts as long as human life on this planet, and if that life lasts as long as scientists now expect, the history of the Church will cover some two thousand million years. Many wounds and scars have been left by the first two thousand years, but if Christians are now daunted by being told to 'spare no effort to make fast with bonds of peace the unity which the Spirit gives . . . until we all attain to the unity inherent in our faith' (Eph 4.3, 13), it may be recalled that at Pentecost Peter is said to have quoted the word of the Lord to the prophet Joel (2.28–29):

> I shall pour out my spirit on all mankind;
> your sons and daughters will prophesy,
> your old men will dream dreams
> and your young men see visions;
> I shall pour out my spirit in those days
> even on slaves and slave-girls.

For further reading

My books on *The Futures of Christianity* (1987) and *Tradition and Truth* (1989)
included bibliographies. Austin Flannery edited *Vatican II: Conciliar and Postconciliar
Documents* (1980) and *Vatican Council II: More Postconciliar Documents* (1982). Karol
Wojtyła (later Pope John Paul II) expounded *Sources of Renewal* (in English, 1980) and
B. C. Butler *The Theology of Vatican II* (revised, 1981). The studies by Avery Dulles
of *Models of the Church* (1976) and *The Catholicity of the Church* (1985) provide a good
background, as does the *Encyclopaedia of Theology* translated from German sources
which Karl Rahner edited in English (1975). Aidan Nichols, *The Shape of Catholic
Theology* (1991), is more conservative. *The New Jerome Biblical Commentary*, edited by
Raymond E. Brown and others (1989) is a standard work by RC scholars. *Mary's
Place in Christian Dialogue*, edited by Alberic Stacpoole (1982), and John Macquarrie's
Mary for All Christians (1991) treated a relevant question in a biblical context.
Marina Warner, *Alone of All Her Sex* (1976), was a feminist critique. Oscar Cullmann
discussed *Peter: Disciple, Apostle, Martyr* (in English, 1953). RC scholars have
explored many other fields, including Francis Sullivan, *Magisterium: Teaching
Authority in the Catholic Church* (1983), J. M. R. Tillard, *The Bishop of Rome* (in
English, 1983), Edward Schillebeeckx, *The Church with a Human Face* (in English,
1985) and Patrick Granfield, *The Limits of the Papacy* (1987). The *Oxford Dictionary of
the Popes* compiled by J. N. D. Kelly (1986) is invaluable. *A Pope for All Christians*,
edited by Peter McCord (1976), is suggestive. A recent history is Bernard
Schimmelpfennig, *The Papacy* (in English, 1992).

Recent scholarly presentations of basic doctrines include Karl Rahner, *Foundations
of Christian Faith* (in English, 1978), James P. Mackey, *The Christian Experience of
God as Trinity* (1983), two books by Walter Kasper, *Jesus the Christ* (in English, 1976)
and *The God of Jesus Christ* (in English, 1983), and two by John Macquarrie, *Principles
of Christian Theology* (revised, 1977) and *Jesus Christ in Modern Thought* (1990).

Publications about sexuality are innumerable, but Theodore Mackin, *Divorce and
Remarriage* (1984), John T. Noonan, *Contraception: A History of Its Treatment by the
Catholic Theologians and Canonists* (1986), John Mahoney, *The Making of Moral
Theology* (1986) and Heinz-J. Vogels, *Celibacy: Gift or Law?* (in English, 1993), were
substantial. Charles Curran collected some of his essays on *The Living Tradition of*

Catholic Moral Theology (1992). A fiercer attack on the old tradition was launched by Uta Ranke-Heinemann, *Eunuchs for the Kingdom of Heaven* (in English, 1990).

The work of the Anglican–RC International Commission was reprinted and put in context by *Growth in Agreement: Reports and Agreed Statements of Ecumenical Conversations on a World Level*, edited by Meyer Harding and Lukas Vischer (1984). The hopes with which it began are on record in *Anglican/Roman Catholic Dialogue*, edited by Alan Clark and Colin Davey (1974). Commentaries include Maria J. van Dyck's *Growing Closer Together*, which ends with the Vatican's cool response (1992), and Hugh Montefiore's *So Near and Yet So Far*, which refers to many Church of England documents (1986). The wider dialogue was surveyed by Bernard and Margaret Pawley, *Rome and Canterbury: A Study of the Relations Between the Church of Rome and the Anglican Churches, 1530–1973* (1974), and G. R. Evans, *Authority in the Church: A Challenge for Anglicans* (1990). Paul McPartlan edited *One in 2000?: Towards Catholic-Orthodox Unity* (1993). RC studies include B. C. Butler, *The Church and Unity* (1979), Yves Congar, *Diversity and Communion* (in English, 1982), George H. Tavard, *A Review of Anglican Orders* (1990), and Aidan Nichols, *Holy Order* (1990). Horton Davies presented 'newer ecumenical perspectives on the Eucharist' in *Bread of Life and Cup of Joy* (1993), P. J. FitzPatrick explored the meaning of *In Breaking of Bread* (1993), and Aram Keshishian studied the thinking of the World Council of Churches about *Conciliar Fellowship* (1992). A commentary on *The Code of Canon Law* was edited by James A. Coriden and others for the Canon Law Society of America (1985). Peter Hebblethwaite's chronicles of recent tensions have included *The New Inquisition?* (1980), *Synod Extraordinary* (1986), *In the Vatican* (1987) and biographies of *John XXIII, Pope of the Council* (revised, 1994) and *Paul VI: The First Modern Pope* (1993). Adrian Hastings edited essays on *Modern Catholicism* (1991). Hans Küng, *The Structures of the Church, Infallible?* and *The Church Maintained in Truth* (in English, 1965–80) had more angry sequels: for example, his own *Reforming the Church Today* (1990) and the essays which he edited with David Tracy, *Toward Vatican III* (1978), and with Leonard Swidler, *The Church in Anguish* (1987). His influence has pervaded the journal *Concilium*, but the more conservative journal *Communio* and Joseph Ratzinger, *Church, Ecumenism and Politics* (in English, 1987), are also noteworthy. David Willey, *God's Politician* (1992), provided a good journalist's assessment of John Paul II's international impact. *The Tablet*, a weekly, is one of the best journals commenting on RC and other literature and affairs. Its independence is specially remarkable. The address for subscriptions is PO Box 14, Harold Hill, Romford RM3 8EQ, England.

Index